International Studies in Educational Achievement

VOLUME 13

The IEA Study of Computers in Education:

Implementation of an Innovation
in 21 Education Systems

International Studies in Educational Achievement

Other titles in the Series include

TRAVERS & WESTBURY
The IEA Study of Mathematics I: Analysis of Mathematics Curricula

ROBITAILLE & GARDEN
The IEA Study of Mathematics II: Contexts and Outcomes of School Mathemat

BURSTEIN
The IEA Study of Mathematics III: Student Growth and Classroom Processes

GORMAN, PURVES & DEGENHART
The IEA Study of Written Composition I: The International Writing Tasks
and Scoring Scales

PURVES
The IEA Study of Written Composition II: Education and Performance
in Fourteen Countries

ANDERSON, RYAN & SHAPIRO
The IEA Classroom Environment Study

ROSIER & KEEVES
The IEA Study of Science I: Science Education and Curricula
in Twenty-Three Countries

POSTLETHWAITE & WILEY
The IEA Study of Science II: Science Achievement in Twenty-Three Countries

KEEVES
The IEA Study of Science III: Changes in Science Education and Achievement:
1970 to 1984

The IEA Study
of Computers in Education:

*Implementation of an Innovation
in 21 Education Systems*

Edited by

WILLEM J PELGRUM

and

TJEERD PLOMP
University of Twente, The Netherlands

Published for the International Association
for the Evaluation of Educational Achievement by

PERGAMON PRESS

OXFORD · NEW YORK · SEOUL · TOKYO

U.K.	Pergamon Press Ltd, Headington Hill Hall Oxford OX3 0BW, England
U.S.A.	Pergamon Press Inc, 660 White Plains Road, Tarrytown New York 10591-5153, U.S.A.
KOREA	Pergamon Press Korea, KPO Box 315, Seoul 110-603, Korea
JAPAN	Pergamon Press Japan, Tsunashima Building Annex, 3-20-12 Yushima, Bunkyo-ku, Tokyo 113, Japan

First edition 1993

British Library Cataloguing in Publication Data
A catalogue record for this book is available from the British Library

Library of Congress Cataloging in Publication Data
A catalogue record for this book is available from the Library of Congress

ISBN 0 08 041935 6

Printed in Great Britain by BPCC Wheatons Ltd, Exeter

Contents

APPENDICES

Foreword

This volume on computers in education is published as part of IEA's study of Computers in Education (Comped).

IEA, the International Association for the Evaluation of Educational Achievement, was founded in 1959 for the purpose of conducting comparative studies focusing on educational policies and practices in various countries and education systems around the world. IEA has grown over the years from a small number of countries to a group of about fifty until today. It has a Secretariat located in the Hague, the Netherlands. IEA studies have reported on a wide range of topics, each contributing to a deeper understanding of educational processes. The Computers in Education study (Comped) is a project, shedding light on the way computers have been introduced in education and are being used nowadays across the world.

The Comped study is a two stage study with data collection for stage 1 in 1989 and for stage 2 in 1992. With the publication of this volume stage 1 of Comped is now completed. The International Coordination Center at the University of Twente, Enschede, the Netherlands, is now working on the analysis of the data of stage 2, about which we can expect a first publication in 1993. The project will be officially finished by the end of 1994, when the data base derived from this study will be made available via the IEA Secretariat and the Volume on stage 2 will be drafted.

IEA is very grateful to the following organizations which are the major contributors to the financing of the international overhead of the study: Ministry of Education and Sciences and the Institute for Educational Research (SVO) of the Netherlands, Commission of the European Community (Brussels), National Institute for Educational Research (NIER) of Japan and the Japan Society for the Promotion of Science (JSPS), and the National Science Foundation of the USA. The Japanese contribution through NIER and JSPS has been received from Fujitsu Ltd., Hitachi Ltd., IBM Japan Ltd., Matsushita Electric Industrial Company Ltd., and Sony Corporation.

This volume is the result of efforts of many individuals. A special thank must go to the staff of the International Coordinating Center under the leadership of Willem J. Pelgrum, which did an excellent job under difficult budgetal conditions. I would also like to express my gratitude to IEA's Publications and Editorial Committee, chaired by dr. Richard M. Wolf, and to the external reviewers: dr. R. Konttinen from Finland, and dr. R.G. Ragsdale from Canada for their constructive comments. Finally, I would like to thank Pergamon Press for their support in realizing this volume.

Those readers wishing additional information on this or other IEA studies may directly correspond to IEA at the following address:

IEA Executive Director
14 Sweelinckplein
2517 GK the Hague
the Netherlands

Tjeerd Plomp
Chairman of IEA

Preface

The IEA Computers in Education study is a major international cooperative effort to describe and analyze the situation with regard to the introduction and use of computers in education systems around the world. The data which were collected in 1989 were described in a first report (Pelgrum and Plomp, 1991). Since then more countries have been included in the database and more indepth analyses were conducted by several authors who contributed to writing this book.

This book is the end product of many years of work by numerous persons. Much of the preliminary work was done by the National Project Coordinators (Appendix D contains their names), who helped in designing the study and collected all the data. Without their commitment the study could not have been completed successfully.

The Steering Committee members (Ryo Watanabe and Dick Wolf) as well as the sampling coordinator (Colm O'Muircheartaigh from the London School of Economics) offered invaluable help in advising the International Coordinating Center and assisted in making (sometimes difficult) decisions. Tjeerd Plomp in his role as supervisor and chair of the Steering Committee professionally guided the processes and progress of the project.

At the International Coordinating Center the data-managers Leendert van Staalduinen and Rien Steen skilfully and patiently constructed the database, while Arjan Schipper and Ria Marinussen conducted many of the required analyses.

A special word of thanks goes to Monique Kole who did much of the graphical work and produced the camera ready manuscript.

Finally we like to thank Richard M. Wolf for his assistance in editing the final draft of this book.

Willem J. Pelgrum (International Coordinator)

Abbreviations for Educational Systems

AUT	Austria
BFL	Belgium-Flemish
BFR	Belgium-French
CBC	Canada-British Columbia
CHI	China
FRA	France
FRG	Federal Republic of Germany
GRE	Greece
HUN	Hungary
IND	India
ISR	Israel
ITA	Italy
JPN	Japan
LUX	Luxembourg
NET	Netherlands
NWZ	New Zealand
POL	Poland
POR	Portugal
SLO	Slovenia
SWI	Switzerland
USA	United States of America

1

Theoretical Framework, Design and Sampling

Aims and character of the study

Many countries throughout the world are facing issues about the role of computers in education: what is the place and role of computers in the schools? Is there a need for separate courses in computer literacy and computer science? How can the computer be used effectively in existing subjects? What will be the effect of computers on student learning, on teachers' behavior, on the school and classroom organization? These are important questions and, although research evidence is accumulating, at present, there is little information available about the situation in the schools which might guide us in answering these questions. Moreover, the introduction of computers in education is probably the first major educational innovation which can be studied systematically almost from its earliest state of development, from which much can be learned about mechanisms of educational change.

These considerations led the International Association for the Evaluation of Educational Achievement (IEA) in 1985 decide to embark on an international comparative study of 'Computers in Education' (Comped) in which, at two points in time, data would be collected regarding the content and outcomes of this innovation in more than 20 educational systems. The Comped study was designed as a two stage study. Stage 1, with data collection in 1989, was aimed at collecting data at the national, school and teacher level. It was a survey, primarily descriptive in nature, focusing on how computers are being used, the extent and availability of computers in schools, the nature of instruction about computers, and estimates of the effects that computers are having on students, the curriculum and the school as an institution, as well as other factors influencing the use of computers in schools.

This chapter was written by Tjeerd Plomp and Willem J. Pelgrum.

The second stage of the study, with data collection in 1992, consisted of two parts. The first part was a follow-up of stage 1, for studying changes over time. The second part of stage 2 involved assessing effects of school variables, teacher and teaching variables on student outcomes in the domain of computer usage in schools (functional computer knowledge and skills).

In principle, both stages were designed as studies, in which countries could decide, per stage, to participate.

More specifically, the aims of stage 1 of the Comped study were (Wolf, Plomp & Pelgrum, 1986):

1. to obtain information about the current status of the use of computers in education, more specifically within schools, which should serve as a valuable source of information for policy makers, teachers, administrators and other educational personnel engaged in planning, implementation and evaluation in the field of computers in education; and
2. to collect baseline information for studying in stage 2 directions of changes and developments in computer usage in education, as well as for analyzing relationships among various factors concerning the use and application of computers in education.

This book describes the empirical findings with regard to major issues related to the introduction of computers in education. It offers an empirical basis for further discussions among educational practitioners and policy makers about the directions of change, and for documenting baseline information which is important to evaluate future developments in this field. It presents analytic and descriptive results of stage 1 of the Comped study and is, in this respect, complementary to the preliminary report of Stage 1 of Comped (Pelgrum & Plomp, 1991). Other results will appear (or have been published) in national reports of the participating countries, and in articles in scientific journals (see the references at the end of this chapter).

In the remainder of this chapter we will give a brief description of the context of the study by providing an overview of the type of arguments for introducing computers in education, and a summary of research findings, which illuminates the difficulties of integrating computers in the schools' curriculum. Next, the conceptual framework and the design of stage 1 of the study will be summarized, followed by an overview of the remainder of the book.

Why are new technologies important for schools?

Many reasons have been presented for introducing computers in education. Hawkridge (1990) summarizes these in four rationales.

Social rationale: children should be prepared to function adequately as citizens in a society permeated with new technologies.

Vocational rationale: children should be prepared to function adequately as professional workers in a technological society. Although the need for well prepared professionals is a societal need, this rationale is called vocational to clearly distinguish it from the preceding one.

Pedagogical rationale: computers may improve the instructional processes and learning outcomes.

Catalytic rationale: the use of computers may accelerate another educational innovation such as more emphasis in the teaching and learning process on information handling and problem solving, and less on memorizing facts; this rationale refers to the possibility that schools can be changed for the better by the introduction of new technologies. Hawkridge (1990) and others refer to possible effects such as improved administrative and managerial efficiency; more emphasis on students learning by collaborating rather than by competing. In this approach computers are seen as catalysts, enabling desired change in education to occur (o.c., p. 5).

Hawkridge (1990) points to two other rationales, which have at present little support in education. The *information technology rationale* supports the idea of stimulating a national computer industry by placing at the government's expense large numbers of nationally produced or assembled computers in the schools. Finally, the *cost-effectiveness rationale* argues that computers can reduce the cost of education drastically as they will allow for a reduction in the number of teachers. This rationale indeed has some validity in the domain of (corporate) training in business and industry, but is not really supported in formal education.

Although Hawkridge presents these rationales as possible answers to the question why Third World countries may want to put computers in their schools, many educators and policy makers in other countries will recognize similar rationales when they recall the discussions on the national, regional, local and/or school level about the introduction of new technologies, in the recent past predominantly computers, in education.

In addition to Hawkridge, one may distinguish some other rationales. Especially in the early 1980s during the initiation stage of introducing computers in education, the *opportunistic rationale* was (informally) mentioned consisting of the expectation that the use of computers in schools may contribute to attract more students to the school. Anderson and Collis (1993) point to another rationale, which is especially popular nowadays, namely the *'functionality'* perspective. This perspective implies that students in schools need to learn to use computers in a way which is functional for the many different tasks they are confronted with; such a perspective refers to the use of computers as a tool for, for example, writing (word processing) and data handling (spreadsheet and database programs).

It is usually not one single rationale which guides policy makers. Often two or three of these rationales are simultaneously referred to as the starting points for policies at whatever level. On the other hand, the selection of one or more rationales as being the dominant ones may determine to a large extent the implementation strategies as well as the budgets needed.

Why is it difficult to integrate computers in the school curriculum?

The introduction of computers in education is a large-scale complex innovation in which many obstacles need to be overcome before a successful implementation can take place. When designing the study during 1985-1987, it was known that in many countries the number of computers in schools had increased considerably over the years (Cerych, 1982). Yet, it was reported that little progress had been made in integrating computers into existing lesson practices: few teachers were actual users, software use was often restricted to drill and practice activities, and the integration in the curriculum was poor (for example, Becker, 1986; Inspectorate, 1986).

Van den Akker, Keursten & Plomp (1992) reviewed the research (of both survey and case study type) and concluded that there is still a long way to go before computer use would be effectively integrated in most schools and classrooms. They concluded that there are four categories of important obstacles for a successful integration of computers in education: national context, school organization, external support, and innovation (product) characteristics.

National context: difficulties may arise if, apart from obvious tasks as investing in hardware, software development, research, teacher training and the like, there is a lack of proclamation of new aims for the educational system and encouragement "from above" for initiatives and activities in the field.

School organization: difficulties may arise if,
- there is a lack of encouragement and support from school administrators and principals, especially in the provision of facilities for training, acquisition of hardware and software, rearrangements of time tables, and other organizational measures;
- the school climate is negative and teachers are not mutually supportive by exchanging ideas and experiences and by providing feedback;
- there is no computer coordinator available;
- there is no long term security of supply and maintenance of hardware and software.

External support: many in-service training programs emphasized too much the technical aspects of computers while paying too little attention to the integration of computers into daily classroom practice and to skills in selecting and evaluating courseware. Teachers need strong support to overcome their (initial) problems of uncertainty and their concerns about changing teacher/student relationships and about accountability. There is a growing consensus about characteristics of in-service training that can increase its effectiveness: appropriate balance between theory and (guided) practice; detailed curriculum guides and plans for the course plus lesson-related materials and hand-outs; clear training objectives; in-service lessons linked to teachers' own instructional practice; peer interaction, including communication during hands-on activities; strategies for teaching heterogeneous groups; follow-up support and guidance.

Innovation characteristics: important concerns and questions related to characteristics of computers for the educational practice are:
- need and relevance: is there a need for using computers? How appropriate are computers for realizing certain goals? What is the priority of introducing computers in comparison with other concerns?
- clarity: how clear are the goals and the essential features of computer use for those who are supposed to work with computers? How clear are the practical implications for the users?
- complexity: how many components of instructional practice are affected, and how drastic are the deviations from existing practice and beliefs? How difficult is it to get familiar with the expected changes?
- quality and practicality: how well developed and tested are the software products? To what extent is the expected impact guaranteed? What is the trade-off between actual benefits and the personal and organizational costs?

These questions are often asked by teachers (and other educational practitioners), who are ultimately the central actors in successfully implementing computers in educational practice. Weaknesses in one or more of the categories referred to above may cause major obstructions in the implementation of computers in educational practice.

Conceptual framework

In order to determine which information needed to be collected in this study, a framework was developed which identified the key factors at which the study was aimed. The framework consists of concepts derived from systems theory, curriculum theory and theories on educational change, as discussed in the previous section.

An educational system is a complex of subsystems at different levels: at the macro level the educational system of a country or state, at the meso level the school, and at the micro level the classroom and the student. On each level, educational decisions are influenced by different actors; for example, at the school level the school board, the principal, the subject matter department, and the teacher. External influences may be exerted by, for example, business and industry, or parents. The output of a subsystem at a certain level can be conceived as the input for the subsystem on the next level. For example, the output at the macro level may consist of policies, intentions and plans of governments, laid down in official documents, or existing as shared conceptions of what is expected from schools. Conceiving this as the input for schools, the output at this level consists of the activities and the practices in the classrooms, the time allocations and the instructional practices with computers of teachers. This is the input at the micro level, resulting in activities, cognitive skills and attitudes of students.

In curriculum theories, a distinction is made between the intended, implemented and attained curriculum. The intended curriculum refers to the curriculum plans (at the macro level), which may be laid down in official documents or which may exist as shared conceptions of what the important curriculum content is. The implemented curriculum (at the meso level) consists of the content, time allocations, instructional strategies, etc. which the teacher is actually realizing in his/her lessons. The attained curriculum (at the micro level) is defined as the cognitive skills and attitudes of students as a result of teaching and learning.

Taking these three curriculum levels as major input/output categories one may wonder how these levels influence each other and which factors may explain the occurrence of discrepancies. The literature on educational change may be used for tracing potential factors (e.g. Fullan,

Miles, & Anderson, 1988). As already mentioned in the previous section, these factors include the quality, clarity and relevance of the objectives and the characteristics of the innovation (content, materials, instructional strategies); support and leadership; staff development; experiences with innovations; and the existence of evaluation and feedback.

This study incorporated the three different perspectives which are described above. The global conceptual framework for the study, in which the three perspectives are related to each other, is depicted in Figure 1.1.

The framework in Figure 1.1 identifies the actors who operate at different levels of decision-making in an educational system. The framework assumes that the decisions taken at different educational system levels influence each other via the curricular products which can be identified at each level. The curricular outputs at the macro and meso level can be conceived as mechanisms for directing the outcomes at student level. Different processes (indicated as influencing factors), derived from the literature on educational change, mediate and determine the characteristics of the curricular products at several levels. The picture illustrates that different sub-systems interact (sometimes mediated via other sub-systems) and that the "behavior" of a certain sub-system can only be understood if context information about "neighbor" sub-systems is available.

Certain factors in the model may be at the same time relevant as primary variables and as context variables. For example, the implemented curriculum may be important in itself when studied from an implementation perspective, but at the same time it may be conceived as context information when one is interested in studying student outcomes.

We have characterized the educational system in terms of levels of decision-making and of factors contributing to effect changes.

The framework reflects the hierarchical structure of most educational systems, but acknowledges that decisions which promote or inhibit the implementation of computer-related curricula are made at all levels and, which may cause discrepancies between the different system levels. An identification of these discrepancies may in itself be an important starting point for improvement measures in education.

The framework as shown in Figure 1.1 has been used as the basis for the instrument development for stage 1 of this study.

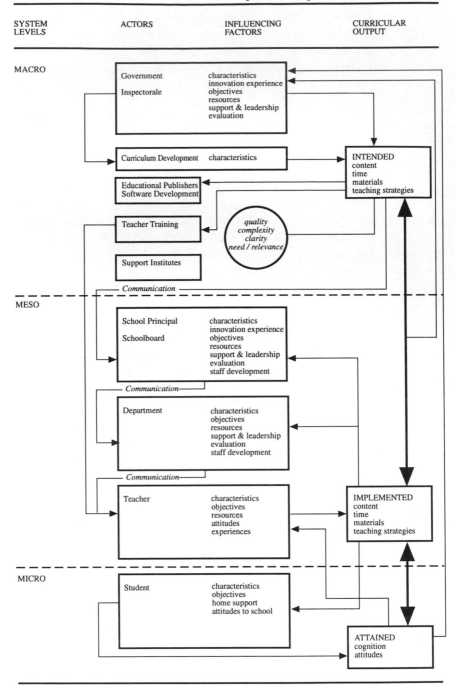

Figure 1.1. Global conceptual framework of the study.

From conceptual framework to indicators

The framework functioned as a guide for the international coordinating center of the study for further elaboration of the research questions and instrumentation by the researchers from over 20 countries who cooperated in this research project. Such cooperation implied that the concrete content of the study was shaped by many actors, who, on the basis of own experiences, national policy concerns and other considerations, gave input to discussions and decision-making with regard to the design and instrumentation. Throughout the whole project the international coordinating center (assisted by a steering committee) took care that data would be collected with regard to a set of indicators which will be briefly summarized below.

Hardware availability: availability was defined as the presence of computers in the school building. With regard to this indicator, several aspects were distinguished, such as type and amount of computers, and peripherals (such as printers, monitors, and mouses).

Software availability: availability of software was defined as the presence of certain types of software in the school building. The major types of software which were distinguished were general purpose software (such as programs for word processing, spreadsheets and data bases), programming languages (such as Basic and Pascal) and instructional tool software (such as programs for drill and practice, tutorials and computer assisted learning).

Type of use: two major aspects were distinguished, namely the computers as object of study (learning about computers) and the computer as tool (learning with computers).

Software use: with regard to software use a distinction was made between use by teachers and students.

Support: with regard to this indicator, a major distinction was made between school internal and external support. External support was further classified in terms of agencies, like Ministry of Education, local educational authorities, universities, etc.

Relevance: this indicator was defined as the attitudes of educational practitioners (school principals as well as teachers) with regard to the potential effects (on students' achievement, motivation and social behavior) of using computers.

Complexity: the complexity of introducing computers was seen as a multifaceted construct. It was mainly defined in terms of problems experienced by educational practitioners with regard to hardware availability and quality, software availability, support, organization, and the integration of computers in the curriculum.

Training: training was conceived in terms of the availability of in-service courses with regard to computers, training need, the content of training received by teachers, and knowledge and skills of teachers.

Participating educational systems

The educational systems which participated in stage 1 of the study are listed in Table 1.1.

Table 1.1
List of participating educational systems

Participating Systems	
Austria	Italy
Belgium-Flemish	Japan
Belgium-French	Luxembourg
Canada-British Columbia	Netherlands
China	New Zealand
France	Poland
Federal Republic of Germany	Portugal
Greece	Slovenia
Hungary	Switzerland
India	United States of America
Israel	

Table 1.1 shows that in the case of Belgium more than one educational system participated in the study and that in other countries only some states or provinces were included (see also Appendix A for more detailed information). Throughout this book we will use both the terms *country* and *educational system* to indicate the participants in this study.

Design: populations, samples and instruments

This section contains a description of the populations, samples and instruments as defined for stage 1 of this study.

Populations of schools and teachers

The populations of interest are located in (1) elementary, (2) lower secondary and (3) upper secondary education. In stage 2 of the study also data on student level will be collected, for which the following (student) population definitions will be used:

Population 1: students in the grade in which the modal age is 10 years (if more than one grade has a modal age of 10 years, the grade with the largest number of 10 year olds should be taken)

Population 2: students in the grade in which the modal age is 13 years (if more than one grade has a modal age of 13 years, the grade with the largest number of 13 year olds should be taken)

Population 3: students in the final year of secondary education

The marker date of age is the middle of the school year.

The data collection in stage 1 was restricted to school and teacher level. Given the global goals of stage 1, namely to provide a description of the status of computer use on school level, it was decided that the data collection in stage 1 should be aimed at grade ranges which contain the stage 2 populations plus and minus one year for elementary and lower secondary schools and minus 1 year for upper secondary schools. This was in particular the case for school level questionnaires and computer education teacher questionnaires.

The following definitions of the populations of schools and teachers to be used in stage 1 are derived from the student population definitions given above:

Population 1 (elementary schools)
- *non-using schools*: all schools which do not use computers for teaching/learning purposes in grades in which the modal age of students is 9, 10 or 11 years.
- *using schools*: all schools in which computers are used for teaching/learning purposes in grades in which the modal age of students is 9, 10 or 11 years.
- *computer using teachers*: all teachers in computer using schools who use computers or teach about computers in grades in which the modal age of students is respectively 9, 10 and 11.
- *non-computer using teachers*: all teachers in computer using schools who don't use computers and do not teach about computers, but are teachers of grades in which the modal age of students is respectively 9, 10 and 11.

Population 2 (lower secondary schools)
- *non-using schools*: all schools which do not use computers for teaching/learning purposes in grades in which the modal age of students is 12, 13 or 14 years.
- *using schools*: all schools in which computers are used for teaching/learning purposes in grades in which the modal age of students is 12, 13 or 14 years.
- *computer using teachers existing subjects*: all mathematics, science and mother tongue teachers in computer using schools who provide lessons in these subjects in which computers are used in grades in which the modal age of students is 13 years.
- *non-computer using teachers existing subjects*: all mathematics, science and mother tongue teachers in computer using schools who provide lessons in these subjects (without using computers) in grades in which the modal age of students is 13 years.
- *teachers computer education*: all teachers in computer using schools who teach about computers in grades in which the modal age of students is respectively 12, 13 and 14.

Population 3 (upper secondary schools)
- *non-using schools*: all schools which do not use computers for teaching/learning purposes in the final and penultimate secondary grades.
- *using schools*: all schools in which computers are used for teaching/learning purposes in the final or penultimate upper secondary grades.
- *computer using teachers existing subjects*: all mathematics, science and mother tongue teachers in computer using schools who provide lessons in these subjects in which computers are used to students who are in their final year of secondary education.
- *non-computer using teachers existing subjects*: all mathematics, science and mother tongue teachers in computer using schools who provide lessons in these subjects (without using computers) to students who are in their final year of secondary education.
- *teachers computer education*: all teachers in computer using schools who teach about computers to students who are in their final or penultimate year of secondary education.

In order to simplify the presentation throughout the rest of this report we will assume that the grade levels in which the modal ages of students are 10 and 13 are respectively grade 5 and 8, and that consequently the grade ranges which need to be considered for elementary and lower educational schools are 4-6 and 7-9.

Samples of schools and teachers

The sampling design for this study, as developed by the International Coordinating Center (ICC), can be summarized as follows:

> *The population of interest was stratified according to dimensions relevant for each participating educational system (and laid down in national sampling plans to be approved by the project's sampling referee). Minimum sample sizes for using and non-using schools (if appropriate) were specified. Oversampling of certain categories of schools was allowed. Schools were selected with probabilities of selection proportional to the size of the school. The selected schools were asked to provide lists of names of the target groups of teachers as defined above. Next, National Centers selected teachers according to specifications provided in a sampling manual.*

For some countries it appeared to be necessary to deviate from this plan for technical and/or practical reasons. For instance, sometimes equal probabilities of selection were used, as it was not possible in some countries to sample schools with probabilities of selection proportional to the size of the school. Such deviations were negotiated with and approved by the International Coordinating Center (after consultation of the sampling referee) before they could be incorporated in a national sampling plan. Appendix A contains an overview of the characteristics of the realized samples per educational system. In order to compensate for different probabilities of selection of schools, weights were calculated and applied for all the school level results reported in this book, except for Canada-British Columbia, the Federal Republic of Germany, Hungary and Italy for which information for weight calculations was not available. This omission is assumed not to affect any of the conclusions reached in this book, as comparisons of weighted and unweighted statistics for the other countries did not change the major trends. All teacher results are unweighted.

Furthermore, the reader should note that, due to the weights that, are applied in this book, percentages should be read as reflecting estimates of the percentages of schools/teachers in the population. Applying weights that reflect the student body represented may increase or decrease certain statistics depending on the correlation between school size and the variable of interest. For example, Table 3.1 (in Chapter 3) contains the percentage of schools using computers for instructional purposes. We found that, if one would apply weights that reflect the student body represented by these schools, the percentage increases with up to roughly 10 % in lower secondary schools in Switzerland and Portugal, due to the fact that large schools are more likely to possess computers than small schools.

Appendix A shows that the sample sizes for computer using schools are in general quite acceptable, except for Greece because only about 5% of the schools in the country use computers. Although the number of schools in Luxembourg may look small, the sample constitutes the whole population.

The number of computer using teachers is rather small for many countries, especially when broken down by subject. This is due to the fact that in those countries only a small group of teachers (in mathematics, science or mother tongue) uses computers for their lessons.

In general, results presented in this book are based on at least fifty schools, unless a particular category includes virtually all respondents in a country.

For most countries, the samples of elementary and lower secondary schools are representative for the whole educational system, with the exception of Switzerland (where three out of 26 cantons were excluded for lower secondary schools and one for upper secondary schools) and the Federal Republic of Germany where not all the Bundesländer took part in this study. For upper secondary schools, the national representativeness of the samples is more often problematic. Some countries (like India and China) selected a few areas/cities, whereas other countries excluded certain school types. For instance, in the Netherlands in upper secondary schools, only teachers from general secondary education are represented and not from vocational or technical education. An overview of the excluded populations is given in Appendix A.

Instruments

As indicated above, the instrumentation for this study was developed on basis of the framework in Figure 1.1 and finalized after pilot testing in 1988.

Table 1.2 contains an overview of the questionnaires for each population. The school and teacher questionnaires contained a part for computer users as well as non-computer users. It should be noted that the teacher questionnaires for the three existing subjects have the same content except for the specification of the subject area and one question about the topics for which computers are used.

Table 1.2
Available instruments per population

Population	Instrument	Respondent
	National questionnaire	National Project Coordinator
1	School questionnaire	Principal
	Technical questionnaire	Technically informed person
	Teacher questionnaire	Teacher grade 4-6
2	School questionnaire	Principal
	Technical questionnaire	Technically informed person
	Teacher questionnaire subject*	Subject teacher grade 8
	Teacher questionnaire computer education	Teacher computer education grade 7-9
3	School questionnaire**	Principal
	Technical questionnaire**	Technically informed person
	Teacher questionnaire subject*	Subject teacher final grade
	Teacher questionnaire computer education	Teacher computer education final/ penultimate grade

Notes: * = subjects are: mathematics, science and mother tongue, ** = probably in most countries integrated with population 2 version.

The technically informed persons mentioned in Table 1.2 will be further referred to as computer coordinators.

Outline of this book

In the remaining chapters of the book several authors present the results of stage 1 of the Comped study. All topics discussed can be placed in the conceptual framework for the study presented in this chapter.

In Chapter 2, the reasons schools put forward for starting to use computers are discussed, as well as the initiator of the schools' involvement in computers.

Chapter 3 discusses some necessary conditions for educational computer use, namely the availability of hardware and software.

In Chapter 4 data on how schools and teachers use computers are presented.

As training is an important factor in the implementation of this new and complex innovation, Chapter 5 is devoted to this issue.

Chapter 6 is devoted to administrative use of computers and some school policies, for example related to gender, are described.

Chapter 7 contains the results of applying LISREL analyses for examining causal relations between innovation strategical variables and computer implementation on school level.

Finally, Chapter 8 contains a summary and a discussion of possible implications of the results.

Within this agreed upon content frame, each author or pair of authors applied their own perspectives in analyzing and discussing the data, resulting in some differences in approaches. As a consequence, Chapters 4 and 6 are descriptive in nature, while Chapters 2, 3 and 5 do present next to descriptions also (cor)relational analyses. Finally, the explanatory LISREL analysis in Chapter 7 provides some sort of integration of the analyses presented in the previous chapters.

A brief characterization of the remaining chapters is given below.

Characterization of chapters

In Chapter 2 the reasons put forward for using computers are discussed as well as the persons initiating the use of computers in the school. It was found that providing students with experience for their future is the most important reason mentioned for starting to use computers. School oriented as well as class oriented reasons are distinguished. School authorities, groups of teachers, and outside school authorities were important responsible groups for the introduction of the computer in the school. An examination of schools which did not use computers in 1989 revealed that many of these schools consider to start using computers.

Chapter 3 discusses hardware and software availability in relation to the integrated use of computers. The trends that are presented show that, although many educational practitioners still experience considerable problems in using computers, the technological innovations of hardware and the increased availability of instructional tool software tend to facilitate the educational use of computers.

Chapter 4 describes the use of computers in educational practice: at the one hand the degree of implementation, at the other hand the types of uses in mathematics, science and mother tongue are presented. In addition, the chapter discusses 'learning about computers' in schools, by presenting data about the context and the topics of computer education. Finally, problems computer using teachers are experiencing, as well as their expectation about the changes computers may bring about education are addressed.

In Chapter 5, the training issue in this complex innovation is dealt with for the teachers of mathematics, science, and mother tongue. It is shown that teacher knowledge is related to the training received and to the amount of integrating the computer in the existing curriculum. The analyses show that coverage of pedagogical/instructional aspects in teacher training covary with the degree of integration of computers in the curriculum.

Chapter 6 presents a large amount of information about administrative policies and practices regarding the educational use of computers, attitudes of principals, and gender issues. The chapter shows that there is a slight social bias with regard to the use of computers in schools, but that school principals have generally favorable attitudes towards computers in education. It also reveals that there is considerable variability between countries regarding the provision of opportunities for males and females.

Chapter 7 contain the results from LISREL analyses, which show that the highest degree of confirmation for the influence of indicators on computer use among countries was found for internal school innovation assistance and teacher competence and readiness.

Most chapters focus on identifying major trends in the available data and by summarizing findings in a condensed way. Authors often had to struggle with finding a compromise between space limitations and the wish to elaborate the description and analyses for the readers interested in more details. Therefore it is not always possible to trace details for each country on every single aspect discussed. For more details (but less trends and analyses) the reader is referred to Pelgrum & Plomp (1991) and to other publications about (inter)national results (see references at the end of this chapter).

The Appendices contain more detailed information about the participating national centers and the characteristics of the national samples.

2

The Decision Phase: Starting to Use Computers

The first phase in an innovation process is the initiation or adoption phase, consisting of the process that leads up to and includes a decision to adopt or proceed with a change (Fullan, 1991). The adoption phase concerning the introduction of computers in education implies that a school or teachers have to decide whether they expect that a computer can be a worthwhile instrument in the educational process and whether they want to invest (in terms of energy, time and finances) in the introduction of computers. The decision to start using computers can be taken by the school administration, as well as by the subject matter departments or individual teachers. The role of policy makers can be crucial, as a proclamation of new aims for the educational system and encouragement 'from above' (Fullan, Miles and Anderson, 1988) for initiatives and activities can be helpful for the many participants in the innovation. Similarly important, is the school administration (including the principal) as they determine the climate and the direction of computer use at the school level and stimulate encouragement or discouragement for those who 'carry' the first introduction of computers in the school (Fullan et al., 1988; van den Akker, Keursten and Plomp, 1992). The way in which this process of deciding about computer use evolves determines for a great deal whether the implementation of the computer in education will become successful.

This chapter deals with the reasons and objectives of schools for starting to use computers and the question of who was responsible for the school getting involved in this new technology. The effect of certain reasons for starting to introduce computers in the school on its actual use in 1989 will be studied, as well as the effect of the type of person or group of persons responsible for the introduction on the type(s) of computer use.

This chapter was written by Ingeborg A.M. Janssen Reinen and Tjeerd Plomp.

19

The outcome of the adoption process may well lead to the conclusion in a school that it is too early to introduce computers or that other activities in the school have a higher priority. Those schools which did not use computers in 1989 were asked whether they were considering starting with this new technology and, if so, for what purposes they intended to use the computer.

Reasons for introduction of the computer

A question in the principal questionnaire dealt with the importance (ranging from 'not important' to 'very important', a score between 0 and 4) of each of the following reasons for introducing computers:
1. Give students experience for the future.
2. Make school more interesting.
3. Attract more students to the school.
4. Improve student achievement.
5. Keep curriculum up-to-date.
6. Promote individualized learning.
7. Promote cooperative learning.
8. School had opportunity to acquire computers.
9. Teachers were interested.

For each population, the median percentage agreement for each item is indicated in Figure 2.1, with the reasons ordered in sequence of importance. This means that the sequence of the reasons need not be identical for all three populations. Next to each reason, the countries with the highest percentage are included, as well as the countries with the lowest percentage. The countries are mentioned as scoring relatively high or low on that particular reason. This does not necessarily imply that, absolutely speaking, when looking at a particular country, this reason is the most or least important for that country.

'Providing students with experience for their future' is, in all populations, the most important reason for the introduction of computers. The reasons dealing with cooperative learning, attracting students and the opportunity to acquire computers are the least important. When looking at the countries with the highest and lowest percentage for each reason, some noteworthy patterns evolve. Belgium-French belongs, at the elementary school level, to the countries with high percentages on many of the reasons (if not belonging to the two highest countries, Belgium-French belongs to the group with the four highest percentages). The same holds for Canada-British Columbia at the secondary school level (both lower and upper). Belonging to the group of countries with lowest percentages is France (for many reasons at the elementary and lower secondary school level) and China (upper secondary school level). 'Promoting cooperative learning' is relatively important in Italy (it scores high in all populations, although at the elementary school level as third highest). The United States of America is one of the countries which, for the different populations, mention the reasons dealing with keeping the curriculum up-to-date and improving achievement as relatively important (relatively when comparing all countries).

In order to find out whether grouping of certain types of reasons is possible, a principle component analysis was done. Two reasons, namely 'the school had the opportunity to acquire computers' and 'teachers were interested', were left out of this analysis because the character of these reasons is somewhat different from the other reasons. Both reasons can be called 'non-educational' reasons for introducing the computer and cannot be seen as a school's aim or strategy to start using the computer. Seen from the perspective of the school, the first reason can be considered as a pressure (and support) for computer use from outside the school. The second reason can be called a pressure from inside the school, from the 'workfloor'. The resulting seven reasons for introducing the computer form two factors, as shown in Table 2.1.

The reliability of the first scale is 0.67 for elementary school, 0.71 for lower and 0.72 for upper secondary school. The second scale has the following reliabilities: 0.45 for elementary school, 0.53 for lower and 0.57 for upper secondary school. The reliabilities of the scales are indicated for the different populations across countries, but within each country the figures are of the same magnitude. The correlation between the two groups of items is 0.40 (in all three populations).

The first factor contains reasons related to the classroom use of computers and is therefore called *'class oriented reasons'*, while the second factor is more related to general purposes at school level of using the computer; this group of reasons is therefore called *'school oriented reasons'*.

Elementary Schools

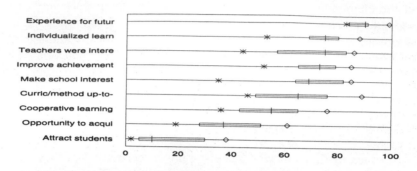

Lower Secondary Schools

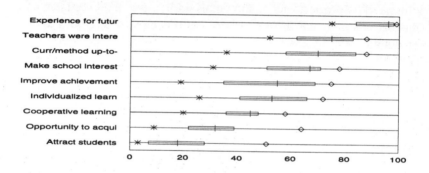

Upper Secondary Schools

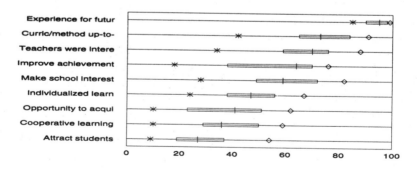

Notes: The complete text for the reasons can be found on page 20.
Legend: 25% Tile [   ] 75% Tile, [   ] Median, * Minimum, ◊ Maximum

Figure 2.1 Boxplots of reasons for introducing computers in computer using schools
the lowest and highest percentage.

LOW	HIGH
ISR / ITA	CBC / NET
FRA / POR	JPN / ISR
FRA / JPN	ITA / NET
FRA / ITA	ISR / USA
ITA / NET	POR / ISR / BFR
FRA / NET	USA / CBC
CBC / NET	BFR / NWZ
ISR / NET	JPN / BFR
CBC / NET	BFR / ISR
FRA / JPN	FRG / AUT / BFR / CBC / NWZ
FRA / GRE	CBC / NET
FRA / LUX	FRG / USA
GRE / SWI	CBC / NWZ
FRG / SWI	CBC / USA
FRG / GRE	FRA / ITA
NET / SWI	ITA / POR
BFL / SWI	CBC / JPN
GRE / SWI	BFR / NET
JPN / POR	BFR / AUT / BFL / CBC / NWZ / SWI
CHI / POR	USA / FRG / ITA
CHI / GRE	CBC / ITA
FRG / SWI	NWZ / USA
CHI / SWI	CBC / ISR
CHI / FRG	CBC / USA
BFL / SWI	HUN / JPN
CHI / NET	IND / ITA
FRG / SWI	ISR / JPN

as indicated by the principal, ranked according to median per cent and countries with

Table 2.1

Loadings for a two factor solution of principals' reasons for introducing the computer in computer using schools

Reasons	Factors	
	1	2
Elementary Schools		
Promote individualized learning	.80	
Improve student achievement	.72	.23
Promote cooperative learning	.64	
Keep curriculum up-to-date	.60	
Give students experience for future		.72
Make school more interes.	.33	.69
Attract students		.56
Lower Secondary Schools		
Promote individualized learning	.84	
Promote cooperative learning	.75	
Improve student achievement	.72	.23
Keep curriculum up-to-date	.47	.29
Make school more interes.	.24	.75
Attract students		.74
Give students experience for future		.53
Upper Secondary Schools		
Promote individualized learning	.81	
Promote cooperative learning	.75	
Improve student achievement	.65	.31
Keep curriculum up-to-date	.60	
Attract students		.86
Make school more interes.		.83
Give students experience for future		.32

To get an impression of the importance of each factor in the different countries, the mean scores on both factors is plotted in Figure 2.2. Because the number of reasons in each of the two scales are not the same, a transformation has been applied so that both class and school oriented reasons are indicated on a ten-point scale.

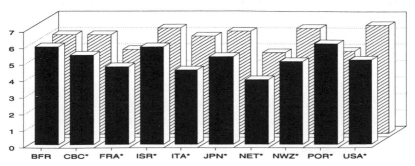

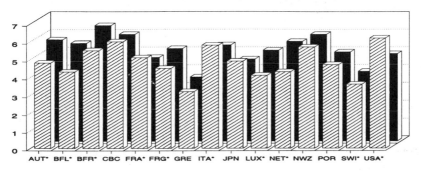

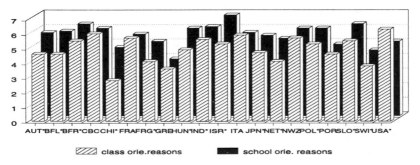

* significant difference between both types of reasons

Figure 2.2 Class and school oriented reasons for introducing computers (each on a 10-point scale) in computer using schools.

Figure 2.2 shows that in both lower and upper secondary schools in (almost) all countries the school oriented reasons were more important for starting to use the computer than class oriented reasons. In elementary schools, the class oriented reasons were more important. As indicated with the asterisks in the figure, in most countries the difference between class and school oriented reasons is significant (t-test with two-tailed probability less than 0.05). Some countries need to be mentioned separately: in Portugal, consistently over all populations the school oriented reasons are more important, while in the United States of America the class oriented reasons for starting to work with the computer at both the elementary and secondary school level are significantly more important, in contrast to most other countries (in lower and upper secondary education). Differences between both types of reasons are relatively small in both France and Italy in lower and upper secondary education and in Japan in lower secondary education.

When discussing all possible reasons for introducing computers above, two reasons were separated from the rest because these had to deal with pressure (from outside or inside the school) for computer use, and not so much with the schools' aims or strategy for introducing computers. In order to explore whether the two 'pressure' reasons ('the school had the opportunity to acquire computers' and 'teachers were interested') are related to the class and school oriented reasons for introducing the computer, the correlations between them are calculated (see Table 2.2).

Table 2.2

Correlation between factor scores (of class and school oriented reasons) and outside or inside pressure in computer using schools

	Pressure	
	Outside	Inside
Elementary Schools		
Class oriented reasons	0.12	0.22
School oriented reasons	0.16	0.16
Lower Secondary Schools		
Class oriented reasons	0.21	0.18
School oriented reasons	0.15	0.15
Upper Secondary Schools		
Class oriented reasons	0.19	0.30
School oriented reasons	0.17	0.17

The results in the table indicate that there is no clear relation across all populations. For elementary schools it was found that pressure from outside the school more often led to school oriented reasons for introducing computers and pressure from inside the school is related to class oriented reasons. This pattern cannot be found in lower and upper secondary education, where outside school pressure is more related to class oriented reasons for introducing the computer. When looking at individual countries, no clear pattern could be found as well.

Reasons for introduction related to years of computer use

At the date of data collection (1989) computers were, in principle, already available in a number of schools for many years. It might be possible that schools that started during the early days of computers in education mention other reasons for introduction than those schools which started working with computers just before 1989. Because developments in the area of computer use were in the beginning not heading towards the use of the computer as a tool (Plomp, 1989), it might be possible that early starters stressed more school oriented than class oriented reasons for introduction.

The correlations between the class and school oriented reasons for introducing computers and the number of years a school works with computers indicate that there is no significant relation between reasons mentioned for the introduction of computers and the number of years a school has been using computers, thus leading to the conclusion that, while the emphasis in educational computer use was different when the early starters began, developments over time did not influence the reasons for starting to work with the computer.

On the other hand, it is possible that reasons for starting to use the computer will differ from reasons for a school to continue working with the computer. Unfortunately, in the Comped project there is not enough information to determine whether shifts in school's aims and strategies for using computers take place over time.

Reasons for use related to type of use

Schools emphasizing class oriented reasons for introduction of the computer probably use the computer for other applications than schools stressing school oriented reasons. As Walker (1986) indicates, the ideological lines followed by the schools in determining the type of reasons why to start using computers determine the type of use of the computer. Traditional educational ideals are represented in computer use directed towards practice of basic skills and fundamental concepts, while progressive educational goals are represented in computer use related to learning to solve problems using software tools and carrying out personal or group projects on the computer.

In order to determine whether there is a relation between reasons of use and types of computer use, the measures developed by Pelgrum and Schipper (1992), which are also discussed in Chapter 3, can be useful. These measures were introduced to characterize two types of computer use, namely 'learning with' (referring to the use of computers as an instructional aid, such as computer-assisted instruction, remedial teaching, enrichment and tests on the computer) and 'learning about' computers (referring to introductory computer education about computers and applications like word processing and databases).

Figure 2.3 shows the relation between the class oriented reasons for introducing computers and the emphasis in the school on 'learning with' computers.

The plots show a trend which indicates that the more schools emphasize class oriented reasons for the introduction of computers, the more they tend to have integrated the computer in their lessons by means of using it as aid in the learning process. The correlation between the two variables is 0.22, 0.38 and 0.34 for the respective populations (across countries). The correlation between the 'learning with' measure and the school oriented reasons for introduction are 0.12, 0.18 and 0.16, indicating a weaker relation. When combining the reasons for introducing computers with the 'learning about' measure, the following correlations are found: the correlation between class oriented reasons and 'learning about' computers is respectively 0.18, 0.13 and 0.16, while the correlation of school oriented reasons with the 'learning about' measure is 0.11, 0.22 and 0.17.

The conclusion from these results is that there is a weak relation between class oriented reasons for introducing computers and applications dealing with 'learning with' computers. Other relations between reasons for use and types of use are far less strong.

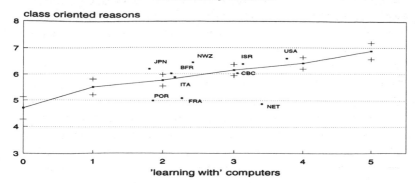

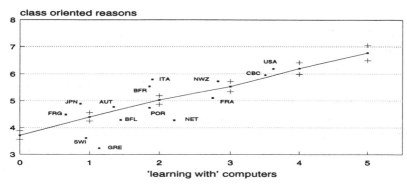

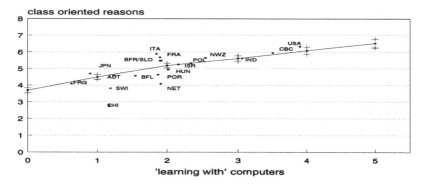

Figure 2.3 Relation between class oriented reasons for introduction of computers and learning with computers (of computer using schools across countries) and scattergram of country means. + = 95% confidence interval.

Reasons for use related to implementation width

One may expect that the more schools mention class oriented reasons for the introduction of computers, the more computer use takes place in different subject matter areas in school. In order to see whether this expectation is correct, a measure of so called 'implementation width' was generated. This measure gives an indication for the number of subject matter areas in which the computer is used in the school. It is not possible to include in this measure the intensity of computer use in the subjects in which the computer is used because these data were not collected in the Comped study. The name for this measure is therefore implementation width and not implementation depth. The measure on implementation width consists of the number of subjects out of the list mathematics, science and mother tongue in which computers are used for instructional or educational purposes. The range of the measure is from 0 to 3.

For each group of schools belonging to a certain degree of implementation width, the mean score on instructional and curricular reasons is calculated. Figure 2.4 gives the results.

For all three populations, the figure shows that the more computers are used in existing subjects, the more class oriented reasons were emphasized when introducing the computer in the school. Insofar as school oriented reasons for introducing computers is concerned, no significant relation was found with the number of existing subjects in which the computer is used.

Responsibility for the introduction

The type and width of computer use in the school and the classroom may be influenced by the person or group of persons who initiated the introduction. As Walker (1986) states, besides advocates of computer use there will be opposition in the school organization against educational innovations.

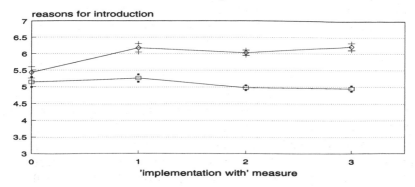

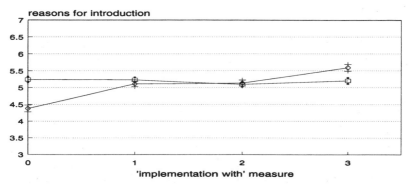

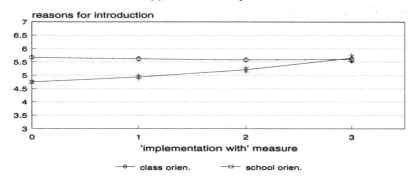

Figure 2.4 Mean score on instructional and curricular reasons for introduction of the computers in computer using schools for the amount of implementation width. + = 95% confidence interval.

The individual or group who initiates the introduction of computers might, in this respect, be very important. A question was included in the principal questionnaire, asking who was responsible for the school getting involved in using computers for teaching and/or learning purposes. The answer options were:

1. outside school authorities;
2. school authorities;
3. a particular department in the school;
4. a group of teachers;
5. an individual teacher;
6. parents;
7. industry;
8. students;
9. others.

Figure 2.5 shows the percentage of principals responding to each answer option. The percentages may exceed 100% because two answers could be given. The category 'others' contains the answer options parents (2% and 1% in lower and upper secondary education), industry (1% in all three populations), students (0%, 1% and 2% in the respective populations) and others/don't know (11%, 6% and 8%).

In all three populations, the most important initiating group is school authorities. Groups of teachers and outside school authorities are second or third most important. In some countries, notable deviations from this general pattern are found. In elementary schools the importance of outside school authorities as the responsible group for initiating computer use is quite high in France (46%), Japan (34%) and the United States of America (40%). In France, this initiating group is the most important one; in Japan school authorities and individual teachers are more important, and in the United States of America outside school authorities is the second most important group responsible for introducing computers (after school authorities).

In lower secondary education, particularly Luxembourg and Greece must be mentioned with percentages of respectively 74% and 55% on outside school authorities being responsible for computer introduction. Although overall not one of the most important initiators, Canada-British Columbia and New Zealand mention the individual teacher as being the second most important initiator of computer use. In upper secondary education, the Federal Republic of Germany and Japan mention (in contrary to the means across countries) a particular department within the school as the most important initiating group, while Italy, the Netherlands and New Zealand stress the importance of a group of teachers.

Elementary Schools   Lower Secondary Schools

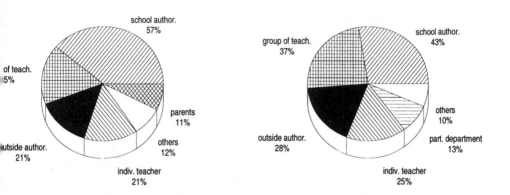

Upper Secondary Schools

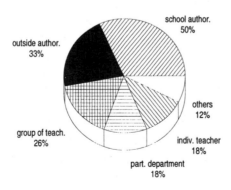

Figure 2.5 Percentage of computer using schools across countries indicating each category of people/agencies responsible for the introduction of the computer.

Whereas principals could indicate a maximum of two individuals or groups as being responsible for the initiation of computer use in the school, in order to be able to address analytical questions, it was necessary to recode these data into one initiating group score for each school. The way of recoding is such that bottom-up initiatives are distinguished from top-down initiatives. The following rule is applied: individuals or groups of people are ordered in a sequence of top-down responsibility and given a score from 1 to 7 (see list in Table 2.3). When a principal indicated that two different individuals or groups were responsible for the introduction, the mean of the scores of both groups were taken, resulting in the matrix in Table 2.3.

Table 2.3

Matrix of recoding initiating groups responsible for introducing computers in computer using schools

Initiating group	Score	Initiating group score						
		1	2	3	4	5	6	7
Outside authorities	1	1	1.5	2	2.5	3	3.5	4
Parents/Industry	2		2	2.5	3	3.5	4	4.5
School authorities	3			3	3.5	4	4.5	5
Particular dept.	4				4	4.5	5	5.5
Group of teachers	5					5	5.5	6
Individual teacher	6						6	6.5
Students	7							7

Within each country, it is useful to examine the resulting measure for top-down initiatives in the sense that the higher the score on the above measure in a country, the more computer use was initiated from the 'bottom' of the school organization (groups of teachers, individual teachers or students). The results are shown in Figure 2.6.

The figure nicely shows that there is a difference among countries in the type of groups who initiated computer use in schools. In elementary education the high score of the Netherlands indicates that in this country responsiblity for the introduction of the computer came more from 'inside' the school than in other countries.

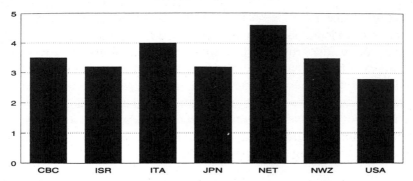

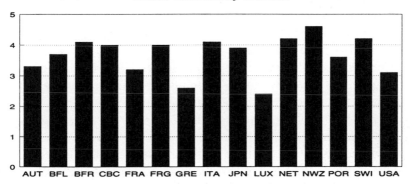

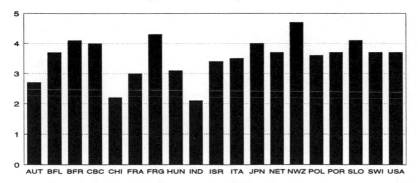

Figure. 2.6 Mean score (recoded) on initiation groups responsible for the introduction of the computer in computer using schools, indicating bottom-up initiatives (only those countries are included with at least 50 valid cases).

In secondary education, countries like Greece and Luxembourg in lower secondary education and China and India in upper secondary education, show clear initiatives from the 'top' of the organization (which is outside authorities, parents, industry or school authorities). In other countries, the groups responsible for the introduction are from the bottom of the organization (particular departments or teachers): examples of these countries are New Zealand, the Netherlands and Switzerland in lower secondary education and the Federal Republic of Germany and New Zealand in upper secondary education.

Responsibility related to years of use

In the early 1980s, when educational computing started to develop, not many countries had policies regarding the introduction of computers in education. These policies were initiated more and more when the relevance and possibilities of computers in education became clearer. One may therefore expect that those schools that were early starters had their initiators among individuals or groups of teachers (and thus scored higher on the recoded initiating scale), while the late starters might have been more influenced by policy from the school or outside school authorities. This possible relation can be studied by correlating the recoded scale of initiating groups with the number of years a school is working with computers.

The correlations between these two variables are for the respective populations -0.08, 0.13 and 0.18, which indicates that there is no (or only a weak) relation between the persons responsible for the introduction and the number of years a school is working with computers.

Responsibility related to implementation width

It is possible that when computer use was initiated by teachers or departments, the actual use of the computer in the existing subjects was greater than when the initiation came 'from above'. On the other hand, the process in the field of computer use in the school since the initiation might be of greater influence on the actual computer use than the person or group who (often a long time ago) started the process and in that sense, there would be no relation between the two variables.

The results show that no strong relationship was found across and within countries between these two variables. This means that our data provide no evidence that the person or group who initiated computer use in the school determined the actual computer use. The strongest relation of this type is found in Switzerland in lower secondary school (r=0.32) and the Netherlands in upper secondary school (r=0.46).

Non-use

In almost all countries participating in the study, there are schools which were not able or have decided not (yet) to start using computers for instructional purposes. When looking at the reasons mentioned in 1989 for not using computers, Pelgrum and Plomp (1991) concluded that the most important reasons were the lack of knowledge of teachers and organizational/financial constraints. In this section we will analyze to what extent schools which did not use computers in 1989 were considering using them for instructional purposes in the near future.

Considerations

Those principals who indicated that their school did not use the computer for instructional purposes in 1989 were asked to answer the question whether the school had considered obtaining computers for
1. teaching students about computers;
2. computer applications in existing subjects;
3. administrative use.

Figure 2.7 shows the results for all three populations on each type of purpose.

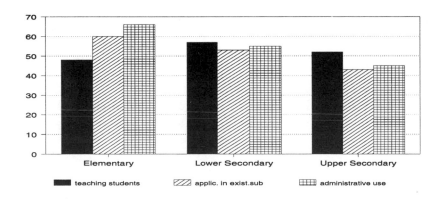

Figure 2.7 Per cent of non-computer using schools which had considered obtaining computers for different purposes.

Teaching students about computers would have been the most important consideration for buying computers for all secondary schools across educational systems, while at the elementary level, administrative use is mentioned as the most likely purpose for acquiring computers. However, in Belgium-French and Portugal, teaching students about computers is mentioned as the most important consideration in elementary education. Computer application in existing subjects is an important consideration in Israel and New Zealand.

In lower secondary schools, only in Austria has this consideration been mentioned as the most important one, while upper secondary schools in Italy indicated this as the most important consideration. Although across countries in upper secondary schools the most important consideration is teaching students about computers, Greece and the Netherlands mention administrative use as the most important possible reason for introducing computers.

Plans for near future

Another question to non-computer using schools was whether non-using schools had plans in 1989 for the introduction of the computer in the educational program within the following three years. Results for this question are presented in Figure 2.8.

In elementary and upper secondary education, non-using schools in 1989 mostly had plans for the introduction of computers in education under discussion or had no plans at all at that time. In lower secondary education, the largest proportion of schools had definite plans. Within countries, sometimes the answers are somewhat more meaningful. In lower secondary education a high percentage for definite plans is reported for Austria (98%), while Greece mentions predominantly no plans in both lower secondary education (68%) and upper secondary education (75%). In the Netherlands a majority of schools in upper secondary education (56%) had the introduction of computers under discussion.

Elementary Schools   Lower Secondary Schools

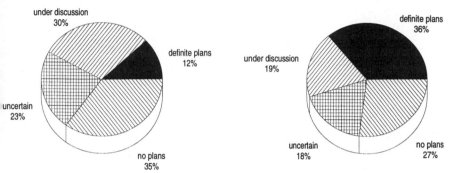

Upper Secondary Schools

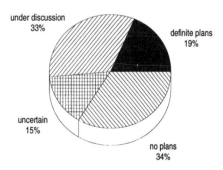

Figure 2.8 Per cent non-computer using schools indicating having plans for introduction of the computer in the period 1989-1992.

Summary

Providing students with experience for their future is at the elementary as well as secondary level the most important reason mentioned by school principals for starting to use computers. In that sense, schools seem to stress the social rationale for using computers (preparing students through computer literacy for their place in society, Plomp and Janssen Reinen, in press), more than emphasizing the pedagogical rationale (which is directed towards using the computer to improve teaching and learning in existing subject matters). This reason is one of the so called 'school oriented' reasons for introducing computers. The other type of reasons that was identified are the 'class oriented' reasons. Although it cannot be said that schools only mention one type of reasons, across countries the school oriented reasons are more important in secondary education, while the class oriented reasons are more emphasized in elementary education.

The relation between the reasons for introducing computers and a number of other variables is studied. The relations found to be noteworthy, deal with the type of use of the computer and the number of subjects in which the computer is used. The results show that there is a relation between class oriented reasons for introducing computers and applications dealing with 'learning with' computers (using the computer as instructional aid, such as computer-assisted instruction, remedial teaching, enrichments and tests on the computer). Furthermore, it was found that the more computers are used in existing subjects (implementation width), the more class oriented reasons were emphasized when introducing the computer in the school.

These results indicate that schools which intended to use the computer for improving the teaching and learning process and not just for a general subject like computer education in daily practice use the computer in more different subjects and for applications directed towards the improvement of the teaching and learning process. These are the schools which deal with the hardest process of introducing the computer: not adding a new subject to the curriculum in which students learn about computers but changing and improving the existing curriculum.

Across countries, school authorities are the most mentioned group that was responsible for the introduction of the computer in the school, while groups of teachers and outside school authorities are also mentioned frequently. When analyzing the influence of the group that was responsible for the introduction on a number of variables, it was found that there is no clear relation between the people responsible and the number of years a school has been using computers. Furthermore, no relation was found between the group who was responsible and the amount of computer use in existing subjects (the implementation width). Most likely, influences other than the individual or group who started the process of working with computers in the school determine the actual use of the computer in the class. Other chapters in this book may shed some light on other factors that influence computer use in the class (like hardware and software availability in Chapter 3 and training in Chapter 5).

Those schools which did not use computers in 1989 sometimes had definite plans for introducing them in the near future (especially in lower secondary education) or had plans under discussion. Possible reasons for acquiring computers would be predominantly for administrative use at the elementary level, while schools at the secondary level mention teaching students about computers most frequently. Again, these results show that schools at the secondary level are more likely to stress the social rationale for using computers than the pedagogical one.

3

Hardware and Software
Provision in Relation to
the Integrated Use of Computers

As indicated in Chapter 1, the availability and quality of hard- and software are seen as major conditions for integrating computers in education. Which type and quantity of computers and which software is needed by schools and teachers depends on the goals which are being pursued. Making students aware of certain basic principles of computer hardware can be achieved with rather simple equipment. However, in order to use computers as an aid in teaching and learning, much greater demands in terms of the quality and quantity of hard- and software need to be fulfilled. Although during the 1980s the developments with regard to the introduction of computers in schools had an explosive character and many schools acquired equipment, still in 1989, in a number of countries computers were not yet available for instructional purposes in all schools (see Table 3.1).

As indicated in Table 3.1, the data from stage 1 of our study show that, in 1989, the situation with regard to the percentage of schools using computers for instructional purposes (teaching about computers or using computers as educational tool) was most favorable in upper secondary schools and least favorable in elementary schools. Although, by 1989, in some countries such as Canada-British Columbia, France and the United States of America, all schools throughout the whole system used computers for educational purposes, this was not yet the case for a number of other countries. Even in a high developed country like Japan, a minority of schools at the elementary and lower secondary levels had access to computers. However, it was also observed (Becker, 1993) that once a few schools in a country started introducing computers, almost inevitably all schools acquired computers within a relatively short time.

This chapter was written by Willem J. Pelgrum.

Willem J. Pelgrum

Table 3.1

Per cent of schools using computers for instructional purposes (adapted from Pelgrum and Plomp, 1991)

Country / Educational System	Elementary Schools	Lower Secondary Schools	Upper Secondary Schools
Austria	-	50	100
Belgium-Flemish	-	78	98
Belgium-French	54	93	93
Canada-British Columbia	99	100	100
China	-	-	64
France	92	99	99
Federal Republic of Germany	-	94	100
Greece	-	5	4
Hungary	-	-	100
India	-	-	8
Israel	62	-	81
Italy	43	58	80
Japan	12	35	94
Luxembourg	-	100	-
Netherlands	53	87	68
New Zealand	78	99	100
Poland	-	-	75
Portugal	29	53	72
Slovenia	-	-	94
Switzerland	-	64	98
United States of America	100	100	100

Notes: - = data not collected.

Figure 3.1 illustrates this trend at the between country level: countries with low percentages of schools possessing computers such as Greece, India, Japan, and Portugal tend to have only recently started introducing computers, while in countries where almost all schools use computers such as Luxembourg, France, and the United States of America, the median number of years since computers were first used was 4 years or more. Hence, we may infer from these data that access to computers is a rapidly changing phenomenon and that it may be expected that in the not distant future, computers will be common in almost all schools.

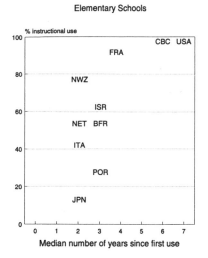

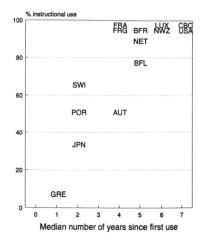

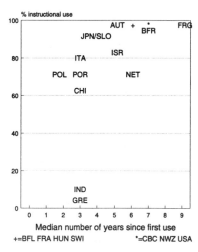

Figure 3.1 Per cent of schools using computers for instructional purposes and median years since start by elementary, lower-, and upper secondary schools per educational system.

A criterion measure for evaluating hard- and software characteristics

In order to evaluate different aspects of hardware and software availability (such as quantity and quality) a criterion measure is needed.

As set out in Chapter 1, a major issue with regard to the introduction of computers in education pertains to the goals which are pursued. This relates to the question of how computers are used and whether, analogous to the use of computers in work settings, the educational use of computers has led to the replacement of old tools and instructional approaches for new ones. Pelgrum and Plomp (1991) showed that this doesn't yet seem to have occurred to a substantial degree. Rather, it seems that the most popular use of computers in secondary education is simply as an add-on to the already existing curriculum in the form of teaching students **how** to use computers. Most secondary schools in many countries created a new subject (informatics) in which students learn about computers. However, the use of computers as tools in existing subjects was, by the end of the 1980s, still not very widespread in lower secondary schools. This can be shown by pointing to Figure 3.2, which contains, for a few countries in which these data could be collected, the estimates of school officials as to the per cent of teachers using computers in mathematics, science and mother tongue and the frequency of computer use based on the ratings given by these computer using teachers themselves.

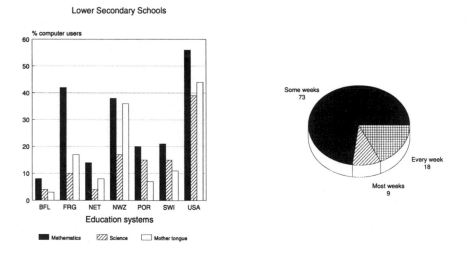

Figure 3.2 Percent of computer using teachers in computer using lower secondary schools for the subjects mathematics, science and mother tongue (according to school officials) and frequency of use by mathematics teachers.

It should be noted that the estimates from school principals in Figure 3.1 are likely to be inflated, not only because principals may be inclined to also count teachers who "talk" about computers instead of using them, but also because teachers from existing subjects are counted who teach *about* computers (which is especially common in Federal Republic of Germany) instead of using computers as tools in their subjects. Furthermore, it should be noted that Figure 3.2 is based on computer using schools and, hence, does not contain estimates for the percentage of all teachers for each subject in a country who use computers. Keeping these caveats in mind, it is evident from Figure 3.2 that the percent of teachers using computers is, in general, quite low and that the group of intensive computer using teachers at best does not exceed 15%. It probably is even worse than that, as more in depth analyses for the United States of America (which has relatively high percentages in Figure 3.1) show that "*the proportion of exemplary teachers* [that is, teachers who integrate computers to a substantial extent] *among all teachers of the studied subjects* [Mathematics, Science, Mother Tongue] *and grade levels is only 3%*" (Becker, 1992).

The limited integration of computers into existing curricula may also be seen as a result of the dominant way of thinking about educational computer use that has prevailed in the past decade. Hebenstreit (cited by Makrakis, 1988) makes a distinction between two main approaches, namely (1) the technical approach, and (2) the pragmatic approach. The first approach advocates the importance of learning about computers (via subjects like informatics) and emphasizes the need for teaching programming, while the second approach emphasizes the importance of learning with computers via applications (by using databases in history and geography, simulations in sciences, spreadsheets in mathematics, etc.). Criterion measures that would reflect this distinction might be useful for evaluating hardware and software characteristics. Such measures were constructed by Pelgrum and Schipper (1992), who analyzed the data collected in stage 1 of the Comped study and demonstrated that an indicator could be constructed for measuring the relative emphasis in schools on learning with and learning about computers. This indicator was based on a number of ratings by school principals regarding the ways computers were used in the school. The items which were rated were: students play games, computer-assisted instruction, demonstration, word processing/desk top publishing, introductory courses about computers, computer science, catching-up/remediation, enrichment, tests on computer. Factor analyses of these ratings showed two clearly interpretable dimensions, which were labelled as *learning with computers* (students play games, computer-assisted instruction, catching-up/remediation, enrichment, tests on computer; further abbreviated as USEWITH) and *learning about computers* (word processing/desk top publishing, introductory courses about computers, computer science; further abbreviated as USEABOUT). The plots in Figure 3.3 offer a basic description of the country positions on these two dimensions. It shows, amongst other things, that across populations a quite consistent picture emerges: Canada-British Columbia and the United States of America are located high and Japan low on both dimensions; Austria, Greece, Switzerland and the Federal Republic of Germany pay much attention to learning about computers, but do not integrate computers to a large extent. The differences between countries in terms of USEWITH are quite systematic: if one correlates the country positions on each dimension between population 1, 2 and 3 the correlations between population 2 and 3 for USEWITH are very high (>.90) and somewhat lower (.75) between population 1 and 2. This means that there is considerable stability across educational levels and countries in the amount of emphasis on computer integration which may point to differences in underlying philosophies about computer related goals. This systematic difference is also, to a lesser extent, the case for USEABOUT (for which the correlations are near to .60).

In analyzing the data that were collected with respect to hardware and software, we will focus especially on the question how these data can shed light on the issue of computer integration (that is, the computer as a tool or learning with computers) versus computer as object of study (learning about computers) and whether there are any indications that the kind of hardware and software provisions are related to these ways of using computers.

Hardware quantity

Type of hardware

In the early 1980s, when the first schools started introducing computers, the available equipment was, compared to the current standards, of low quality. Processing and storage capacities were low, the screen quality usually was bad, and, above all, the machines were difficult to operate, while easy-to-use software was hardly available and very expensive.

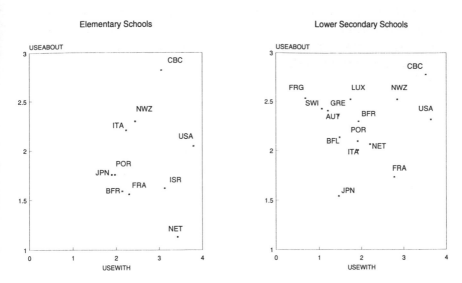

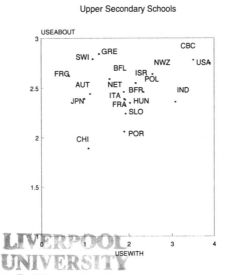

Figure 3.3 Plots of country means for each population on learning with computers (USEWITH) and learning about computers (USEABOUT).

These hardware characteristics as well as the limited availability of sophisticated educational software, almost automatically stimulated educational practices like programming and the development of usually low quality software by teachers. Anderson and Collis (1993) state

"*..one often had to write a program in Basic, Fortran or Pascal to accomplish a computer related task*". This situation changed drastically during the 1980s, when new generations of computer hardware and software appeared in cycles of less than two years. By the end of the 1980s, at relatively low costs, high powered machines were available that could handle very sophisticated software packages. The technological innovations continued, and we are now clearly in the midst of the multimedia-wave and recently many futuristic speculations have been put forward about further revolutionary developments with respect to hardware.

The technological developments with regard to computer equipment in the 1980s certainly had consequences for schools and one may argue that those schools which started recently introducing computers are much better off than the early pioneers who had to invent much of the educational computer-wheel. How these developments in the 1980s have affected the situation in the schools by the end of the 1980s can be illustrated with some results (Table 3.2).

Table 3.2 shows some statistics related to the amount of hardware in schools (in terms of number of computers and the student:computer ratio) as well as the type of equipment which is available. During the data collection, the type of equipment was coded in terms of the following processor types: 1: IBM 8086, etc.; 2: Z-80, etc.; 3: other 8-bit processor; 4: IBM 80286, etc.; 5: Motorola 68000 ; 6: IBM 80386, etc.; 7: Motorola 68000+, etc; 8: other processor types. Categories 1-3 concern 8-bit machines, while categories 4-7 can be characterized as more up-to-date machines. The types of equipment in Table 3.2 are defined as follows: IBM-8-bits: category 1; Other 8-bits: category 2 and 3; IBM-16-bits: categories 4 and 6; Atari/Mac: categories 5 and 7.

Table 3.2 shows considerable variation between as well as within countries in terms of the mean percentage of available equipment in schools. The table shows that, in 1989 in most countries, the majority of equipment consisted of 8-bit computers (IBM-like or other). Only in Japan (in all populations), and upper secondary schools in Switzerland were a substantial percentage of IBM-like 16-bit computers found, whereas the availability of Atari/Mac type of equipment was minor in most countries (with the exception of upper secondary schools in Greece, and lower and upper secondary schools in Switzerland).

Homogeneity of equipment

In order to obtain an indication of the amount of variation in the types of equipment available in schools, we calculated a so-called hardware-homogeneity index which is the variation between the percentages of different types of equipment (in terms of the equipment-types as defined above) in a school. This index is 1 if a school has only one type of equipment and the index reaches a value of 0 if all types of equipment are available in equal proportions. Country means for this index are also included in Table 3.2.

The homogeneity of equipment in schools is relatively low in secondary schools in France, upper secondary schools in the Federal Republic of Germany, lower secondary schools in the Netherlands and upper secondary schools in Slovenia. There is a clear trend within countries that the homogeneity increases from upper secondary to lower secondary and elementary schools. This is not strange, as upper secondary schools started earlier to introduce computers than lower secondary and elementary schools and, hence, one would expect a greater variety of hardware types in these schools.

Student:computer ratio

The student:computer ratio (as shown in Table 3.2) is calculated by taking the total number of students in a school divided by the total number of computers that are available in that school. This is a rough indicator for the accessibility of computers by the student body in the school. It does not indicate how many students actually share computers, because schools may have a policy to restrict access only to certain groups of students or to limit the access-time per student. As was shown by Pelgrum and Plomp (1991) schools usually organize computer use such that 1-2 students (in India 5 and in Poland 4 students) share a computer.

For **elementary schools** the student:computer ratio varies substantially between approximately 15-25 in Israel, Japan, France and the United States of America and almost three to four times as much in countries like the Netherlands and New Zealand. Exceptional is Portugal with a student:computer ratio of 301.

The student:computer ratio tends to be more favorable in **secondary schools** than in elementary schools. There are, again however, large differences between countries, showing that the United States of America and Switzerland have the most favorable ratio while in many other countries the ratio's are almost two to three times as high.

Table 3.2

Mean percentage of available equipment and median student:computer ratio's in computer using schools per country and level

Country/Level	# comp.	Other-8	IBM-8	IBM-16	AtaMac	Hom	Rat
Elementary Schools							
Belgium-French	9	90	10	0	0	.94	28
France	4	95	5	0	0	.91	23
Israel	15	78	20	0	2	.93	25
Italy	4	69	29	2	1	.88	116
Japan	13	44	0	56	0	.90	14
Netherlands	3	83	10	1	6	.91	63
New Zealand	3	87	5	0	8	.98	62
Portugal	4	38	59	3	0	.80	301
United States of America	18	90	8	0	2	.92	23
Lower Secondary Schools							
Austria	9	10	69	19	2	.84	29
Belgium-Flemish	14	32	64	3	1	.77	28
Belgium-French	13	60	38	1	1	.70	34
France	16	73	26	0	0	.55	31
FR-Germany	13	44	44	9	3	.78	47
Greece	7	8	92	0	0	.98	52
Italy	5	67	30	1	3	.89	90
Japan	13	20	0	80	1	.89	143
Luxembourg	22	81	9	11	0	.78	45
Netherlands	19	31	68	1	0	.64	26
New Zealand	18	83	12	1	4	.81	34
Portugal	6	34	63	2	0	.78	287
Switzerland	11	23	30	11	36	.86	21
United States of America	22	88	11	0	1	.86	18
Upper Secondary Schools							
Austria	14	18	61	20	1	.70	46
Belgium-Flemish	14	28	67	3	2	.72	35
Belgium-French	14	51	45	3	1	.69	38
China	22	97	3	0	0	.96	43
France	30	30	56	13	1	.52	26
FR-Germany	15	45	38	13	4	.66	48
Greece	16	21	52	0	27	.69	44
Hungary	18	97	0	3	0	.93	27
India	4	73	26	1	0	.92	95
Israel	23	40	52	6	2	.67	29
Italy	20	11	72	16	1	.72	36
Japan	31	28	0	72	0	.82	32
Netherlands	32	13	81	5	1	.72	34
New Zealand	20	79	12	4	5	.77	38
Poland	10	98	2	0	0	.98	53
Portugal	6	31	67	2	0	.76	289
Slovenia	14	59	23	17	0	.56	50
Switzerland	24	8	42	33	18	.74	21
United States of America	35	76	21	0	3	.75	15

Notes: Other-8: 8-bit machines other than IBM-8 bits; Hom: Homogeneity-index (see text); Rat: Student:computer ratio. The table contains only data for countries with sufficient valid cases (missing cases <20%).

Changes over time

From the outset of this study it was hypothesized that time would be an important factor that should be taken into account in interpreting the situation with regard to the introduction of computers in education. It was not only expected that certain descriptions (for instance, the percentage of schools using computers, available computer types, etc.) would be outdated by the date the results were published, but time was also seen as a variable (closely connected to the construct 'experience' in the conceptual framework) which could play a role in interpreting the results. Therefore, in this section we will examine to what extent time covaries with student:computer ratios and type of equipment.

In Figure 3.4 one can observe that the quantity of hardware (expressed as the median student:computer ratio per country) tends to increase with the number of years of using computers. Although the figure suggests that, in general, obtaining more computers is a matter of time, it also shows that in some countries (like elementary schools in Japan and lower secondary schools in Switzerland) the development was relatively fast, while the progress in other countries (like lower secondary schools in Luxembourg and upper secondary schools in the Federal Republic of Germany) was relatively slow.

The technological developments with regard to hardware quality in the 1980s is reflected in the type of machines available in schools (Figure 3.5): schools which started using computers recently have a higher proportion of 16-bit machines than do schools which started earlier, although, as the figure shows, the recent starters did not acquire only high powered machines (the average percentage is only 35), which is understandable because these machines were still quite expensive in 1989.

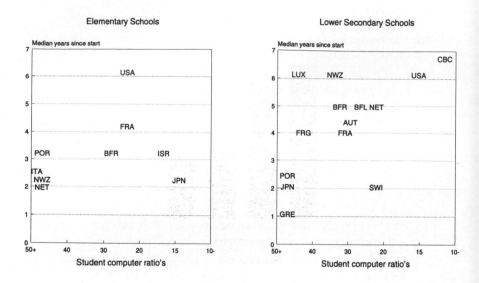

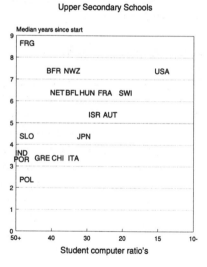

Figure 3.4 Median student computer ratio's and median years of working with computers for computer using schools per country.

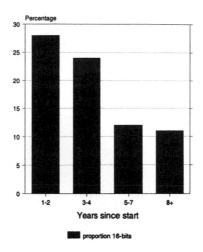

Figure 3.5 Proportion of 16-bit machines plotted against years since start of computer use across countries for lower secondary schools.

Hardware quality, satisfaction and integration

One of the interesting questions related to technological innovations of hardware is whether more sophisticated hardware tends to be associated with a higher level of satisfaction by users and especially whether there are any indications that more sophisticated hardware tends to increase the integrated use of computers in the curriculum of schools (that is, emphasis on learning with computers). Given the design of the study, this question can only be analyzed by comparing groups of schools that are mainly equipped with one particular type of hardware. Moreover, such an analysis can not be conducted within countries because the number of schools which are equipped mainly with one particular type of computer is usually too low. Even across countries, these numbers tend to be low for certain types of equipment (see Table 3.3). Especially for the Atari/Macintosh type of equipment, it was hardly possible to find schools with more than 80% of the equipment consisting of these machines. Therefore, the results in Figures 3.6-3.8 should be interpreted with caution.

Table 3.3

Number of schools in the sample with more than 80% of a particular type of equipment across countries per population

| Population | Type of equipment | | | |
	Other 8-bit	IBM 8-bit	IBM 16-bit	Atari/ Macintosh
Elementary Schools	1439	158	123	30
Lower Secondary Schools	1143	914	294	180
Upper Secondary Schools	1775	976	519	60

Figure 3.6 clearly shows that the percent of computer coordinators who experience the limitations of computers as a serious problem covaries with the type of hardware that is available in the school. This is especially so in schools that are mainly (more than 80% of the available hardware) equipped with 8-bit machines other than the IBM-type. Computer coordinators in these schools mention the limitation of the hardware more frequently as a serious problem than other groups. However, the differences between IBM-8 bits and IBM-16 bits (as well as the differences between the IBM-16 bits group and Atari-MacIntosh group) are hardly noteworthy, which indicates that increasing power of equipment in itself does not seem to directly reduce the number of computer coordinators perceiving the available equipment as being too limited in capacity.

With regard to the comparisons in Figure 3.6, it should be noted that the groups not only differ with regard to the equipment that is mainly available, but also on other characteristics (as illustrated in Figures 3.7 and 3.8) which may affect the perception of problems that occur in introducing computers in the school.

Figure 3.7 shows that elementary and lower secondary schools which differ in terms of availability of one particular type of computer also differ in the years of experience using computers. Elementary schools which mainly possess Other-8-bit machines started, on the average, 4.5 years ago introducing computers, while the schools that mainly possess Atari-Mac types of machines started about 2.5 years ago. For lower secondary schools, the difference between these groups is about 1.5 years. Interestingly, the trend for upper secondary schools is in the opposite direction. This may be due to a renewal effect because these schools started earlier using computers and, hence, may have replaced a lot of the old equipment.

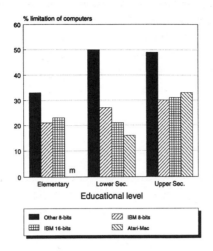

Figure 3.6 Percentage of computer coordinators expressing dissatisfaction with quality of hardware by type of equipment mainly (>80%) available in a school.

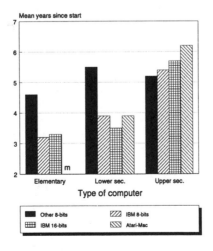

Figure 3.7 Mean year since start by type of equipment mainly (>80%) available in a school.

Figure 3.8 shows that, on average, the schools which mainly possess Atari/Mac types of machines have a relatively low number of computers compared to schools that are equipped with other machines. Hence, although differences in the extent to which computer coordinators experience problems with regard to the limited capacity of hardware can be observed between groups using different computer types, it is not clear whether these differences can be attributed to other factors.

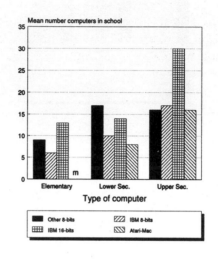

Figure 3.8 Mean number of computers by type of equipment mainly (>80%) available in a school.

Moreover, it should be noted that, in 1989, most respondents appeared to be more concerned with the shortage of hardware than its quality. As further documented in Chapter 4, shortage of hardware is one of the most prominent problems experienced by all respondents.

With regard to the question of whether more sophisticated hardware tends to increase the integrated use of computers, the analyses did not show a clear trend.

Location of computers

From the outset of this study, it was hypothesized that the location of computers may be a complicating factor in accessing computers by teachers and students. Niederer and Frey (1992) state: *"If school computers are available only in specially designed rooms, teachers are compelled to do their teaching in these rooms. This is more likely to preclude a short sequence of instruction involving computers than if computers are on the spot in the classroom".* One may expect that the integrated use of computers is enhanced if computers are located inside, instead of outside classrooms (for instance, in computer labs). Moreover, one might hypothesize that, especially in situations where - due to a lack of available equipment-, only a part of a class can use the computers at a time in a separate room, a possibly complicating element is introduced in the organization of lessons which may lead to withdrawal behavior of teachers in terms of integrating computers into their existing lesson practices. This hypothesis is not very well supported by the available data as 39% of the teachers that use computers in classrooms indicate that the difficulty of the lesson organization increased. In contrast, 33% of the teachers who use computers in computer rooms report this as a difficulty. Rather, it seems that some other problems are more clearly associated with the location of computers: 72% of the teachers using computers in the classroom versus 44% of the teachers using computers in computer rooms indicate that they do not have enough computers, and 30% of the computer-classroom teachers report that they do not have enough space compared to only 13% for the computer-room-teachers.

Table 3.4 contains some overall statistics regarding the location of computers, which shows that, in the majority of schools in almost all countries, computers are mainly located in special computer rooms. Exceptions are elementary schools in Belgium-French, France and New Zealand where, in a considerable number of schools, computers are mostly located in classrooms. There is a clear trend that elementary schools are more inclined to locate computers in classrooms than secondary schools.

One may expect that the location of computers is related to how they are used. If computers are located in classrooms, the number is usually low (about 2-3 on the average) and, consequently, only a few students at a time will be able to use the available equipment. This may lead to more individual approaches compared to situations where computers are placed in special rooms and the whole class can work at the same time.

Table 3.4

Per cent of schools with computers only (100%) and mostly (70%) in classrooms or special computer rooms

Country/level	Location			
	Class 100%	Comp.room 100%	Class 70%	Comp.room 70%
Elementary Schools				
Belgium-French	15	35	16	50
Canada-British Columbia	4	13	13	48
France	47	25	48	30
Israel	3	70	4	88
Italy	13	47	13	54
Japan	4	24	7	60
Netherlands	10	4	12	5
New Zealand	38	2	40	4
Portugal	4	35	5	41
United States of America	6	6	26	23
Lower Secondary Schools				
Austria	1	58	4	85
Belgium-Flemish	6	40	8	73
Belgium-French	12	53	14	73
Canada-British Columbia	3	3	9	54
France	11	41	17	61
Federal Republic of Germany	1	48	1	87
Greece	7	80	8	84
Italy	4	51	5	61
Japan	1	15	1	55
Luxembourg	11	30	26	63
Netherlands	1	28	3	75
New Zealand	4	16	8	70
Portugal	6	37	7	48
Switzerland	8	21	13	52
United States of America	5	9	14	44
Upper Secondary Schools				
Austria	0	57	1	91
Belgium-Flemish	6	36	8	75
Belgium-French	3	61	6	78
Canada-British Columbia	3	3	9	55
China	4	84	4	92
France	20	26	35	40
Federal Republic of Germany	0	29	1	90
Greece	3	87	3	94
Hungary	1	24	3	70
India	5	84	6	85
Israel	4	49	6	78
Italy	1	35	4	70
Japan	1	17	3	68
Netherlands	0	23	3	68
New Zealand	0	20	4	75
Poland	3	61	3	83
Portugal	4	36	7	48
Slovenia	8	21	23	51
Switzerland	4	20	10	66
United States of America	7	2	21	27

In order to investigate whether the location of computers covaries with the way of use in schools, a number of analyses were performed. First, a distinction was made between schools where the majority of computers (more than 70% of the available hardware) was located in special computer rooms and schools in which almost all computers were located in classrooms. A total of 2416 lower secondary schools from all countries (74% of the total sample) fit into one of these categories. For elementary and upper secondary education these figures are, respectively, 1113 (58% of total sample) and 3634 (77% of total sample). It should, however, be noted that the number of lower and upper secondary schools which only have computers located in classrooms is very small (7-8% of the total samples across countries), whereas for elementary schools this figure is 22%. Figure 3.9 presents some statistics taken from the principal and teacher questionnaires regarding the integrated use of computers by schools and teachers depending on where computers are mainly located. Included in the charts are the indicator of integration at the school level by principals (further abbreviated as USEWITH), as well as indicators for integrated use at the class level, namely the average percentage of subject matter topics for which teachers use computers (further abbreviated as TOPWITH), the per cent of teachers indicating student use of tutorial (in the Figure abbreviated as TUTOR) and simulation programs (SIMUL), and the percent of teachers indicating that they use computers for CAI (CAI), remediation (REMED) and/or enrichment (ENRICH). The chart illustrates that schools which mainly have computers in classrooms tend to show more signs of integrated use than schools which have computers located only in special computer rooms. The differences between the groups on each variable in Figure 3.9 are statistically significant for lower secondary schools. This does not hold for elementary schools for the variables USEWITH and TOPWITH, and also not for Tutorial Software, Enrichment and Remediation in upper secondary schools. Especially noteworthy is that teachers who use computers in classrooms tend to use computers much more for enrichment and remediation activities than teachers who use computers in special computer rooms.

These results are rather meaningful and indicate that, although in 1989 it was quite an infrequent practice of schools to locate computers in classrooms, this practice tends to covary with the integrated use of computers.

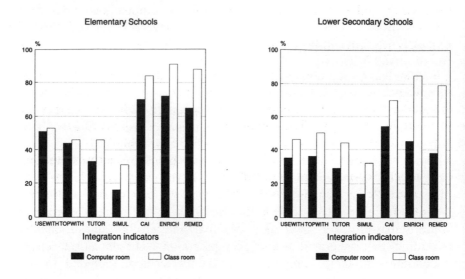

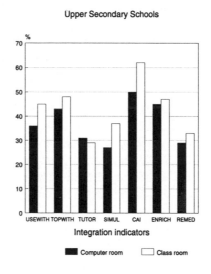

Figure 3.9 Percentage of responses by school principals and teachers on indicators for integrated use of computers if computers are used mainly in classrooms or in special computer rooms.

Especially noteworthy is the finding that teachers who mainly use computers in their classrooms tend to use computers very frequently for remediation and enrichment, which is understandable as these activities can be undertaken by students on an individual basis without disrupting the class activities.

Software quantity and quality

Beside hardware, the availability of instructional tool software is another necessary condition for using computers in schools. Therefore, this survey contained a number of questions about the availability of software in the schools. The computer coordinators were asked to check which of 23 types of software were available in the school.

This list together with the boxplots of the percentages across countries of computer coordinators indicating that a particular type of software was available in the school is presented in Figure 3.10 for each population.

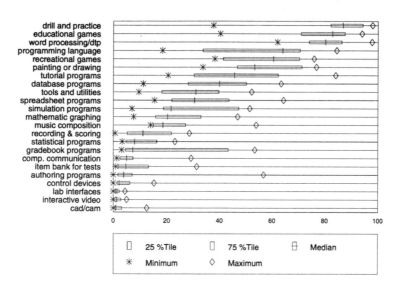

Figure 3.10 (cont.) Boxplots of the country percentages of computer coordinators indicating that a particular type of software was available in the school.

Lower Secondary Schools

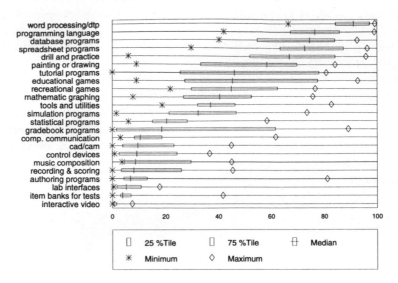

Upper Secondary Schools

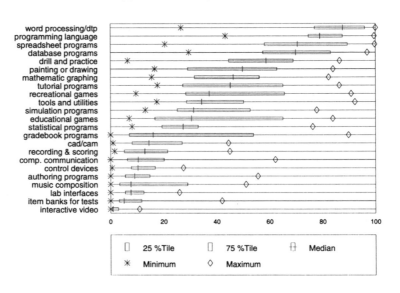

Figure 3.10 Boxplots of the country percentages of computer coordinators indicating that a particular type of software was available in the school.

Figure 3.10 shows that there is considerable variation between countries with respect to the availability in schools of particular types of software. The medians show that educational tool software (drill/practice, tutorial and educational games) as well as general purpose programs (word processing and database programs) are in the top ten of available types of software in all populations. There is a clear difference between elementary education (with drill/practice and educational games at the top) and secondary education (with general purpose and programming languages at the top). Furthermore, it is interesting to note that item banks for testing students (a potentially powerful application of computers) were hardly available in schools.

A very interesting finding is that a factor analysis of the ratings by computer coordinators (from lower secondary schools) of available software types results in clearly interpretable factors (see Table 3.5): General purpose software, Instructional Tool software, Test software, Specific Application software and Laboratory software.

Table 3.5

Loadings for a 5 factor varimax solution of lower secondary school coordinators'
ratings of available software

	Factor Loadings				
Software	1	2	3	4	5
Word processing	.67	.22	-.05	.06	.07
Spreadsheet	.78	.06	.09	.13	.01
Database	.76	.01	.17	.12	.01
Programming languages	.57	.04	-.11	.18	.08
Drill and practice	.04	.59	.03	.36	.04
Tutorial programs	.10	.45	.22	.34	.06
Painting or drawing	.41	.44	.09	.04	.09
Music composition	.11	.56	.13	-.14	.18
Recreational games	.08	.69	.04	.05	-.04
Educational games	.04	.72	.14	.18	.02
Item banks	.03	.06	.64	.17	.09
Record/score tests	.01	.12	.72	.13	.03
Grade book	.01	.18	.68	.12	.04
Simulation	.14	.34	.14	.48	.19
Mathematics graphing	.30	.20	.00	.62	.06
Statistics	.14	.06	.21	.59	-.00
CAI authoring	.11	.04	.22	.56	.03
Autom. data acquisition	-.01	-.05	-.06	.40	.54
Control devices	.07	.10	-.15	.13	.64
Control interact.video	-.05	.07	.19	-.08	.52
CAD/CAM	.23	.05	.30	-.07	.45
Computer communication	.23	.03	.28	.14	.40

Table 3.6

Reliabilities per country for WITHSOFT (WI) and ABOUSOFT (AB) per population

Country/level	WI	AB
Elementary Schools		
Belgium-French	.64	.68
Canada-British Columbia	.40	.37
France	.47	.57
Israel	.55	.72
Italy	.57	.56
Japan	.52	.64
Netherlands	.34	.62
New Zealand	.52	.57
Portugal	.58	.81
United States of America	.39	.70
Lower Secondary Schools		
Austria	.62	.50
Belgium-Flemish	.65	.82
Belgium-French	.61	.80
Canada-British Columbia	.51	.49
France	.45	.61
Federal Republic of Germany	.58	.59
Greece	.71	.76
Italy	.65	.52
Japan	.59	.67
Luxembourg	.38	.88
Netherlands	.52	.58
New Zealand	.49	.57
Portugal	.54	.76
Switzerland	.62	.65
United States of America	.54	.72
Upper Secondary Schools		
Austria	.62	.55
Belgium-Flemish	.57	.64
Belgium-French	.60	.69
Canada-British Columbia	.52	.51
China	.71	.68
France	.65	.62
Federal Republic of Germany	.58	.59
Greece	.10	.71
Hungary	.53	.76
India	.69	.58
Israel	.65	.60
Italy	.47	.61
Japan	.56	.60
Netherlands	.67	.16
New Zealand	.48	.19
Poland	.66	.71
Portugal	.58	.76
Slovenia	.39	.65
Switzerland	.49	.68
United States of America	.52	.58

For the purpose of this chapter, it is particularly interesting to note that this factor solution reflects a distinction between software that is suited for learning with computers (Factor 2, further abbreviated as WITHSOFT) and software which tends to be associated with learning about computers (Factor 1, further abbreviated as ABOUSOFT). Although general purpose software (word processing and data bases) generally is seen as an application tool, this result might indicate that, in 1989, the main focus was still on learning to handle this software rather than applying it.

The result of the factor analysis was used to create the scales WITHSOFT (consisting of items which load higher than .44 on Factor 2, reflecting the availability of software that is suited for learning with computers) and ABOUSOFT (consisting of the items with loadings greater than .44 on Factor 1, reflecting the amount of software for learning about computers). The total score for these items was standardized on a scale from 0 to 100. Most reliabilities of these scales within countries vary from moderate to reasonable (see Table 3.6). Some very low reliabilities (such as .10 for the WITHSOFT scale in Greece-upper secondary schools) are due to a lack of variance in some of the items constituting the scale. However, for analysis purposes, the reliabilities are acceptable, although some caution is required in interpreting the results for elementary schools (as the relatively low reliabilities in Table 3.6 indicate).

Figure 3.11 shows the plot of country means on both scales.

Figure 3.11 shows that in lower secondary education the country means for some countries (New Zealand, Canada-British Columbia, Netherlands and France) are relatively high on both scales whereas other countries are typically high on one type of software (for instance the United States of America is high on WITHSOFT, while Greece and the Federal Republic of Germany have high scores on ABOUSOFT). Thus, the conditions with regard to the integrated use in terms of the availability of instructional tool software in schools seems to be much better in some countries than in others. Hence, one may hypothesize that this may have positive effects on the degree of integration of computers.

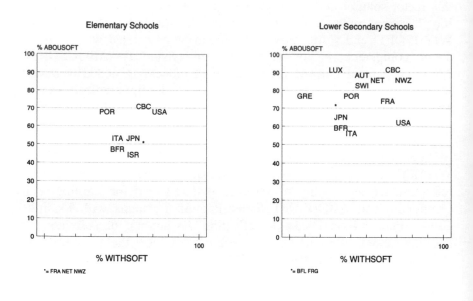

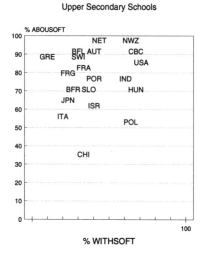

Figure 3.11 Country positions on the scales WITHSOFT and ABOUSOFT (see text).

The tenability of such a hypothesis is confirmed by Figure 3.12, which shows that emphasis on learning with computers at the school level (USEWITH) as well as at the teacher level (TOPWITH, which is the number of subject topics for which computers are used) tends to be associated with the availability of instructional tool software

(WITHSOFT) in the schools. The country means show this association rather clearly.

Despite the fact that schools and countries are quite different in terms of the availability of instructional tool software, there is little indication that the software needs of schools tend to be satisfied more in the countries with greater software supplies. Rather, it seems that the lack of high quality instructional tool software (see Chapter 4) is one of the problems experienced as most serious by a majority of educational practitioners (school principals as well as teachers) around the world.

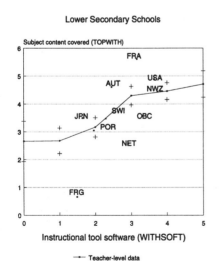

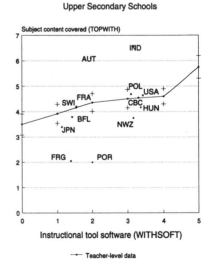

Figure 3.12 Emphasis on learning with computers (mean values) at school level (USEWITH) and teacher level (TOPWITH) plotted against the availability of instructional tool software (WITHSOFT). + = 95% confidence interval.

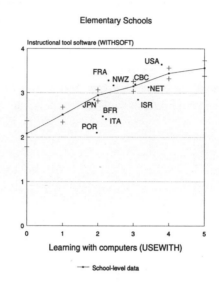

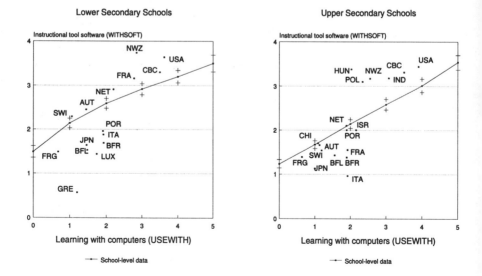

Figure 3.12 (cont.) Emphasis on learning with computers (mean values) at school level (USEWITH) and teacher level (TOPWITH) plotted against the availability of instructional tool software (WITHSOFT). + = 95% confidence interval.

Discussion

The results presented in this chapter show that, in most countries by the end of the 1980s, the introduction of computers in education was well underway. Some countries were still in an early stage of development with a clear emphasis on learning about computers, while in other countries the integration of computers into the existing educational classroom life seems to have developed to a considerable extent. The trends that were presented showed that, although many educational practitioners still experience considerable problems in using computers, certain facilities (such as availability of instructional tool software and location of computers in classrooms) tend to facilitate the educational use of computers. On the other hand, one must also note that some countries lag behind considerably in integrating computers into the curriculum. In the final chapter the question will be addressed as to what implications these findings may have for future action.

4

Implementation and Educational Uses of Computers

The end result of policy decisions and staff development in regard to computer use is its integration into the curriculum, and into daily practice. The complete investigation of computer use requires in-depth observation and interviews. This clearly is not possible in a survey study such as this. However, valuable information can be obtained for determining the broad directions of computer use in schools. For example, one can examine the relative use of computers for drill as opposed to their use as a tool, e.g. word processing; or, one can examine the most salient difficulties encountered in the integration of computers in school life from the point of view of principals, teachers and computer coordinators. Hopefully, such examinations will help in developing policy for future implementation and its improvement.

In a series of survey studies, Becker (1990) examined the development of school computer use in the United States of America. He found an increase in use of computers from 1983 to 1985 and to 1989 (the latter study examined the United States of America results for this survey). However, he concluded that very few teachers or students could be defined as "major users" in 1989. The question of interest is whether other participating countries were in a similar position, or possibly more advanced in the integration of computers into instruction.

In this chapter we examine the integration of computers in the school curriculum. This includes: the use of computers in various subject matters, computer education, how computers are used, and problems encountered in using computers. As an aid for interpreting the findings we also examine: perceived changes due to computer use and expenditure priorities.

This chapter was written by Dan Davis.

Our main emphasis is on providing an estimate of worldwide use of computers, in which we focus on the degree of similarity or dissimilarity among the countries in terms of their emphases.

For each variable we summarize the distribution of results over countries with box plots in which the international median, minimum, maximum, and quartial points are represented. In the rather long lists of uses or subjects we rank the results and present them according to the rank order of the international medians. This is done so that the reader can see the relative importance of the various categories at a glance. The specific results for the participating countries are lost, but in some cases these can be found in the first report of this study (Pelgrum & Plomp, 1991). Also, at the side of some of the plots we present the countries which stand out for the specific variable.

Use of computers in various subject matters

The use of computers in subject matters was examined in two ways: first, the computer coordinator was asked to indicate how many teachers used computers in each of eleven subject matters; second, teachers in elementary schools as well as teachers of mathematics, science, and of mother tongue in lower and upper secondary schools were asked how often they used computers in these three subjects. We first present the results of coordinators, who indicated use of computers at the school level. Then we present the results of teachers, who indicated use of computers at the class level.

The questions for both coordinators and teachers allowed for gradations of use. However, most of the variability was between "no use" and the other categories. As a result, we were able to simplify by presenting percent of schools or teachers reporting at least some use. Conceivably, a country could have high implementation at the school level (most schools report some use in a subject), and low implementation at the class level (few teachers use computers in that subject).

In Figure 4.1 we present the results at the school level, in the form of box plots. For each country we calculated for each subject the percent of computer using schools in which at least one teacher used computers. Then for each subject we calculated the median, minimum, maximum, 25% tile, and 75% tile values over countries. At the right side of each box plot we present the four highest countries in percent of schools using computers, for that subject, in alphabetical order.

Figure 4.1 provides information of use, only in schools where the subject was taught. As a result there will be differences with the information in Table 3.4 of Pelgrum and Plomp (1991) where the system-wide frequency of use is given.

A problem we faced was that for some subjects in some countries very few schools reported teaching a subject, so that the sample size for calculating percent of use was very small. We decided to include data only where at least 25 schools reported. However, in small countries where the population of using schools was very small (around 30 schools), we eased the restriction to at least 15 schools: Luxembourg in lower secondary schools and Greece and Slovenia in upper secondary schools (in Luxembourg and Slovenia the population of using schools was close to that of all schools, but in Greece this represented only about five percent of schools).

The results indicate that in elementary schools the predominant subject matter was mathematics followed by mother tongue and informatics. In lower and upper secondary schools the predominant subject was informatics followed by mathematics and commercial studies.

Worth noting was the relative emphasis of mother tongue and science. A natural expectation just a few years ago would have been for much greater use in science. However, we see that in elementary schools there was much greater use in mother tongue, while in lower secondary schools there was approximately equal use. Only in upper secondary schools was there greater use in science versus mother tongue. The results were apparently due to the increasingly wide spread use of word processors in general and the relative emphasis on the two subject matters in the various grade levels.

Variability among countries tended to be large. For example, in lower secondary schools, computers were used in mother tongue classes in 83% of the computer using schools in New Zealand and in none of the computer using schools in Belgium-Flemish. On the other hand, there was relatively low variability in the most emphasized subjects. In elementary school mathematics, seven of the eight countries reported use in 80% to 91% of the computer using schools. In lower secondary school informatics, twelve of the fifteen countries reported use in 75% to 100% of the schools. And, in upper secondary school informatics, all twenty countries reported use in 67% to 100% of the schools.

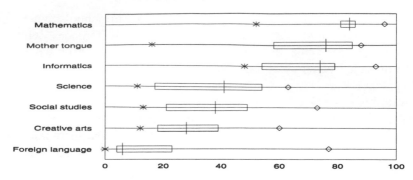

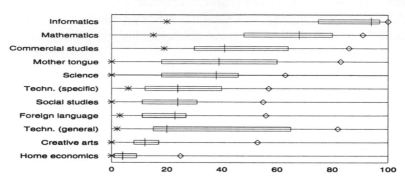

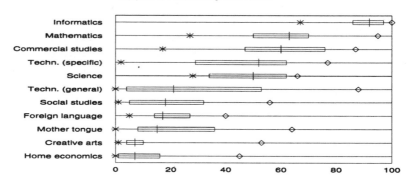

Legend: 25% Tile [ ]   75% Tile, [|]   Median, * Minimum, ◊ Maximum

Notes: + = only five countries with valid data.

Figure 4.1 Percent computers using schools in a country where at least one teacher

Four highest countries

CBC / FRA / ISR / JPN

CBC / FRA / NWZ / USA

BFR / FRA / ITA / NWZ

CBC / FRA / JPN / USA

CBC / FRA / JPN / USA

CBC / FRA / NWZ / POR

ISR / ITA / POR / USA[+]

AUT / GRE / LUX / SWI
FRA / FRG / ITA / NWZ
CBC / FRA / FRG / NWZ
CBC / FRA / NWZ / USA
AUT / CBC / FRA / JPN
CBC / FRA / NET / USA
CBC / FRA / NWZ / USA
AUT / FRA / JPN / SWI
AUT / CBC / FRA / ITA
CBC / FRA / NWZ / SWI
CBC / FRA / JPN / USA

BFL / FRG / IND / ISR
FRG / ITA / NWZ / USA
CBC / FRA / NWZ / USA
BFR / FRA / HUN / SWI
CBC / FRG / IND / ITA
CBC / FRA / HUN / JPN
CBC / FRG / NET / NWZ
BFL / FRA / HUN / NET
CBC / FRA / NWZ / USA
CBC / IND / NWZ / USA
CBC / JPN / POL / USA

Comparison of country profiles

We turn now to the question of uniformity across countries in the relative emphasis of the subject matters. We examine this in two ways:

1. looking at the correlations among countries over the percents of the various subjects;

2. looking at the number of countries agreeing on the highest ranked subjects.

The second way provides a check on the possibility that correlations were inflated by some subjects having zero percent use in all countries.

In the eight countries providing full data in elementary schools, four ranked mathematics first, three ranked it second and one ranked it third. In seven of the eight countries the first two highest ranked subjects were some combination of mathematics, informatics and mother tongue. In the only exception, Israel, foreign language was second after mathematics, and was followed by mother tongue and informatics.

uses computers.

In lower secondary schools informatics was the most emphasized subject in 8 of the 11 countries providing full data over the subject matters. In 8 of the 11 countries informatics and mathematics were the two most emphasized subjects. In the three other countries the emphasis was as follows: in Canada-British Columbia informatics was first, followed by commercial studies; in New Zealand mathematics was first, followed by mother tongue, while in Portugal mathematics was first, followed by commercial studies.

In upper secondary schools informatics was the most emphasized subject in 14 of the 16 countries providing full data, in one country it was ranked second, and in one country it was ranked third. In 13 of the 16 countries the two highest ranked subject matters were some combination of informatics, commercial studies and mathematics. Exceptions are China and India where informatics was ranked first, followed by science just before mathematics and Japan where general technology was first, followed by informatics.

An index of the degree of similarity among countries in their rankings of the subjects can be obtained by correlating percent use over topics for each pair of countries. In Table 4.1 we present a summary of these between country correlations. It can be seen that all correlations were positive and that in lower and upper secondary schools most correlations were significant ($p<.05$). In elementary schools about a third were significant. The two analyses demonstrate consistent emphases of computer use in the subject matters across countries.

Table 4.1

Summary of between-country correlations (of percent of schools using computers, over the subject matters)

Population	Median corr.	Minimum corr.	Maximum corr.	Number of significant corr.
Elementary Schools	.65	.06	.99	9/28
Lower Secondary Schools	.75	.34	.94	41/55
Upper Secondary Schools	.77	.30	.97	99/120

Notes: Corr. = correlations.

"Major" and "Universal" use of computers in the subject matters

We turn to examining the absolute investment of countries in computer use. We define "universal" use of computers in a subject to exist in a country when at least 80% of the schools report computer use in that subject. We define "major" use of computers in a subject to exist in a country when 50% to 79% of the schools report computer use in that subject. The number of countries with major or universal use as a function of subject matter is presented in Table 4.2.

Mathematics and Informatics. Major or universal use was found in most or all countries in each of the three school populations; universal use was found in at least 3 countries in each population. For these subjects, use of computers at the school level could be described as universal over the set of countries in this study.

Mother Tongue and Science. Major use was found in at least 3 countries for each of the 3 school populations. For these subjects, the sample of countries was approaching universal use of computers.

Foreign language. In elementary schools only Israel reported major use; in lower secondary schools Austria and France reported major use; in upper secondary no countries reported major use.

General and Specific Technology. Relatively few countries provided enough data for these courses. For specific technology only the Netherlands among 11 countries reported major use of computers in lower secondary schools while 8 out of 16 countries reported major use in upper secondary schools. In general technology, France reported universal use and Austria, Canada-British Columbia and Italy reported major use out of 9 countries in lower secondary schools; Japan reported universal use and Hungary and Canada-British Columbia reported major use out of 11 countries in upper secondary schools.

Creative arts. Only Canada-British Columbia reported major use - in each of the three populations.

Home economics. No countries reported major use.

We turn now to the question of which countries use computers the most for the different subjects. At the right hand side of Figure 4.1 we have listed the four countries with the highest percent use of computers for each subject matter. We counted the number of times each country appeared over the subjects and it was found that in each of the three school levels Canada-British Columbia and France were the two highest users followed by New Zealand and the United States of America.

Table 4.2

Number of countries with major use and with universal use of computers at the school level (major use - 50% to 79% of schools; universal use - 80% + of schools)

Subject/Level	Number of Countries Universal use	Major use	Number of Countries
Elementary Schools			
Mathematics	7	1	(8)
Mother tongue	3	3	(8)
Informatics	3	4	(9)
Science	0	3	(8)
Social studies	0	2	(8)
Creative arts	0	1	(8)
Foreign language	0	1	(5)
Lower Secondary Schools			
Informatics	10	3	(15)
Mathematics	4	6	(14)
Commercial studies	1	3	(11)
Mother tongue	1	3	(14)
Science	0	5	(15)
Technology specific	0	1	(11)
Social studies	0	2	(14)
Foreign language	0	2	(14)
Technology general	1	3	(9)
Creative arts	0	1	(14)
Home economics	0	0	(13)
Upper Secondary Schools			
Informatics	16	4	(20)
Mathematics	3	12	(19)
Commercial studies	4	8	(17)
Technology specific	0	8	(16)
Science	0	10	(19)
Technology general	1	2	(11)
Social studies	0	2	(18)
Foreign language	0	0	(18)
Mother tongue	0	3	(18)
Creative arts	0	1	(18)
Home economics	0	0	(15)

Computer use at the class level versus the school level

Estimating the percent of teachers using computers (in computer using schools) required random selection of teachers in schools. Unfortunately, complete random selection was not maintained in a number of countries. For this reason, the estimate could be made at the elementary level in three countries, at the lower secondary level in nine countries, and at the upper secondary level in twelve countries. Also, in those countries where random selection of teachers was maintained, we suspect that computer using teachers were more likely to return the questionnaires than were non-using teachers. This would lead to an inflated estimate of percent of teachers using computers.

In Table 4.3 we present the median percents of schools across countries using computers and of teachers using computers. It can be seen that in elementary schools percent use was about the same at the two levels, indicating that use was distributed over most or all of the teachers in computer using schools. This pattern is probably a result of the fact that drill was the predominant use, in which all children were sent to the computer for short periods. On the other hand, in lower and upper secondary schools, the percent use reported by teachers was considerably lower than the percent use of schools. In these levels computer use in the three subjects was restricted to a small group of teachers. For example, in lower and upper secondary schools about 67% of the schools used computers, but of these schools only about 30% of the teachers reported use. If non-computer users were less likely to complete and return questionnaires, then 30% can be viewed as upward biased estimate.

In lower secondary schools, while 7 out of 9 countries reported major or universal use at the school level, only one country (United States of America) reported major use at the class level. In upper secondary schools, 9 out of 12 countries reported major or universal use at the school level, but only 3 reported this at the class level (the Netherlands, New Zealand and the United States of America). It is clear that integration of computers into mathematics, science and mother tongue education at the lower and upper secondary levels had not progressed to include a significant number of teachers.

Table 4.3

Median percent use of computers across countries at the school level and at the class level

Subject/Level	Median-Percent Schools	Median-Percent Teachers
Elementary Schools		
Mathematics	83	83
Science	34	39
Mother tongue	78	83
Lower Secondary Schools		
Mathematics	75	25
Science	37	16
Mother tongue	39	10
Upper Secondary Schools		
Mathematics	64	31
Science	54	21
Mother tongue	18	4

Use of computers in Specific Mathematics, Science and Mother Tongue Topics

Subject matter teachers in lower and upper secondary schools, and class teachers in elementary schools were asked to indicate whether computers were used for selected topics within mathematics, science, and mother tongue. In Tables 4.4, 4.5, and 4.6 we present median percent use for each topic and rank the topics according to the median. Because relatively few teachers used computers in lower and upper secondary schools, we were faced with many cases of low sample size. We present results only for countries where at least 25 teachers responded and where at least three countries met this criterion. Also, teachers were not asked to indicate whether the topic was taught. Therefore, the median percent of teachers presented for a particular topic indicates the likelihood of encountering use of computers in that topic over all computer using teachers.

Use of computers in mathematics education

In this section we examine use of computers in various mathematics topics. The first section of Table 4.4 shows the percent of teachers reporting use in general mathematics topics. The following sections of Table 4.4 present percent use of computers in sub-topics within each of the general topics.

General mathematics topics (Table 4.4a). In elementary schools 78 percent of the teachers reported use of computers in arithmetic and about a third reported use in measurement and geometry. In lower secondary schools 70, 61 and 59 percent of teachers reported use in arithmetic, algebra, and geometry, in that order. In upper secondary schools, about half of the teachers reported use in algebra and elementary functions; followed by sets and relations and geometry with a reported use of about 40%; and, about a third reported use in probability/statistics.

From the point of view of sub-topics taught in all populations we see that for geometry most use was in lower secondary schools: 59% versus 30% and 37% in elementary and upper secondary schools. For algebra, virtually no use was made in elementary schools and somewhat greater use was made in lower versus upper secondary schools: 61% versus 51%. For probability/statistics, use increased from being virtually nil in elementary schools to a maximum of 30% in upper secondary schools.

Arithmetic (Table 4.4b). In both elementary and lower secondary schools most teachers reported use of computers in natural/whole numbers and in common fractions. About half of elementary and about a third of lower secondary teachers reported use of computers in teaching decimal fractions. On the average, teachers indicated using computers in two of the seven topics in elementary schools and in two of the eight topics in lower secondary schools. (Based on median percents shown at the bottom of each list of topics.)

Algebra (Table 4.4c). In lower secondary schools, teachers were most likely to use computers for instruction of integers and for equations and inequalities (about 40%). On the average, computers were used in two of the eight topics. In upper secondary schools, the emphasis was on equations and inequalities with 69% of teachers reporting use of computers.

We also present, without comment, results for measurement (Table 4.4d), geometry (Table 4.4e), and functions (Table 4.4f).

Table 4.4

Median percent of computer-using mathematics teachers across countries reporting computer use in various topics

4.4a General Topics

Elementary Schools	%	Lower Secondary Schools	%	Upper Secondary Schools	%
Arithmetic	78	Arithmetic	70	Algebra	51
Measurement	35	Algebra	61	Elementary functions	48
Geometry	30	Geometry	59	Sets, relations	42
Probability	6	Measurement	28	Geometry	37
Algebra	2	Probability	19	Probability	30
				Number systems	21
				Finite mathematics	4
BFR, CBC, FRA, ISR, JPN NET, NWZ, USA**		AUT, FRA, FRG, JPN, NWZ, SWI, USA**		BFL, FRA, FRG, HUN, IND, JPN, NWZ, POR, SWI**	

Notes: * = The numbers in parentheses are: minimum, median, and maximum of median percent topics per country in which computers were used. ** = Countries included in calculations.

4.4b Arithmetic

Elementary Schools	%	Lower Secondary Schools	%
Natural and whole numbers	86	Natural and whole numbers	71
Common fractions	62	Common fractions	71
Decimal fractions	52	Decimal fractions	34
Number theory	17	Powers and exponents	27
Ratio, proportion, percentage	9	Ratio, proportion, percentage	24
Powers and exponents	2	Square roots	16
Square roots	2	Number theory	12
		Dimensional analysis	0
(21, 27, 36)*		(23, 31, 45)*	
BFR, ISR, JPN, NWZ, USA**		AUT, FRA, NWZ, SWI, USA**	

Notes: * = The numbers in parentheses are: minimum, median, and maximum of median percent topics per country in which computers were used. ** = Countries included in calculations.

4.4c Algebra

Lower Secondary Schools	%	Upper Secondary Schools	%
Integers	42	Equations and inequalities	69
Equations and inequalities	41	Polynomials	40
Formulas	34	Systems of equations	35
Relations/functions	30	Roots and radicals	33
Rationals	18	Matrices	24
Polynominals	14	Quotients of polynominals	13
Integer exponents	7		
Finite sets	0		
(20, 24, 39)*		(27, 38, 41)*	
AUT, FRA, JPN, NWZ, SWI, USA**		FRA, HUN, IND, JPN, SWI**	

Notes: * = The numbers in parentheses are: minimum, median, and maximum of median percent topics per country in which computers were used. ** = Countries included in calculations.

4.4d Measurement

Elementary Schools	%		
Estimation	57		
Standard measurement units	40		
Determination of measures	36		
Approximation	11		
(27, 34, 42)*			
ISR, JPN, NWZ, USA**			

Notes: * = The numbers in parentheses are: minimum, median, and maximum of median percent topics per country in which computers were used. ** = Countries included in calculations.

4.4e Geometry

Elementary Schools	%	Lower Secondary Schools	%	Upper Secondary Schools	%
Classification	42	Coordinates	40	Trigonometry	50
Geometric construction	26	Geometric construction	34	Analytic plane	
Congruence/plane fig.	22	Pythagorean triangle	29	geometry	43
Properties/plane fig.	17	Properties/plane fig.	28	Vector methods	33
Similarity/plane fig.	16	Spatial visualisation	26	Euclidean geometry	21
Spatial visualisation	16	Classification	18		
Coordinates	12	Similarity/plane fig.	11		
Orientation	6	Congruence/plane fig.	8		
Informal transformation	6	Orientation	8		
Solids (symmetry)	3	Simple deductions	6		
Simple deductions	0	Solids (symmetry)	4		
Pythagorean triangle	0	Informal transformation	2		
(11, 16, 22)*		(15, 20, 21)*		(34, 38, 41)*	
BFR, ISR, JPN, NWZ, USA**		AUT, FRA, JPN, NWZ, SWI**		FRA, HUN, IND, JPN, SWI**	

Notes: * = The numbers in parentheses are: minimum, median, and maximum of median percent topics per country in which computers were used. ** = Countries included in calculations.

4.4f Functions

Upper Secondary Schools	%
Elementary functions	48
Properties of functions	42
Integration	34
Limits and continuity	29
Differentiation	24
Application of derivative	16
Application of integration	13
Techniques of integration	10
Differential equations	5
(21, 24, 27)*	
BFL, FRA, HUN, IND, JPN, NWZ, SWI**	

Notes: * = The numbers in parentheses are: minimum, median, and maximum of median percent topics per country in which computers were used. ** = Countries included in calculations.

Use of Computers in Science Topics

In Table 4.5 we present data provided by science teachers concerning their use of computers. There was negligible use in elementary schools. In lower and upper secondary schools most use was in physics (73% of teachers and 52% of teachers, respectively). There was relatively little use in biology - about 25% in these populations.

Within physics, in lower secondary schools the clear emphasis was electrical current (Table 4.5b); in upper secondary schools use occurred in a wide variety of topics. In earth sciences in elementary schools (Table 4.5c), the only use was in the study of the solar system.

Table 4.5

Median of percent computer-using science teachers across countries reporting computer use in various topics

4.5a General Topics

Elementary Schools	%	Lower Secondary Schools	%	Upper Secondary Schools	%
1 Earth science	12	1 Physics	73	1 Physics	52
2 Biology	5	2 Earth science	42	2 Chemistry	33
3 Physics	3	3 Chemistry	38	3 Biology	22
4 Chemistry	1	4 Biology	27	4 Earth science	2
BFR, CBC, FRA, ISR, JPN, NET, NWZ, USA**		AUT, FRA, JPN, USA**		CBC, FRA, HUN, IND, JPN, NWZ, POL, SWI, USA**	

Notes: * = The numbers in parentheses are: minimum, median, and maximum of median percent topics per country in which computers were used. ** = Countries included in calculations.

4.5b Physics

Lower Secondary Schools	%	Upper Secondary Schools	%
Current electricity	67	Time and movement	46
Measurement	36	Wave phenomena	44
Forces	21	Measurement	32
Time and movement	15	Dynamics	23
Light	15	Vibration and sound	22
Change of state	8	Forces	22
Energy	7	Kinetic theory	21
		Light	19
		Energy	19
		Electromagnetism	19
		Molecular/nuclear physics	16
		Static electricity	15
		Current electricity	14
		Electronics	12
		Introductory heat	10
		Change of state	10
		Spectra	8
		Machines	8
		Mechanics of fluids	4
		Theoretical physics	4
(7, 13, 13)*		(15, 20, 28)*	

FRA, JPN, USA**	FRA, HUN, IND, JPN, POL, SWI, USA**

4.5c Earth science

Elementary Schools	%
Solar system	66
Stellar system	8
Meteorology	8
Earths constitution	6
Physical geography	6
Soil sciences	2
(20, 22, 22)*	

JPN, NWZ, USA**

Notes: * = The numbers in parentheses are: minimum, median, and maximum of median percent topics per country in which computers were used. ** = Countries included in calculations.

Computer Use in Mother Tongue Education

In Table 4.6 we present the percent of mother tongue teachers reporting use of computers in various topics. In elementary schools there was a clear emphasis on reading skills followed by written composition and writing skills. However, in lower secondary schools there was a clear emphasis on written composition followed by writing skills. In both populations little was done with oral communication. The emphasis on literature increased from only 7% reporting use in elementary schools to 21% in lower secondary schools.

There was no consistent pattern over the topics in elementary schools: Belgium-French, United States of America, and Israel emphasized reading first, followed by one of the writing topics in the case of Belgium-French and the United States of America, and followed by linguistics/grammer in the case of Israel. New Zealand emphasized the two writing activities followed by reading; the Netherlands emphasized writing skills followed by linguistics/grammer.

On the other hand, in lower secondary schools, countries generally agreed in the ranking of the topics: four of the five countries clearly emphasized written composition which was always followed by writing skills (Canada-British Columbia, New Zealand, Switzerland, United States of America). In France there was a strong emphasis on linguistics/grammer which was followed by reading skills.

Table 4.6

Percent computer-using mother tongue teachers reporting use in various topics

Elementary Schools	%	Lower Secondary Schools	%
Reading skills	63	Written composition	78
Written composition	43	Writing skills	53
Writing skills	40	Linguistics/grammar	41
Linguistics/grammar	35	Reading skills	38
Literature	7	Literature	21
Oral communication	6	Oral communication	5
(20, 29, 38)*		(26, 32, 41)*	
BFR, ISR, JPN, NET, NWZ, USA**		CBC, FRA, NWZ, SWI, USA**	

Notes: * = The numbers in parentheses are: minimum, median, and maximum of median percent topics per country in which computers were used. ** = Countries included in calculations. Upper secondary schools not included because only two countries with sufficient valid cases available.

Computer Education

In this section we examine:

1. The context of computer education (in a special course versus various subject matter courses).

2. Topics taught in computer education (Computers and Society-4 topics; Applications-14 topics; Problem Analysis and Programming-5 topics; Principles of Hardware and Software-3 topics).

3. Software use in computer education (students' use of 21 types of software).

4. Frequency of computer use in computer education.

Context of Computer Education

In both lower and upper secondary education most countries reported that most of the computer education instruction took place in a separate course. The subject matter most used as the context for computer education in both populations was mathematics (median ≈ 5%). All the other subjects were rarely the context for most computer education (median ≈ 0%). It is interesting to note that little computer education occurred in science as compared to technology and commercial studies.

France, Japan and Italy stand out in both populations as providing most computer education in subject matter courses:

France-lower secondary: general technology (54%), mathematics (13%), separate course (10%); upper secondary : commercial studies (42%), separate course (25%), specific technology (15%).

Japan-lower secondary: separate course (33%), general technology (30%), mathematics (24%); upper secondary: separate course (30%), commercial studies (28%), mathematics and general technology (18%).

Italy-lower secondary: mathematics (46%), general technology (39%), separate course (8%); upper secondary: mathematics (63%), separate course (25%).

Also, notable are Portugal and the United States of America. Portugal was the only country in which a significant amount of computer education occurred in informal frameworks (30% of lower secondary schools). In the United States of America about half the computer education occurred in a separate course with the remainder taking place in mathematics, mother tongue, commercial studies and "other".

Topics Taught in Computer Education

Computer education teachers in lower and upper secondary schools and class teachers in elementary schools were asked to indicate which of a set of topics were taught by them. The topics were divided into four areas: computers and society, applications, problem analysis and programming and principles of hardware and software structure.

Computers and Society

The subtopics included in this topic are: history/evolution of computers, relevance of computers, impact of computer applications, ethical issues.

The results in Figure 4.2 indicate that in elementary schools these four topics were rarely taught. There were no countries in which more than 24% of schools reported instruction in any of the four topics. Ethical issues was the least taught topic in all three school populations: the international medians were 8%, 26%, and 30% of respectively elementary, lower secondary, and upper secondary schools. The three remaining topics were not very different in the degree to which they were taught in either lower or upper secondary schools. However, history/evolution was the most taught topic in upper secondary schools (median = 55%), while impact of computer applications and relevance of computers were the most taught in lower secondary schools (median = 45%).

The particularly low percent of schools dealing with ethical issues concerning copyright and privacy is troubling since these are of particular importance in computer use.

From the list of four highest countries it is seen that those most emphasizing these topics included Canada-British Columbia, France, New Zealand, and the United States of America in elementary schools; Austria in lower secondary schools; and New Zealand in upper secondary schools.

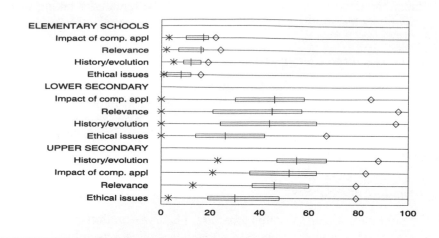

Legend: 25% Tile [   ]   75% Tile, [   ]   Median, * Minimum, ◊ Maximum.

Figure 4.2 Computers and Society: percent of teachers reporting that a topic is taught.

Applications which were taught as part of computer education

In the first part of Figure 4.3 we present box plots for the applications which were most taught as part of computer education. In the second part we list all 14 applications according to the size of the international medians.

Word processing. This was clearly the application most taught over the three school populations. It was well above all other topics in lower and upper secondary schools with medians of 79% and 63% respectively; in elementary schools its median, 34%, was lower than that for games, but the overlap of the two distributions was high and they both stood out above the other applications.

Drawing/painting and Educational/recreational games. Each of these was among the first three applications in elementary and lower secondary schools, but were fourth and fifth in upper secondary schools.

Database and Spreadsheets. These were the second and third most taught applications in upper secondary schools and were fourth and fifth in lower secondary schools. There was very little teaching of these topics in elementary schools.

Models and simulation. This application was taught in around 10% of schools in each of the three school populations.

Four highest countries

CBC / FRA / JPN / NWZ
CBC / FRA / NWZ / USA
BFR / CBC / FRA / USA
CBC / JPN / NWZ / USA

AUT / CBC / GRE / USA
AUT / CBC / GRE / NWZ
AUT / GRE / ITA / USA
AUT / CBC / GRE / USA

CHI / HUN / NWZ / SLO
AUT / CHI / NWZ / POR
HUN / NWZ / POR / SLO
AUT / CBC / FRG / NWZ

The following eight remaining applications were rarely taught in the three school populations: telecommunications/networks, authoring languages, statistical applications, CAD/CAM/robotics, music generation/applications, scanning/image processing, laboratory instrumentation, artificial intelligence.

The range in percent of teachers teaching a particular application tended to be large: for example, the percent of upper secondary teachers reporting instruction in word processing varied from 15% in China to 99% of teachers in New Zealand. Of interest are topics which were rarely taught in most countries, but were taught in a significant number of schools in a few countries. For example, in upper secondary schools laboratory instrumentation was rarely taught in all countries but Japan, where 22% of teachers reported teaching it. In telecommunication/networks Canada-British Columbia and New Zealand stand out with 34% and 48% of teachers reporting instruction. In lower secondary schools almost all countries reported that less than 10% of teachers taught CAD/CAM/robotics versus Austria with 36%.

The countries most emphasizing instruction in computer applications were Canada-British Columbia and New Zealand in elementary schools; Austria and Canada-British Columbia in lower secondary schools; and Canada British-Columbia, Slovenia and New Zealand in upper secondary schools.

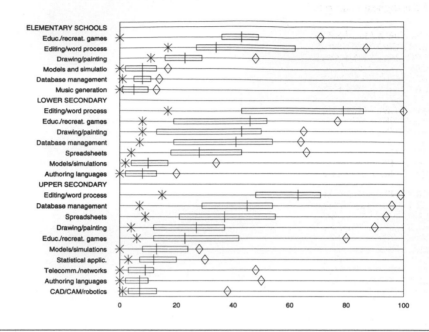

Legend: 25% Tile [   ] 75% Tile, [|] Median, * Minimum, ◊ Maximum

Median Percentages

Elementary Schools	%	Lower Secondary Schools	%	Upper Secondary Schools	%
Educ./recreat. games	43	Editing/word process	79	Editing/word process	63
Editing/word process	34	Educ./recreat. games	46	Database management	45
Drawing/painting	23	Drawing/painting	43	Spreadsheets	37
Models and simulation	8	Database management	41	Drawing/painting	27
Database management	8	Spreadsheets	28	Educ./recreat. games	23
Music generation, appl.	5	Models and simulation	10	Models and simulation	13
Telecom/networks	3	Authoring languages	8	Statistical application	12
Spreadsheets	3	Statistical application	5	Telecom/networks	9
Authoring languages	2	Telecom/networks	4	Authoring languages	7
Scanning/image process	1	Music generation, appl.	4	CAD/CAM/robotics	7
Statistical application	1	CAD/CAM/robotics	4	Artificial intell.	3
Artificial intell.	0	Scanning/image process	2	Music generation, appl.	3
Laboratory instrument	0	Laboratory instrument	1	Scanning/image process	3
CAD/CAM/robotics	0	Artificial intell.	1	Laboratory instrument	2

Figure 4.3 Computer applications: percent of computer education teachers across countries reporting that an application is taught and all 14 applications ranked according to size of international medians (including four countries with highest %).

Four highest countries

CBC / FRA / ISR / NWZ
BFR / CBC / JPN / NWZ
CBC / FRA / JPN / NWZ
CBC / JPN / NWZ / USA
BFR / CBC / ISR / NWZ
CBC / FRA / JPN / NWZ

AUT / CBC / LUX / SWI
AUT / NET / SWI / USA
AUT / NWZ / POR / SWI
AUT / CBC / GRE / LUX
AUT / CBC / NET / SWI
JPN / NET / NWZ / USA
CBC / GRE / JPN / LUX

CBC / NWZ / SLO / USA
AUT / BFL / CBC / NWZ
CBC / NWZ / POL / SWI
HUN / NWZ / POL / SLO
HUN / IND / POL / SLO
FRG / HUN / ITA / NWZ
CHI / HUN / IND / ITA
BFL / CBC / NWZ / USA
BFR / CBC / JPN / SLO
AUT / JPN / NWZ / SLO

Problem Analysis and Programming

The subtopics included in this topic were: general concepts, general procedures, structure of programs, programming languages, problem analysis.

As expected, these five topics were rarely taught in elementary schools and were most often taught in upper secondary schools (Figure 4.4a).

Programming languages and general concepts (e.g. file, variable) were the first and second most taught topics in both lower and upper secondary schools (over 80% of upper secondary and over 40% of lower secondary teachers).

Program structure (e.g. input, output) and problem analysis (e.g. flowchart, algorithms) were the next most taught topics. Program structure was more emphasized in lower secondary schools while problem analysis was more emphasized in upper secondary schools.

General procedures such as debugging was the least emphasized topic in both lower and upper secondary schools.

The countries most emphasizing these topics were Belgium-French and the United States of America in elementary schools; Greece and Italy in lower secondary schools; and New Zealand in upper secondary schools.

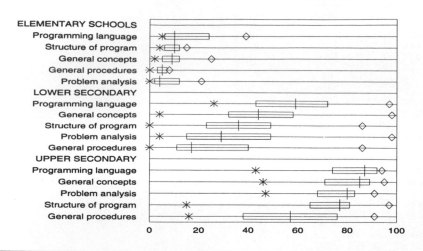

Figure 4.4a Problem analysis and programming: percent of teachers reporting that a
with highest percent.

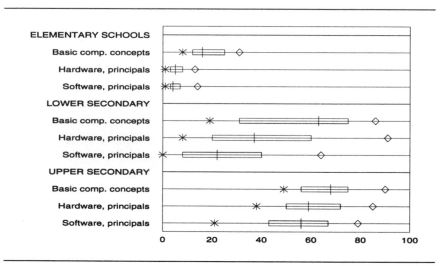

Legend: 25% Tile [   ] 75% Tile, [|] Median, * Minimum, ◊ Maximum.
Figure 4.4b Principles of hardware and software: percent of teachers reporting that a
with highest percent.

Four highest countries

BFR / FRA / JPN / USA
BFR / CBC / ISR / USA
BFR / FRA / JPN / USA
BFR / JPN / NWZ / USA
BFR / CBC / FRA / NWZ

AUT / BFR / GRE / ITA
AUT / GRE / ITA / USA
AUT / BFL / GRE / ITA
BFL / BFR / GRE / ITA
CBC / GRE / ITA / USA

AUT / NWZ / POL / SLO
FRG / HUN / NWZ / POL
BFR / HUN / POL / SLO
CBC / FRG / HUN / NWZ
CBC / CHI / FRG / NWZ

topic is taught and four countries

Four highest countries

CBC / JPN / NWZ / USA
BFR / CBC / JPN / USA
BFR / CBC / JPN / USA

BFL / GRE / ITA / NWZ
AUT / BFL / GRE / ITA
AUT / BFL / GRE / USA

IND / JPN / NWZ / SLO
HUN / ITA / NWZ / SLO
AUT / HUN / ITA / NWZ

topic is taught and four countries

Principles of Hardware and Software Structure

The subtopics included in this topic are: basic concepts, hardware, software.

In Figure 4.4b it can be seen that in all school populations the topic most taught was basic concepts, followed by hardware principles and then software principles. The countries most emphasizing these topics were Canada-British Columbia, Japan and the United States of America in elementary schools; Belgium-Flemish and Greece in lower secondary schools; and New Zealand in upper secondary schools.

Comparison of Country Profiles over all 26 Topics.

In elementary schools, in all eight countries word processing was ranked first or second (four for each). Educational/recreational games was ranked first by four countries; second by two countries; and, third by one country.

In nine of the fourteen countries reporting in lower secondary schools word processing was ranked first. It was ranked second by one country. Programming languages was ranked among the first three emphasized topics in nine countries.

In upper secondary schools twelve of the nineteen countries ranked programming languages as the most taught topic. An additional four countries ranked it second or third. All countries except for France most strongly emphasized the five programming and analysis topics. France emphasized applications.

These results show that in all three populations there was similar emphasis among the topics. This is reinforced by the intercorrelations, shown in Table 4.7, of the percentage use between countries over the 26 topics. In all three populations all correlations were positive and most were significant.

Table 4.7
Summary of between country correlations (of percent of teachers teaching a topic over 26 topics)

Population	Median corr.	Minimum corr.	Maximum corr.	Number of significant corr.
Elementary Schools	.75	.27	.96	25/28
Lower Secondary Schools	.63	.18	.91	79/91
Upper Secondary Schools	.82	.53	.95	171/171

Notes: Corr. = correlations.

Students' Use of Software

Computer education teachers and elementary school teachers were asked to indicate whether their students used various types of software from a list of 21.

In Table 4.8a it can be seen that in elementary schools most use was of drill programs (median = 71% of teachers).

In lower secondary schools most use was of word processing programs (77%).

In upper secondary schools most use was of Basic and word processing programs (about 55% of teachers reported use of each).

It is interesting to note that relatively little use was made of tutorial programs (35%, 27% and 19% in elementary, lower and upper secondary schools, respectively).

Basic was still the predominant programming language, especially in lower secondary schools where 48% of teachers reported use by students (as opposed to Logo with 31% and other languages with 3%). As mentioned above, in upper secondary schools Basic was the most used software (56% versus 34% for other languages and 7% for Logo). Even in elementary schools there was significant use of Basic (18% versus 22% for Logo and 2% for other programming languages).

In all three populations there was virtually no use made of: lab interfaces, interactive video, CAD/CAM, computer communication, statistical programs, control devices, music composition.

Some notable exceptions were in lower secondary schools: 34% use of CAD/CAM in Austria, 20% computer communication in Canada-British Columbia; in upper secondary schools: 21% use of control devices and 26% use of computer communication in New Zealand.

The countries reporting most use over all the software types were: the United States of America and New Zealand in elementary schools; Austria and the United States of America in lower secondary schools; and New Zealand, Canada-British Columbia, and Hungary in upper secondary schools.

Comparison of country profiles

Almost all between-country correlations were positive and most were significant (Table 4.8b). It is clear that there was uniformity among the countries in their emphases on computer program use.

Table 4.8a

Median percent of teachers across countries reporting software use by their students and four countries with highest percent

Software/Level	Median	Minimum	Maximum	Four highest countries
Elementary Schools				
Drill/practice	71	52	88	FRA ISR NET USA
Educational games	59	18	86	FRA NET NWZ USA
Recreational games	43	19	60	FRA NET NWZ USA
Tutorial programs	35	15	58	CBC NET NWZ USA
Word processing	32	2	85	CBC FRA NWZ USA
Logo	22	6	73	BFR CBC FRA NWZ
Painting/drawing	19	14	29	CBC FRA JPN NWZ
Basic	18	6	50	BFR FRA NWZ USA
Simulation	14	6	43	CBC JPN NWZ USA
Math. graphing	8	3	19	BFR FRA NWZ USA
Database	6	1	20	CBC ISR NWZ USA
Music composition	5	1	16	CBC FRA JPN NWZ
Tools/utilities	4	0	14	FRA NET NWZ USA
Spreadsheet	3	1	6	CBC FRA NWZ USA
Control devices	2	0	6	CBC NET NWZ USA
Other prog. lang.	2	0	5	CBC ISR NWZ USA
Statistics	1	0	7	FRA JPN NET NWZ
Comp. communic.	1	0	6	CBC FRA NWZ USA
CAD/CAM	1	0	4	CBC ISR JPN NWZ
Lab interfaces	1	0	3	BFR CBC FRA ISR
Interact. video	0	0	2	CBC JPN NWZ
Lower Secondary Schools				
Word processing	77	0	95	AUT CBC LUX NWZ
Basic	48	8	86	FRG GRE ITA USA
Drill/practice	45	11	78	CBC FRG ITA USA
Database	42	2	60	CBC GRE LUX NET
Recreational games	32	8	71	AUT NWZ SWI USA
Spreadsheet	32	1	61	AUT CBC FRG SWI
Logo	31	2	94	AUT BFR LUX NWZ
Educational games	30	11	67	AUT NET NWZ USA
Tutorial programs	27	3	64	CBC NET NWZ USA
Painting drawing	26	4	63	AUT CBC NWZ SWI
Simulation	14	4	39	CBC NET NWZ USA
Math. graphing	12	0	23	AUT NWZ POR SWI
Tools/utilities	9	0	23	CBC NWZ POR USA
Music composition	4	0	16	AUT NWZ SWI USA

(Continued on next page)

Table 4.8a (continued)
Median percent of teachers across countries reporting software use by their students and four countries with highest percent

Software/Level	Median	Minimum	Maximum	Four highest countries
Lower Secondary Schools				
Statistics	4	0	16	AUT BFL NWZ POR
CAD/CAM	3	0	34	AUT CBC NWZ SWI
Other prog. lang.	3	0	27	AUT BFL CBC NET
Control devices	3	0	15	BFL FRG NET USA
Comp. communic.	2	0	20	CBC NET NWZ USA
Lab interfaces	0	0	6	BFL ITA NET USA
Interact. video	0	0	2	AUT ITA NET USA
Upper Secondary Schools				
Basic	56	11	95	CHI HUN ISR NWZ
Word processing	54	4	99	CBC ITA NWZ USA
Spreadsheet	36	2	95	CBC FRA NWZ SWI
Other prog. lang.	34	4	87	AUT BFL CBC ITA
Database	33	1	97	AUT BFL CBC NWZ
Recreational games	31	5	76	HUN IND POL SLO
Drill/practice	28	16	56	HUN IND POL SLO
Painting/drawing	23	5	69	CBC HUN NWZ POL
Educational games	22	5	60	HUN IND NWZ POL
Tutorial programs	19	7	63	CBC NWZ POL USA
Math. graphing	17	4	53	IND ITA NWZ POL
Tools/utilities	15	1	59	AUT CBC NWZ POR
Simulation	12	0	48	HUN IND NWZ POL
Logo	7	0	73	IND ISR NWZ POL
Statistics	7	1	24	HUN IND NWZ SLO
Control devices	4	0	23	CBC HUN NWZ USA
CAD/CAM	4	0	19	AUT CBC NWZ SLO
Music composition	3	0	45	HUN IND NWZ POL
Comp. communic.	2	0	26	CBC ITA NWZ POL
Lab interfaces	2	0	7	CBC HUN ITA NWZ
Interact. video	0	0	4	CBC HUN NWZ USA

Table 4.8b

Summary of between-country correlations (of percent teachers indicating student-use of software, over software types)

Population	Median corr.	Minimum corr.	Maximum corr.	Number of significant corr.
Elementary Schools	.77	.60	.95	28/28
Lower Secondary Schools	.69	-.09	.94	75/91
Upper Secondary Schools	.64	-.04	.92	132/171

Notes: Corr. = correlations.

Frequency of computer use in computer education

In Table 4.9 it is seen that in most countries in all three populations computers were used every week or almost every week in computer education. Regular and frequent use of computers would seem to be beneficial. However, it is clear that the way in which the computers are used is critical. Investigation of this is beyond the capability of this survey study.

Table 4.9

Median percent of schools across countries reporting computer use in computer education lessons every or almost every week and four countries with highest percent

Population	Median	Minimum	Maximum	Four highest countries
Elementary Schools	70	23	96	CBC FRA ISR NET
Lower Secondary Schools	92	19	100	AUT FRG LUX NET
Upper Secondary Schools	88	57	100	AUT CBC NWZ POL

How computers are used

In this section we examine how frequently computers are used in various ways: CAI or Drill, a programming or computer science unit or course, an introductory unit or course, tools (word processor, database, spreadsheet), games as a reward or motivator, enrichment for certain students, catching up for certain students, testing, demonstration before a class.

All of the above, except for demonstration, refer to student activities. For each activity computer coordinators were asked to indicate either: no use, some weeks, most weeks, or every week. We prefer to focus on consistent, systematic use of computers, and in Table 4.10 present the ordered data for percent of computer coordinators indicating use most weeks or every week.

The three school populations differed in terms of the most emphasized way of use: in elementary schools most emphasis was given to CAI/Drill; in lower secondary schools most emphasis was given to an introductory course or unit; while in upper secondary schools most emphasis was given to a programming or computer science course.

In elementary schools, the international medians of percent use every or almost every week were 47% and 25% for CAI/Drill and tools, respectively. For all other ways, the international median was less than 20% of schools.

In lower secondary schools, the median for introductory unit was 46% followed by tool-use, programming unit and CAI/Drill. The international median was less than 20% for all other ways.

In upper secondary schools there was much more regular use: 61% reported weekly use in a programming unit; 53% in an introductory unit; 49% reported weekly tool use; followed by CAI/Drill, computer club and demonstration use. The international median was less than 20% for all other ways.

The overall ranking of ways was similar in lower and upper secondary schools: Most regular use was in programming, introductory units, tool use and CAI/Drill. Least regular use was in: games, enrichment, catching up, and testing. Elementary schools differed in that CAI/Drill and games were ranked higher and programming unit was ranked lower.

Worth noting is that little regular use of the computer was made for enrichment and for catching up for particular children: the respective international medians were 14 percent and 11 percent in elementary schools; 9 percent and 5 percent in lower secondary schools; 7 percent and 4 percent in upper secondary schools. The countries standing out on these activities were Canada-British Columbia, Israel, and the Netherlands with usage in these ways in the 15 to 35 percent range.

These aspects of individualization require more than sitting each child in the class before a computer. Achieving such individualization will only occur when classroom management allows it. The question of interest is whether use of computers per se can bring about a change in classroom management. The data indicate that for the countries in this study this probably has not yet occurred.

Dan Davis

Table 4.10

Ways of computer use according to computer coordinator - percent across countries reporting use every or almost every week and four countries with highest percent

Subject/Level	Median	Minimum	Maximum	Four highest countries
Elementary Schools				
CAI/Drill	47	18	87	CBC FRA ISR NET
Use as tool	25	14	86	CBC ITA NWZ POR
Play games	16	7	36	CBC FRA ISR NWZ
Introductory course	16	4	35	BFR ISR ITA POR
Computer club	15	0	68	CBC ISR JPN POR
Enrichment	14	4	34	CBC ISR NET POR
Show on computer	12	4	21	CBC ISR ITA USA
Catching up	11	1	45	CBC FRA ISR NET
Programming course	10	3	39	BFR FRA ISR POR
Test on computer	5	0	12	BFR ITA NET USA
Lower Secondary Schools				
Introductory course	46	16	74	BFR CBC GRE NET
Use as tool	42	14	97	AUT CBC LUX NWZ
Programming course	35	10	79	BFR CBC FRG LUX
CAI/Drill	34	8	57	BFR CBC FRA GRE
Computer club	13	1	55	CBC FRA JPN NWZ
Show on computer	12	2	30	CBC GRE ITA USA
Enrichment	9	0	21	BFL CBC FRA NWZ
Play games	6	0	16	CBC FRA NWZ POR
Test on computer	6	0	12	CBC FRA ITA USA
Catching up	5	0	26	BFL CBC FRA NET
Upper Secondary Schools				
Programming course	61	27	89	FRG GRE ISR POL
Introductory course	53	26	77	BFL HUN ISR SWI
Use as tool	49	6	97	CBC FRA NWZ SWI
CAI/Drill	38	3	75	BFR GRE HUN ISR
Computer club	20	1	63	CHI HUN JPN POL
Show on computer	20	6	39	BFL CBC GRE ITA
Enrichment	7	1	25	CBC IND ISR ITA
Play games	6	0	53	CBC HUN IND SLO
Test on computer	5	0	25	AUT IND ITA USA
Catching up	4	0	15	CBC IND ISR NET

Countries with most frequent use over approaches

From the list of countries at the side of Table 4.10 it can be seen that Canada-British Columbia appeared as one of the most frequent users over the list of approaches in all three populations. Israel matched Canada-British Columbia in elementary and in upper secondary schools.

Comparison of country profiles

In elementary schools CAI/Drill was the most frequent use in five of the nine countries, and was the second most frequent use in three countries. Japan and Portugal stand out in that the most frequent use by far was in a computer club: about 65% in each country reported this use most weeks or every week.

In lower secondary schools tool use was the most frequent use in six of fourteen countries. It was the third most frequent use in another five countries. An introductory course was the most frequent use in four countries, and was the second or third most use in another eight countries.

In upper secondary schools a programming course was the most frequent use in nine of the nineteen countries and was second or third in another eight countries. Tool use was the most frequent use in seven of the nineteen countries and was second or third in another five countries. An introductory course was among the three most frequent uses in eighteen of the countries.

A summary of the correlations among country rankings of the various uses is found in Table 4.11. In elementary schools three negative correlations occurred for Japan and Portugal where club activities was the most frequent use. This accounts for the fact that only 8/36 of the correlations were significant. In lower and upper secondary schools most correlations were significant.

The pattern of the highest ranked uses and the intercorrelations indicate strong agreement among countries in lower and upper secondary schools and moderate agreement in elementary schools.

Table 4.11

Summary of between-country correlations (of percent of schools using the computer in a certain way, over the ten ways of use)

Population	Median corr.	Minimum corr.	Maximum corr.	Number of significant corr.
Elementary Schools	.37	-.31	.92	8/36
Lower Secondary Schools	.70	-.10	.98	50/91
Upper Secondary Schools	.69	.21	.97	104/171

Notes: Corr. = correlations.

An additional set of activities by teachers and/or students was investigated. As in the above set, we examined percent of computer coordinators reporting weekly or almost weekly use of computers. The activities are: writing for school newspaper or year book, using a subject related information database, using an external database via network, exchanging files or messages on an internal network, exchanging files or messages on an external network.

Table 4.12 shows that there was little regular use of computers for the above activities. The international medians for writing for school newspaper and using a subject related database were around 10% in all three school populations. For all the other activities the median was below 5%.

Some noteworthy exceptions are listed below.
Weekly use for school newspaper. Japan stood out in all three school populations: about 50% of schools reporting use. The only case where another country was close to this was the United States of America in upper secondary schools with 41% of schools.
Weekly use of subject related database. France stood out with 40% of upper secondary schools.
Weekly use of internal e-mail. Canada-British Columbia stood out with 17% of schools at both secondary levels. Slovenia was also prominent at the upper secondary level - 21% of schools.
Weekly use of external e-mail. Canada-British Columbia stood out with 21% of schools at both secondary levels.
Weekly use of external databases. Luxembourg stood out in lower secondary schools with 22% of schools.

Table 4.12

Computer activities often used according to computer coordinator

Subject/Level	Median	Minimum	Maximum	Four highest countries
Elementary Schools				
School newspaper	13	1	45	ITA JPN NET POR
Subject database	10	4	14	CBC FRA ISR POR
E-mail internal	3	0	9	BFR CBC NWZ POR
E-mail external	1	0	13	CBC FRA POR USA
External database	0	0	3	CBC FRA JPN USA
Lower Secondary Schools				
Subject database	12	2	21	AUT CBC LUX SWI
School newspaper	8	0	60	CBC JPN NWZ USA
E-mail internal	2	0	17	BFL BFR CBC POR
E-mail external	1	0	21	BFR CBC FRA LUX
External database	1	0	22	BFR CBC LUX USA
Upper Secondary Schools				
Subject database	13	0	40	AUT CBC FRA IND
School newspaper	7	0	46	CBC JPN SLO USA
E-mail internal	4	0	21	CBC NET POL SLO
E-mail external	2	0	21	AUT CBC FRA USA
External database	1	0	9	CBC JPN NET USA

Problems in Implementing Computer Use

In this section we examine problems encountered by school personnel in the implementation of computer use. Principals, coordinators and teachers were presented with a list of possible problems which might occur in the implementation of computer use in schools. The complete list of 28 problems is shown in Table 4.13. The respondents were asked to indicate which problems were serious and which were the five most serious. For each problem we calculated the percent of respondents who included it among their five most serious. The detailed country results are presented in Tables D.1 to D.11 in Pelgrum and Plomp (1991). We have summarized those tables by calculating the median percent of each problem over countries for each respondent and then replacing the actual percent by its rank over the set of problems.

There was general agreement among the rankings for a given group of respondents over the three populations. Based on this we calculated the median percents for each type of respondent over the three populations and ranked them. The results over countries are seen in Table 4.14 and the most prominent problems are: (1) too few computers and (2) too little instructional software. These were the two most cited problems by coordinators, existing subject teachers, and computer education teachers (about 41%, 42%, and 35% respectively). Principals cited 'too few computers' most often (49%), but too little instructional software was the third most cited problem (35%).

This indicates that lack of a basic infrastructure for using computers was seen as the most major problem facing school staff in implementing their use.

(3) lack of teacher skills in using computers was seen as a major problem by principals, coordinators and existing subjects teachers who, ranked it second, third, and fifth respectively. As might be excepted, computer education teachers rarely ranked this as a serious problem.

(4) insufficient time to develop computer based lessons was ranked third by existing subjects and computer education teachers and was ranked fourth and sixth by coordinators and principals, respectively. It was thus, seen as a major problem from all points of view.

(5) inadequate financial support was ranked fourth by principals, fifth by coordinators, fifth by computer education teachers, and seventh by existing subjects teachers.

(6) insufficient training opportunities was ranked fifth by principals, sixth by coordinators, ninth by computer education teachers, and eleventh by existing subjects teachers.

(7) too few peripherals was ranked fourth by computer education teachers but only ninth or tenth by other staff.

(8) difficulty in integrating computers into classroom practices of teachers was ranked seventh or eighth by principals, coordinators, and existing subjects teachers. Interestingly, computer education teachers rarely saw this as a serious problem.

(9) problems in scheduling enough computer use was ranked fourth by existing subjects teachers, ninth by principals, and twelfth and thirteenth by computer education teachers and coordinators.

Table 4.13
Master list of problems in using computers

Hardware
1. insufficient number of computers available
2. insufficient number of peripherals (e.g. printer)
3. difficulty in keeping computers and peripherals in working order
4. limitations of computers (e.g. out-of-date, incompatible with current software, to slow, insufficient memory, etc.)

Software
5. not enough software for instructional purposes available
6. software too difficult or too complicated to use
7. software not adaptable enough for this school's courses
8. manuals and support materials poorly designed, incomplete or inappropriate
9. lack of information about software or its quality
10. most of the software is not available in the language of instruction

Instruction
11. not enough help for supervising computer using students/teachers
12. difficult to integrate computers in classroom instruction practices of teachers
13. integration of computer use in the existing prescribed (school/class) curriculum is difficult
14. computers are inappropriate for the age level of students
15. teachers lack knowledge / skills about using computers for instructional purposes
16. insufficient expertise / guidelines for helping teachers use computers instructionally

Organization / administration
17. no room in the school time-table for students to learn about or to use computers
18. not enough space to locate computers appropriately
19. not enough technical assistance for operating and maintaining computers
20. computers are only available outside the school or the school building
21. problems in scheduling enough computer time for different classes / this class
22. computers not accessible enough for teachers' / my own use
23. insufficient training opportunities for teachers
24. lack of administrative support or initiatives from a higher level of school administration
25. inadequate financial support
26. computers do not fit in the educational policy of the school

Miscellaneous
27. not enough time to develop lessons in which computers are used
28. lack of interest / willingness of teachers in using computers

Table 4.14

Median overall percentage of respondents across countries and populations who included a problem in their top five selection of serious problems in using computers

Principals	Median	Coordinators	Median	Subject teacher	Median	Comped teacher	Median
Insuff. computers	49	Insuff.softw.	45	Insuff.softw.	44	Insuff.softw.	37
Teachers lack knowl.	42	Insuff. computers	38	Insuff. computers	41	Insuff. computers	34
Insuff.softw.	35	Teachers lack knowl.	33	Time develop less.	35	Time develop less.	29
Inadeq.fin. supp.	34	Time develop less.	31	Schedule time	25	Insuff. periph.	26
Insuf. training	24	Inadeq.fin. supp.	28	Teachers lack knowl.	21	Inadeq.fin. supp.	26
Time develop less.	22	Insuf. training	27	Insuff. time learn	19	Limitations comp.	21
Integr. instruc.	20	Teach. lack inter.	20	Inadeq.fin. supp.	17	Poor qual. manuals	21
Insuff. exp. help	18	Integr. instruc.	20	Integr. instruc.	16	Diffic. mainten.	19
Schedule time	17	Insuff. exp. help	18	Insuff. periph.	15	Insuf. training	15
Insuff. periph.	16	Insuff. periph.	16	Lack info. softw.	14	Lack info. softw.	13
Teach. lack inter.	14	Limitations comp.	16	Insuf. training	13	Insuff. exp. help	13
Computer location	14	Insuff. time learn	14	Limitations comp.	12	Schedule time	12
Insuff. time learn	12	Schedule time	13	Softw. not adapt.	12	Techn. operat.ass.	11
Limitations comp.	12	Computer location	13	Integr. curric.	11	Teach. lack inter.	10
Integr. curric.	11	Techn. operat.ass.	12	Not enough superv.	11	Insuff. time learn	10
Softw. not adapt.	11	Lack info. softw.	11	Insuff. exp. help	11	Computer location	10
Lack info. softw.	10	Not enough superv.	11	Diffic. mainten.	9	Not enough superv.	8
Diffic. mainten.	8	Softw. not adapt.	9	Computer location	9	Softw. not adapt.	8
Techn. operat.ass.	8	Diffic. mainten.	9	Techn. operat.ass.	8	Softw.not in lang.	8
Not enough superv.	7	No admin. support	8	Teach. lack inter.	8	Teachers lack knowl.	7
No admin. support	7	Poor qual. manuals	8	Access teachers	6	Integr. curric.	6
Access teachers	6	Access teachers	6	Poor qual. manuals	6	No admin. support	6
Poor qual. manuals	4	Softw. difficult	5	Softw. difficult	4	Integr. instruc.	5
Softw.not in lang.	3	Softw.not in lang.	3	No admin. support	4	Access teachers	5
Softw. difficult	3	No fit school pol.	3	Softw.not in lang.	2	Softw. difficult	4
No fit school pol.	1	Comp. outside school	1	Comp. outside school	1	Comp. outside school	0
Comp. outside school	0	Inappr.stud. age	0	Inappr.stud. age	0	Inappr.stud. age	0
Inappr.stud. age	0	Integr. curric.	0	No fit school pol.	0	No fit school pol.	-

In summary, all staff saw basic infrastructure as the key problem: coordinators, existing subjects teachers, and computer education teachers all ranked insufficient computers and insufficient software as the two key problems. Principals and coordinators saw teachers' lack of knowledge of skills about using computers in instruction as the key problem, while subject and computer education teachers saw lack of time to develop computer based lessons as the key problem. These problems are more of the 'getting started' kind as opposed to those encountered in the course of continued use. The results are an indication that, in fact, the utilization of computers in schools was very much in the 'start up' phase in 1989.

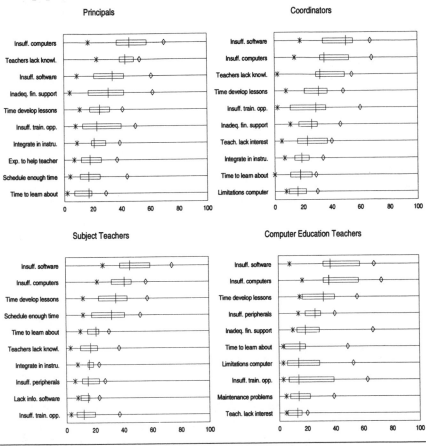

Legend: 25% Tile [ ] 75% Tile, [ ] Median, * Minimum, ◊ Maximum

Figure 4.5 Percent of staff across countries including a problem among their five most serious in using computers (lower secondary schools).

In Figure 4.5 we present the ordered box plots for the ten highest ranked problems in lower secondary schools separately for each category of respondents (the results in elementary upper and secondary schools were similar).

There was a great deal of overlap in the distributions, raising the question that individual countries might have very different orders in the rank of the problems. However, we found very high, significant correlations among countries in their rating of problems (Table 4.15). Particularly impressive was the fact that almost all countries gave the first two or three ranks to the same problems. For principals and coordinators at least 2/3 of the countries in each population included two of the following three problems among the three most serious: insufficient computers, insufficient software, and teachers lack of knowledge.

For subject teachers and computer education teachers at least 2/3 of the countries in each population included two of the following three problems among the three most serious: insufficient software, insufficient computers, and lack of time to develop lessons.

Table 4.15

Summary of between-country correlations (of percent of respondents who indicated a problem as serious, over the 28 problems)

Respondent	Median corr.	Minimum corr.	Maximum corr.	Number of significant corr.
Principal	.66	-.02	.91	90/105
Coordinator	.67	.16	.89	90/105
Subject teacher	.73	.39	.94	28/28
Computer-Ed. teacher	.55	-.10	.81	46/55

Student/computer ratio and the extent to which "too few computers" was seen as the key problem

There was large variation in the student/computer ratio over countries (in computer-using schools). In elementary schools the ratio varied from 17 students per computer in Israel to over 100 students per computer in Italy and Portugal. In lower secondary schools it varied from 12 in Canada-British Columbia to over 100 in Portugal. In upper secondary schools it varied from 12 in Canada-British Columbia to well over 100 in India and Portugal.

Presumably, the problem of "insufficient number of computers" should decrease in importance as the number of students per computer decreases. We examined this proposition by dividing the countries into those with few students per computer (below the median ratio), and those with many students per computer (above the median ratio).

For each of these groups we ranked the problems according to the procedure for Table 4.14. In Table 4.16 we present the rank for "too few computers" for low student/computer ratios and for high student/computer ratios. It can be seen that in elementary schools this was the most serious problem for both low and high ratio groups and for all three respondents. Roughly speaking, the difference of 64 to 23 in student/computer ratio was not associated with a difference in the saliency of the problem, "too few computers".

In lower and upper secondary schools there was little difference between low and high ratio schools in the rankings over respondents. The difference of 49 to 25 in student/computer ratio in lower secondary schools, and the difference of 49 to 27 in upper secondary schools were not associated with a difference in the saliency of the problem "too few computers".

Table 4.16

Median rank of the problem "insufficient computers" as a function of student/computer ratio ("1" indicates highest percent indicated this as a problem)

Respondent	Elementary		Lower Secondary		Upper Secondary	
	Low ratio	High ratio	Low ratio	High ratio	Low ratio	High ratio
Principal	1	1	2	1	1	1
Coordinator	1	1	3	2	2	2
Existing subject teacher	1	1	2	4	2	3
Computer-Ed. teacher	-	-	1	2	1	2
Median student/ computer ratio	23	64	25	49	27	49

The results indicate that within the variation of this sample of countries "too few computers" was considered a serious problem both in countries with relatively few students per computer and in countries with many students per computer. Apparently, the "critical mass" of number of computers needed for orderly integration of computers in the curriculum was not reached. This claim is backed up by the finding of Johnson and Ross (1989) that even with a ratio of three students per computer within the classroom, much of their energy went into procedural and organizational rather than pedagogical matters.

Expenditure priorities

Computer coordinators were asked to indicate which three among nine possibilities have the highest priority for use of available budget: (1) more computers in lab, (2) more computers in class, (3) more powerful computers, (4) network for shared disk storage, (5) network for integrated system of instructional software, (6) more printers or other peripherals, (7) greater variety of instructional software, (8) more tool software, (9) other.

For each expenditure we calculated the percent of coordinators in each country including it among the top three expenditures. We then calculated the median percent over countries for each population. In Table 4.17 we list the expenditures according to the median percent.

There was a high degree of agreement in the rankings over the three school populations. All three ranked, greater variety of software first and the two types of networking and "other" expenditures last. Second or third place was given to "more computers" (in labs for lower and upper secondary schools and in classrooms for elementary schools). More peripherals were ranked fourth in secondary education and third in elementary education. In fifth or sixth place were "more powerful computers".

It is clear that most coordinators would have used their budget for more software first and then for more computers or peripherals. Relatively low priority was given to purchasing more powerful computers or developing networking capabilities. Thus, priority was given to strengthening the present infrastructure rather than upgrading. This is congruent with the fact that the most salient problems were essentially concerned with infrastructure and strengthens the view that computer implementation was still at the beginning stages.

Comparison of country profiles

Agreement among countries was high: "more variety of software" was ranked first by 8/9 countries, 13/15 countries, and 13/20 countries in the three school populations. In Table 4.18, it is seen that most correlations were positive and significant for elementary schools. For lower and upper secondary schools fewer correlations were significant and some were negative. This is associated with Canada-British Columbia which ranked "more computers in laboratories" first; and with Slovenia which ranked "more powerful computers" first.

Table 4.17

Extent to which expenditures are mentioned among the three with highest priority by computer coordinators across countries

Subject/Level	Median	Minimum	Maximum
Elementary Schools			
More variety software	74	48	91
Computers in class	46	18	65
More pheripherals	37	22	52
Computers in lab setting	35	4	68
More tool software	33	25	67
More powerful computers	24	14	39
Integrated system network	13	5	20
Share disk network	10	2	22
Other expenditure	6	4	11
Lower Secondary Schools			
More variety software	64	36	82
Computers in lab setting	46	14	71
More tool software	44	34	72
More peripherals	32	12	46
Computers in class	30	12	52
More powerful computers	28	8	43
Share disk network	11	0	43
Integrated system network	10	1	29
Other expenditure	7	3	33
Upper Secondary Schools			
More variety software	56	19	83
More tool software	47	30	63
Computers in lab setting	43	22	72
More peripherals	38	17	49
More powerful computers	33	14	55
Computers in class	19	4	54
Share disk network	18	4	43
Integrated system network	13	0	29
Other expenditure	9	3	21

Table 4.18

Summary of between-country correlations (of percent of coordinators including an expenditure among the three with highest priority, over ten expenditures)

Population	Median corr.	Minimum corr.	Maximum corr.	Number of significant corr.
Elementary Schools	.74	.16	.90	21/36
Lower Secondary Schools	.77	-.33	.99	65/105
Upper Secondary Schools	.67	-.24	.98	89/190

Teachers estimates of changes resulting from computer use

Computer-using teachers were asked to estimate the extent to which computer use led to changes in:

1. students' behavior:	-interest in work
	-mutual help
	-academic achievement
2. classes' work pattern:	-time spent on individual work
	-time spent on small group work
	-time spent on whole class work
3. curriculum progress	-availability of feedback on students' achievement
	-content covered
4. curriculum organization	-lesson preparation time
	-difficulty in organizing lessons

For each variable teachers were asked to indicate: no change; small or large decrease; small or large increase. For presenting results, we used three categories: decrease, no change; increase. We calculated the percent of teachers in each country who indicated each response and then averaged the percents over countries. The results are shown in Figures 4.6 and 4.7.

1. Students' behavior. In Figure 4.6a it is seen that most teachers reported increases in all three behaviors: over the three school populations the percent of teachers reporting increases in students' interest ranged from 72% to 78%; the percent reporting increases in mutual help ranged from 61% to 69% and, the percent reporting increases in achievement ranged from 44% to 58%. In all three school populations the teachers were most likely to report changes in interest and least likely to report changes in achievement. It was reasonable to expect the large percent reporting increases in students' interest. What is interesting is the large percent of teachers reporting increases in mutual help, and the fact that this percent is higher than that associated with increases in students' achievement. This result is consistent with the growing number of reports in the literature on the computer as social facilitator (Hannafin, 1989; Watson, 1991).

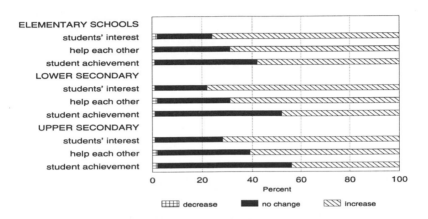

Figure 4.6a Teachers' estimates of changes in students' attributes as a result of computer use.

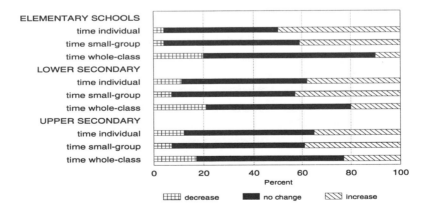

Figure 4.6b Teachers' estimates of changes in time spent during lessons as a result of computer use.

We note with interest that in Chapter 2 of this volume it was shown that when principals indicated reasons for introducing computers in their school, they were equally likely over the three school populations to mention "improving achievement" and "making school more interesting." They were much less likely to indicate "increasing cooperative learning" as a reason. If we compare these results with teachers' estimates of changes we can claim that the expectations concerning students' interest were met; that the increase in mutual help was a bonus; and, that expectations concerning achievement were not met. In fact, upper secondary school teachers were more likely to indicate no change in achievement than an increase in achievement. If we take into account the fact that upper secondary principals were more likely to report improving achievement than increasing interest as the reason for introducing computers, it is reasonable to expect some disappointment in this school population concerning the effect of computers on achievement.

2. *Classes' work patterns.* In Figure 4.6b it can be seen that, in general, the expectations for significant increases in individual and small group work as a result of using computers were not met. The percent of teachers reporting increases in individual work were 50, 38, and 35 percent in elementary, lower secondary, and upper secondary schools, respectively. Most of the remainder reported no change. Similarly, reports of increases in small group activity were about 41 percent in the three populations. Almost all teachers reported no change or a decrease in whole class activities.

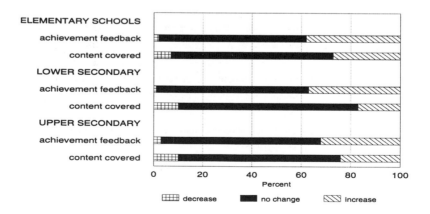

Figure 4.7a Teachers' estimates of changes in curriculum progress as a result of computer use.

3. Curriculum progress. In Figure 4.7a, it is seen that in all three school populations most teachers reported no change in achievement feedback and no change in content covered. The hope that computer use would bring teachers into closer contact with their students' academic performance was not met. With respect to content covered, less than 30 percent of the teachers reported an increase while 10 percent reported a decrease. These findings reflect the growing awareness that realizing the full potential of computers is not easily achieved (Johnson & Ross, 1989).

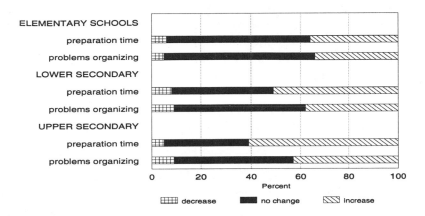

Figure 4.7b Teachers' estimates of changes in curriculum organization as a result of computer use.

4. Curriculum organization. In Figure 4.7b we see that in lower and upper secondary schools most teachers reported an increase in preparation time (51 and 61 percent) while in elementary schools most teachers reported no change (58 percent). This result is probably due to the fact that in elementary schools the emphasis was more on drill and games which require less investment by the teacher. On the other hand, relatively few teachers reported an increase in organizational difficulties around lessons: 34, 38, and 43 percent in elementary, lower secondary, and upper secondary respectively. About 10 percent of teachers reported a decrease in organizational problems.

In summary, teachers saw the main effects of computers in the motivational and social spheres, and less in the academic achievement sphere. Most teachers did not see an increase in individual and small group work. Most teachers saw no change in the feedback they receive on students' achievement and most saw no change in content covered. Most teachers saw no increase in organizational problems, but most lower secondary and upper secondary teachers reported an increase in preparation time.

Comparison of country profiles

Agreement among countries in the percent of teachers indicating a positive change was high: among the ten aspects, the highest percent of teachers indicating a positive change was for, "students' interest", (7/8, 7/10, 8/16 countries in the three school populations. In countries which did not rank this first, it was usually second. In Table 4.19, it is seen that most country correlations were positive and significant. The Netherlands stood out by its relatively high ranking of "increased preparation time", and "increase in organizational problems".

Table 4.19

Summary of between-country correlations (of percent teachers indicating positive change in some aspect of their work, over ten aspects)

Population	Median corr.	Minimum corr.	Maximum corr.	Number of significant corr.
Elementary Schools	.71	.08	.97	15/28
Lower Secondary Schools	.63	-.02	.95	23/45
Upper Secondary Schools	.66	-.15	.96	65/120

Summary and discussion

1. *Subject matter use.* In elementary schools most use was in mathematics followed by comped/informatics and mother tongue. In lower secondary schools the predominant use was in comped/informatics followed by mathematics. In upper secondary schools the predominant use was in comped/informatics followed by mathematics and commercial studies.

Table 4.20 shows the fraction of countries with universal or major use of computers by schools (at least 50% of schools in a country).
It should be noted that these data relate only to schools where a subject is taught, so that 'major' or 'universal' use will not refer to the entire set of schools when a subject is not taught everywhere.

Table 4.20

Fraction of countries with universal or major use of computers by schools (at least 50% of schools in a country)

Subject	Elementary Schools	Lower Secondary Schools	Upper Secondary Schools
Comped/informatics	7/9	13/15	20/20
Mathematics	8/8	10/14	15/19
Science	3/8	5/15	10/19
Mother tongue	6/8	4/14	3/18
Specific technology	--	1/11	8/16
General technology	--	4/9	3/11
Commercial studies	--	4/11	12/17

It is seen that most countries made major or universal use of computers in mathematics and comped/informatics in all populations; in science, upper secondary; in mother tongue, elementary; and in specific technology and commercial studies, upper secondary. This clearly indicates that computer use was well beyond being a fad in a few countries or in a few schools in a country.

However, in lower and upper secondary schools only a small group among mathematics, science, and mother tongues teachers reported use, indicating that implementation was far from complete. In elementary schools, use by a school usually meant that most teachers used computers. Therefore, it can be argued that in elementary schools major or universal use of computers existed for comped/informatics, mathematics and mother tongue over countries, schools, and classes.

It appears that even in elementary schools computer use was far from being integrated into instruction. The predominant uses were for drill and for educational and recreational games; and computer use was generally outside the regular classroom (see also Chapter 3).

Also, Davis, Vinner, Finkelstein, and Regev (1985) found that usage of the small number of computers in each school was spread over all children in most grade levels, so that each child was allotted a short period of computer use each week. While they do not guarantee it, these factors are likely to lead to a certain break between the computer and classroom environments.

2. *Computer education.* In most countries the context of computer education was a separate course. In elementary schools there was little computer education as such, and the topics most emphasized were

educational/recreational games and word processing. In lower secondary schools word processing was the topic most emphasized. In upper secondary schools the problem analysis and programming topics were most emphasized.

In general, lower secondary schools emphasized applications and upper secondary emphasized programming. Basic was clearly the most used programming language in both lower and upper secondary schools. Even in elementary schools it was not far behind Logo in frequency of use. The countries were highly uniform in their emphases among the various topics.

Little attention was given to ethical issues. This is particularly disturbing in light of its importance.

3. *Computer approaches and activities.* In elementary schools the most regularly used approach was CAI/Drill. In lower secondary schools it was an introductory course followed by use as a tool. In upper secondary schools it was a programming course followed by an introductory course and tool use.

There was little regular use of computers for school newspapers, data bases, and electronic mail.

4. *Integration of computers into school life.* This was still at the beginning stages, even in the most advanced countries. This is illustrated by the fact that in most countries, the most serious problems cited by staff concerned infrastructure rather than operation. In particular, "insufficient number of computers" and "too little variety of software" were consistently among the most cited problems: by all school staff, in all school populations, and in all countries.

Also, there was little difference between countries with high and low student/computer ratios in terms of the extent to which insufficient number of computers was a serious problem. Finally, priority for expenditures as expressed by computer coordinators was for strengthening the present infrastructure rather than upgrading equipment or introducing new structures such as networking.

5. *Use in school subjects.* There was a high degree of consistency over countries in terms of which school subjects use computers, how the computers are used, problems most encountered, the priorities for expenditures, and what changes occurred as result of computer use.

6. *Effects on students.* Most teachers saw improvements in students' motivation, cooperative behavior, and achievement, in that order. Most interesting was the reported increase in cooperative behavior, an indication of the social facilitation role of the computer.

7. *Individual instruction.* Computer use did not realize its full potential in individualizing instruction. This is illustrated by the fact that most teachers saw no change in the amount of time children spend in individual or small group activities. Also, computer coordinators indicated that very little use of computers was made for helping specific groups of children through enrichment and remedial activities.

In conclusion, it is clear that computers were widely used at the country and school levels, but not at the class level. They were not yet integrated into the instructional life of the class. It may be that the "critical mass" of numbers of computers and of variety of software were not reached, and that when this occurs, integration will be achieved. It may be that use of advanced technologies such as multi-media will bring about greater integration. We doubt it. The problem is probably more pedagogical than technological.

Acknowledgement

I would like to thank Dr. H. Hansen, Dr. M. Setinc, and Dr. J. Kolenc for comments on early drafts.

A special word of thanks I owe to Drs. Arjan Schipper, who did all the data processing for this chapter.

5

Educating the Educators

The present generation of teachers did not grow up with computers as a normal and integral part of society; and certainly not of school life and classroom practices. They did not receive their first computer experience in elementary or secondary school and a majority was not trained in computer use during their initial, pre-service training. On the other hand, teachers are ultimately the ones charged with the implementation of computers in educational practice and therefore 'education of the educators' or teacher training is an important aspect of the introduction of computers in schools. In this chapter we will address what the knowledge and skills level of teachers is (in other words whether they need training) and what training in the field of computer use was received by teachers until 1989. Not only the teacher perspective will be taken into account; some attention will be paid to the school (transcending) perspective.

The context of this chapter
Defining 'training'

In the literature, several terms are used all referring to teacher training, such as professional development, in-service training or in-service education, with the term chosen more a matter of author preference than of any significant difference in meaning. In the context of this book, training is defined as:

programs or activities that are based on identified needs; that are collaboratively planned and designed for a specific group of individuals; that have a very specific set of learning objectives and activities; and that are designed to extend, add, or improve immediate job-oriented skills, competencies, or knowledge" (Orlich, 1989, p. 5).

Although Orlich uses this description to define the term in-service education, and thus relates it to programs or activities that take place when a teacher is already qualified to teach, conceptually the definition can be used as well for initial or pre-service education.

This chapter was written by Ingeborg A.M. Janssen Reinen and Tjeerd Plomp.

Using the Comped data, it is not possible to distinguish between computer related training received during in-service training or during pre-service education. In the context of this chapter, training will be conceived of as educating the educators in the field of computers and their use in the school, taking place either in pre-service or in-service situations.

The existing subject perspective

Since the introduction of the computer in education, many authors claim that important beneficial aspects of computer use in education are related to the integration of computers in the existing subjects (e.g. Collis, 1988, Hunter, 1984). However, as stated in Chapter 3 (see page 47) and shown in Table 5.1, the use of computers as aid in teaching and learning in existing subjects is limited.

Table 5.1
Percentage of teachers of existing subjects using computers in computer using schools
Source: Pelgrum and Plomp, 1991

	BFL	FRG	IND	ISR	LUX	NET	NWZ	POL	POR	SWI	USA
Elementary Schools											
	-	-	-	96	-	74	92	-	-	-	76
Lower Secondary Schools											
Mathematics	8	42	-	-	8	14	38	-	20	21	56
Science	4	10	-	-	m	4	17	-	15	15	39
Mother tongue	3	17	-	-	7	8	36	-	7	11	44
Upper Secondary Schools											
Mathematics	30	28	44	5	-	61	64	28	9	45	61
Science	21	22	53	6	-	32	37	11	7	31	58
Mother tongue	5	4	10	2	-	8	12	1	2	10	47

Notes: - = Data not collected, m = insufficient number of cases (n<50 or missing cases >20%).

In most countries participating in this study, introduction of the computer in schools is happening predominantly through the introduction of a new subject like computer education or informatics, while the use of computers in existing subjects is still an activity of a rather small group of teachers. The group of intensive computer using teachers did not, at the best, exceed 15% (see Chapter 3, page 47).

One may argue that computer use in existing subjects is not fully integrated because this form of computer use is the most complex part of the innovation (Walker, 1986): this type of computer use requires (unlike the introduction of a new and additional subject like computer education) a change in the role of the teachers and adaptations of the existing curricula. As Tobin (1988) states, *"... adequate hardware, high-quality courseware and administrative support are important, but the teachers' attitude and consequent behavior will determine the impact of the microcomputer in the classroom"*. This leads to the conclusion that the limited use of computers in the different subjects may only be partly explained by the limited availability of hardware and educational software in a particular grade or subject, but that other factors also contribute to the low use of computers in existing subjects. Training is such a factor, but one other factor certainly needs to be mentioned here as well. It is namely found that time is also an important factor (Janssen Reinen and Plomp, 1993). It cannot be expected that teachers, who are completely new in the field of computer use in education, will adopt this innovation and fully integrate it into their curriculum within only a few years. Teachers need time to get to know this technology, to find out what the potential advantages are to integrate the computer in their teaching, and to learn working with the courseware that is available for their subject matter area. It is beyond the scope of this book to study the time factor in detail.

Within the limitations of this chapter and the importance of obtaining a greater understanding of factors influencing the potential benefits of the use of computers in existing subjects, we discuss the training issue only from the perspective of existing subject teachers (computer education teachers will not be taken into account).

In order to be able to relate training to the desired effects in terms of integration of computers in existing subjects, a distinction needs to be made between different categories of teachers indicating different degrees of computer use in their teaching.

The measure for computer integration

It is important to study how exemplary teachers (teachers who are reputationally expert computer-users in their school, Becker, 1992) came to use computers differently from other teachers; whether this be their personal background, their beliefs and philosophy of education, or characteristics of their work environment. Eventual differences will help us to understand the barriers that exist for many teachers to use the computer (Becker, 1992).

To operationalize exemplary (and other categories of) teachers, a measure for integration is used, developed by Pelgrum and Schipper (1992). Computer using mathematics, science and mother tongue teachers marked in a list of possible topics for which they could use computers, for which topics they actually used the computer in their lessons. Pelgrum and Schipper (o.c.) defined a 10-point scale based on the number of subject matter topics indicated by the teachers using computers. In this context three categories of computer using teachers can be defined: low integrators (with scores of 1, 2 or 3 on the 10-point scale of number of topics for which they use computers), the medium integrators (with score 4, 5, 6, or 7) and the high integrators (with score 8, 9 or 10). This last group can be regarded as 'exemplary teachers'. Besides these three groups, the group of teachers not using the computer in their teaching of existing subjects are included in our analyses. The number of respondents in each group is indicated in Table 5.2. The table shows teachers across all countries; however, in some countries (e.g. the Netherlands and France in lower secondary education and Belgium-French, the Federal Republic of Germany, India, Portugal and Slovenia in upper secondary education) a number of cases (10-30%) were excluded from this analysis because the coding of the variables on which the measure is based in these cases deviated from the international version.

Table 5.2
Number of cases in each group of existing subject teachers

| | Number of cases | | | |
| | Lower Secondary Schools | | Upper Secondary Schools | |
Group of teachers	n	%	n	%
Non-users	4667	81	6859	84
Low integrators	565	10	600	7
Medium integrators	352	6	437	5
High integrators	167	3	276	3

For elementary education, it was not possible to develop an identical measure because not enough information was received from the respondents. Therefore, elementary school teachers were not included in the analyses on teacher level.

Knowledge and skills

Teachers who are willing to integrate computers in their subject matter area need knowledge about and skills on how to use computers. In order to find out what teachers themselves think they know about or can do with computers, so-called self-rating scales were included in the teacher questionnaire consisting of three scales with yes/no questions (the complete list of self-rating items is included in Appendix B.
- knowledge scale: 9 questions about knowledge of hardware and software;
- programming scale: 5 questions about programming skills;
- capability scale: 8 questions about the ability of using the computer as a tool for, for example, word processing and computer assisted instruction.

The validity and reliability of these scales seem to be fairly good, as explained by Pelgrum and Plomp (1991).

When considering the four distinct subgroups of teachers (non-users, low integrators, medium integrators and high integrators) and looking at the mean number of all self-rating items each respondent filled in, it was found that using teachers in existing subjects know more than their non-using colleagues (see Figure 5.1).

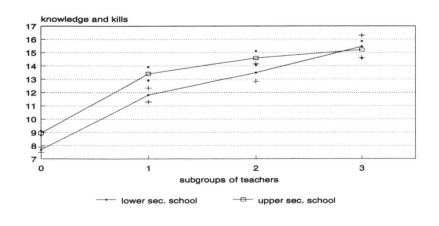

Legend: 0 Non-users; 1 Low integrators; 2 Medium integrators; 3 High integrators

Figure 5.1 Mean number of knowledge and skill self-rating items for each subgroup of teachers including. + = 95% confidence interval.

In lower secondary education, all three subgroups of using teachers and the group of non-using teachers differ significantly on the self-rating scales, indicating that the group of high integrators had the highest level of knowledge and skills. Within upper secondary education, no significant difference was found between medium and high integrators.

For each self-rating item, a test on differences of means for the subgroups of teachers was performed. For lower secondary education each pair of subgroups of teachers differ significantly on two items, namely 'I am capable of adapting instructional software to my needs' and 'I am capable of writing courseware for my own lessons', indicating that the more teachers use the computer in their subject, the more they are capable of adapting instructional software or writing courseware. Furthermore, 20 items show a difference between the using and the non-using group. Of these 20 items, 15 items are also significantly different for the low integrators in comparison with the high integrators.

For upper secondary education the following was found: on only one item ('I can write a program for storing data on a disk drive') a significant difference is found for all four groups of existing subject teachers. 21 items differ between the using and non-using teachers, of which 7 also differ for low and high integrators.

These results indicate that, particularly in lower secondary education, capability items as well as items referring to programming are important in distinguishing low and high integrators. Given these findings, one may conclude that knowledge and skills in general, and these types of knowledge and skills particularly are important for a teacher to be able to integrate computers in their lessons. A logical next step is to examine how teachers received their knowledge and skills.

The role of training

Knowledge and skills can be acquired either by some kind of training or by self-study of the teachers. As the contribution of self-study activities to the knowledge and skill base of teachers can not be determined from the Comped stage 1 data, we restrict ourselves to training.

The overall correlation between participation in training (yes/no) and the knowledge / skill base of teachers is 0.60 (lower secondary education), and 0.57 (upper secondary education), indicating that there is an association between training and knowledge base. This correlation is significant for all subgroups of teachers in both lower and upper secondary education. This means that it is likely that teachers do receive part of their knowledge and skills via training (next to self-study activities). In the context of implementing computers in education, this means that the training component in the innovation process is relevant and contributes to the integration of computers in existing subject matter areas. Given this finding, it is interesting to examine the training component more closely.

Teachers in the Comped project were asked which computer-related topics were covered during their initial or in-service teacher training. The questionnaire listed 31 topics (see Appendix C) within five main categories:
- computers and society (4 topics);
- applications (14);
- problem analysis and programming (5);
- principles of hard- and software structure (3);
- pedagogical/instructional aspects (5).

Pelgrum and Plomp (1991) report that computer education teachers studied more topics during their training than teachers of existing subjects, and that computer using teachers of existing subjects learned more during training than their non-using colleagues.

A breakdown for the question whether training was received or not (regardless the number of topics covered in the training) for the four subgroups of existing subject teachers (non-users, low integrators, medium integrators and high integrators), shows that in lower secondary education 89% of the users and 68% of the non-users have had some form of training; this difference is significant ($p<0.01$). For upper secondary schools these percentages are about 86% for the users and 64% of the non-users; again this difference is significant. No significant difference was found for either population between the three distinct user subgroups. This finding means that having had some training is no indication for the degree of integration of the computer in the existing subject matter area; it only distinguishes the group of users from non-users. A closer look at the curriculum of teacher training, in terms of the number of topics covered and the content of the training, may differentiate between the three user groups.

Figure 5.2 shows the results of a breakdown of the number of topics covered in teacher training by the degree of computer integration.

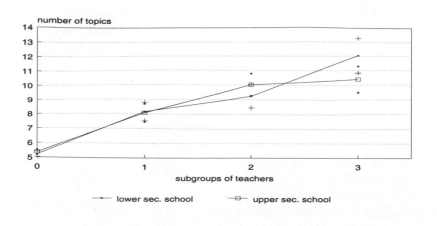

Legend: 0 Non-users; 1 Low integrators; 2 Medium integrators; 3 High integrators

Figure 5.2 Mean number of topics covered in (pre- or inservice) training for each subgroup of teachers.+ = 95% confidence interval.

The subgroups of existing subject teachers differ significantly on the number of topics covered in their training, except in lower secondary education between low and medium integrators and in upper secondary education between medium and high integrators. This means that, where having had training in general does not distinguish the using subgroups, the amount of training (in terms of number of topics) to some extent does because in both populations at least low and high integrators differ significantly on the amount of training received. This finding means that when introducing computers in education, it is not enough to give all teachers a course on how to use computers, dealing with only a few topics. The number of topics covered in teacher training also influences the amount of computer integration.

The question that immediate arises is what are the important topics to be covered in teacher training. The relevance of this question can be illustrated by a quote from Stasz and Shavelson (1985) that *'there is a lack of knowledge and agreement on the topics for and organization of staff development programs'*.

However, it seems relevant to examine the content of training only if training in some sense is related to the actual use of the computer in the class. This relation was already studied above in terms of the relation between the number of topics taught in teacher training and the degree of computer integration but a closer look is possible.

Relation training and actual use of computers in the classroom

In many schools, computer related topics are taught outside formal computer education classes as teachers in existing subjects are addressing them. Teachers of existing subjects were asked to indicate which computer related topics they teach in their subject matter class. The list of topics used for this question was a subset of the list of topics which could be part of teacher training and consisted of four categories:
- computers and society;
- applications;
- problem analysis and programming;
- principles of hard- and software structure.

The correlation between the number of topics covered in training and the number of computer topics taught in the class is for lower and upper respectively 0.39 and 0.35 for all existing subject teachers. For each subject separately, the correlations are respectively 0.36 and 0.28 (mathematics), 0.37 and 0.36 (science) and 0.42 and 0.41 (mother tongue).

Table 5.3 gives the overlap of computer topics taught in the classrooms and the topics covered in teacher training courses.

Table 5.3

Median per cent of topics covered in training, given the computer topics taught in the existing subjects

Teachers	Median %	
	Lower Secondary Schools	Upper Secondary Schools
Overall	69	75
Mathematics	75	80
Science	67	67
Mother tongue	67	75

These results show that a majority of computer topics which are taught in the subject matter class, were also included in the training teachers received. A conclusion from this finding is that the content of training is apparently an important reference for what is actually taught in the lessons. On the other hand, we must be careful to conclude that whatever is taught about in teacher training will also be covered in the instructional practice of the teacher in the class. It was found that of all topics included in the question about teacher training content, 18% in lower secondary education and 25% in upper secondary education (across all subject matter areas) were also taught in the classrooms. The implication of these findings is that it seems important to carefully consider which topics to include in training and which not. This finding, together with the earlier expressed interest to find out what topics were actually covered in teacher training, leads to the following section.

Content of training

Pelgrum and Plomp (1991) note that applications and problem analysis and programming are the most important topics dealt with during teacher training. Pedagogical / instructional aspects are the least mentioned topics of training, but computer using teachers mention the inclusion of these aspects in training more often than non-users. As instructional computer use does not belong to the 'standard repertoire' of most teachers, it may be expected that those teachers who have had some training in the pedagogical/instructional aspects of computer use tend to use the computer more for instructional purposes compared to those who did not receive training in this area.

To investigate this assumption, a test of differences of means for all four subgroups of teachers was done on all 31 training topics. For lower secondary education, 27 training topics show a difference between the non-using group and the users. From these topics, 23 also show a difference between the group of low integrators and high integrators. Only on one training topic was a difference for all four subgroups of teachers found ('evaluation of software'). In upper secondary education also 27 training topics show a difference between non-users and all using groups. From these topics, 14 also show a difference between the group of low and high integrators.

In general, all topics in the categories 'problem analysis and programming', 'principles of hard- and software structure', and 'pedagogical / instructional aspects' distinguish low from high integrators in lower secondary education. Also, when looking at upper secondary education, items in these categories distinguish low and high integrators. However, items in the category pedagogical / instructional aspects (and particularly evaluation of software), contribute the most when distinguishing different groups of integrators. Thus, the initial idea is confirmed that being trained in pedagogical / instructional aspects of computer use can be considered an indicator of the amount of computer use in existing subjects. Because these topics were the least mentioned by teachers as being covered in training, an important conclusion from these findings is that pedagogical and instructional aspects need to be included much more in teacher training activities. Other activities which seem to be relevant for distinguishing different subgroups are some topics related to applications, problem analysis and programming and principles of hardware and software structures, but these topics are often already included in the daily training practice.

Training from school (transcending) perspective

Besides examining training from the perspective of the existing subject teacher, it is possible to discuss this issue from other perspectives. Data obtained from computer coordinators and principals are important sources for a picture of training and support for training given at school and school transcending level.

Computer coordinator perspective

Computer coordinators were asked to indicate whether training activities were made available to the school and through what agencies they were made available (school, local educational authorities or other external agencies).

Figure 5.3 shows for each of the three agencies school, local educational authorities and others to what extent they make training activities available to the school. The median percentage of making an activity available is indicated.

Per type of training activities, the agencies that make this activity available differ. Other agencies than schools or local educational authorities are less important for introductory and application courses in all populations (except to some extent in elementary education), but in making computer science and micro-electronics cources available, they are the most important.

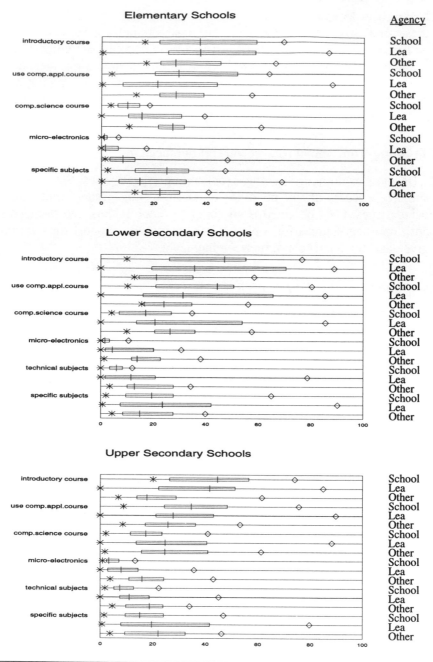

Legend: 25% Tile ▢ 75% Tile, ▢ Median, * Minimum, ◊ Maximum

Figure 5.3 Per cent of different training activities per agency providing it (as indicated by the computer coordinator).

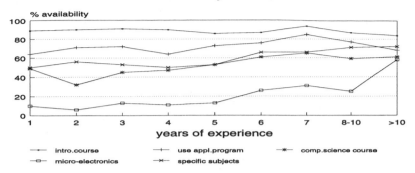

Elementary Schools

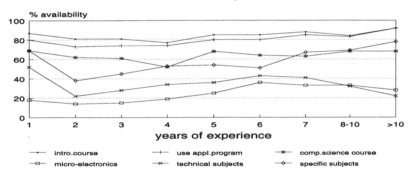

Lower Secondary Schools

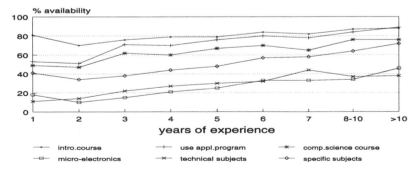

Upper Secondary Schools

Figure 5.4 Per cent schools across countries indicating availability of training activities in the school (according to the computer coordinator), given the number of years of experience with computers.

As the involvement of schools with computers increased during the 1980s, the availability of training activities for the school may have changed over the years; this is the reason why an analysis has been done on this relation. Figure 5.4 shows the relation of staff development activities with the years of computer use of schools. For each staff development activity, the percentage of computer coordinators indicating that this activity is available at school, no matter who (school, lea or others) is responsible for making it available, is broken down for the number of years that schools have been working with computers.

The figure shows that no spectacular changes can be observed in availability of certain training activities dependent on the number of years a school works with computers. Schools in elementary and upper secondary education which have worked longer with the computer tend to have slightly more training activities, according to the computer coordinator. Some noteworthy results are the availability of activities related to micro-electronics in elementary education (more available when a school works longer with computers) and courses for technical subjects and special subjects in lower secondary education (more available when a school just recently started working with computers).

School support for training

To study the role of the school in supporting training, the scores on the training activities are recoded in terms of activities supported by the school or by others (for instance local educational authorities). A factor analysis of these data resulted in two factors, showing that, in essence, two different kinds of training are made available by the school. The first factor contains activities such as introductory course, using application programs, computer science course and a course on using computers in specific subjects; this factor will further be called *general training*. The reliability of this scale of activities across countries is for all populations 0.74. The second factor consists of courses on micro-electronics and courses for technical subjects (further called *specialist training*) with a scale reliability across countries of 0.66 (lower secondary schools) and 0.64 (upper secondary schools). In elementary schools, the second factor did not exist because the topic on courses for technical subjects was not included in the question for elementary school coordinators. The correlation between the two scales is 0.23 (lower secondary schools) and 0.38 (upper secondary schools). The results indicate that especially the first factor, general training activities, is a reliable factor. This factor is also used for the LISREL analyses in

Chapter 7.

The question is whether the emphasis on one of the two types of training leads to more use of the computer in existing subjects. In order to answer this question, the measure for implementation width, introduced in Chapter 2 was used. This measure gives an indication of the number of subject matter areas (out of the list of mathematics, science and mother tongue) in which the computer is used in the school. The range of this measure is from 0 to 3.

When relating the two scales of training activities with the implementation width measure, it was found that the overall correlation (across countries) between general training and implementation width was 0.10 (elementary schools), 0.19 (lower secondary schools) and 0.18 (upper secondary schools). This correlation was significant for all populations, which is easily explainable because of the large number of cases. When looking at specific countries, respectively 4 of the 10 countries in elementary school, 7 of the 15 countries in lower secondary school and 13 of the 20 countries in upper secondary school show significant relations between these two variables.

The correlation between the availability of specific types of training (the second factor of the factor analysis) and the implementation width measure is in both lower and upper secondary education 0.04.

Overall, the conclusion based on these findings is that there is no strong relation between the amount of general training activities made available by the school and the degree of computer use in existing subjects. The relation with the amount of specific training activities is virtually zero.

Principal perspective

The principal was also asked which people or agencies support the school with training activities. This question to the principal contains more detailed information about what external agencies support the school. The principal of each school was asked to indicate whether support was given to the school concerning the use of the computer and by what external people or agencies this support is given. Across countries and populations, between 7 and 8% of the principals indicated that no support at all was received by the school, in no area and by none of the external agencies. In only a few countries does this percentage exceed 10%, namely in elementary education in Belgium-French (14%), Italy (20%), Japan (24%) and Portugal (13%), in lower secondary education in Italy (20%), Japan (28%) and Portugal (19%) and in upper secondary education in India (12%), Japan (31%), Portugal (16%) and Slovenia (16%).

Pelgrum and Plomp (1991) concluded that, *'...although educational systems differ in the way training is organized,... authorities are quite supportive to training, not only at school level, but also at the school transcending level (local, state, provincial, national). In each country, quite a number of other agencies such as universities and teacher training colleges, business and industry, associations and teachers of other schools are relatively important supporters of staff development as well'.*

The relative importance of each agency can be derived from Figure 5.5. Next to each agency the countries with the highest and lowest percentage are included. These countries are mentioned as relatively scoring high or low on this question. This does not necessarily imply that, absolutely speaking when looking at a particular country, this agency is the most or least supporting staff development activities.

For the group of parents, no countries are included in the figure because the scores in most countries are extremely low.

Figure 5.5 shows that the Ministry of Education was the important supporter of teacher training in lower and upper secondary education. In elementary education, teachers of other schools and local educational authorities played a more important role. Clearly, support from parents for teacher training was the least important in all populations.

Some deviations from these results across countries can be reported when looking at specific countries. The importance of the Ministry of Education was particularly stressed (with percentages of support indicated by the principal far more higher than the median percentage for this agency across countries) in Austria (67% in upper secondary education), France (59% in elementary education, 77% in lower secondary education and 72% in upper secondary education), the Federal Republic of Germany (81% in lower secondary education and 83% in upper secondary education), Israel (45% in elementary education and 58% in upper secondary education), Greece (83% and 90% in respectively lower and upper secondary education), Luxembourg and Switzerland (respectively 89% and 74% in lower secondary education) and Italy (86% in upper secondary education).

The local educational authorities were especially important in Austria (50% in lower and 74% in upper secondary education), Canada-British Columbia (74% in elementary education and 66% in both lower and upper secondary education) and the United States of America (64%, 56% and 65% in the respective populations).

Universities and colleges played a relatively important role (compared to other countries) in Austria (33% in lower secondary education, Israel (44% in upper secondary education) and the United States of America (28% and 43% in respectively lower and upper secondary education).

The role of business and industry was relatively important in upper secondary education in Canada-British Columbia (39%), Italy (40%), and the United States of America (40%). Support institutes provide notable assistance in Austria (63% and 55% in respectively lower and upper secondary education), the Netherlands (76% in lower and 52% in upper secondary education), India (59%) and Slovenia (51%; both in upper secondary education). Teachers of other schools were relatively frequently mentioned as supporters in upper secondary education in France (48%), New Zealand (37%) and the United States of America (29%).

Because it is possible that the support agencies change over time, the relationship between these variables and support have been investigated. For this analysis, two subgroups have been determined, namely a group of early starters, working 8 or more years with computers, and a group of late starters, working 2 or less years with computers. Significant differences between the two groups were found for several training support agencies, all indicating that early starters received more support than late starters. This holds in elementary education for local educational authorities, business and industry and teachers of other schools; in lower secondary education for associations (e.g. teacher associations, computer science association), business and industry, and teachers of other schools; and in upper secondary education for associations, business and industry, support institutes and teachers of other schools.

Implications: relating findings with other research

The relevance of looking at training can be derived from earlier research findings as well as from the first results from the Comped study.

Staff development is a basic and necessary component of the continuing development of teachers, administrators and other staff as they extend their professional or technical knowledge (Orlich, 1989) and, as discussed in the introduction, training is an important part of staff development activities.

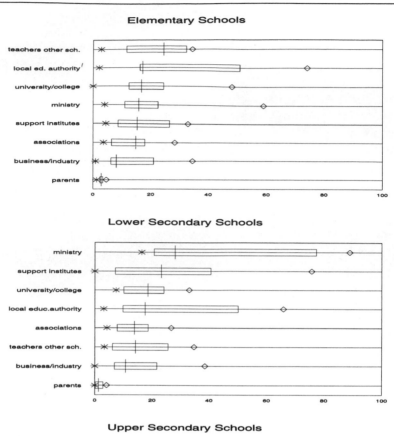

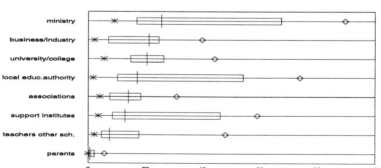

Legend: 25% Tile [   ] 75% Tile, [☐] Median, * Minimum, ◊ Maximum

Figure 5.5 Median per cent of support with teacher training across countries for each countries with the lowest and highest percentage.

LOW	HIGH
ISR / NET	CBC / NWZ
BFR / NWZ	CBC / USA
CBC / NET	FRA / POR
CBC / ITA / POR	FRA / ISR
BFR / POR	ITA / USA
NET / POR	BFR / ITA
NET / POR	ISR / USA
CBC / ITA	GRE / LUX
LUX / GRE / POR	AUT / NET
BFL / GRE / NET	AUT / USA
NWZ / NET / SWI	CBC / USA
AUT / POR	CBC / NWZ
NET / POR	FRA / NWZ
GRE / POR	CBC / USA
IND / POL	GRE / ITA
HUN / POR	ITA / USA
BFL / IND	ISR / USA
NWZ / ISR / SWI	AUT / CBC
IND / NET / POR	CBC / GRE
GRE / POL / POR	AUT / IND
ISR / IND / NET	FRA / NWZ

agency (as indicated by the principal) and

Besides normal updating of knowledge in one's subject, professional development and assistance are important for both the dissemination and implementation of educational innovations (Fullan, 1991). Teachers need to learn new roles in order to work effectively with new programs and technologies. It is therefore not surprising that training is considered one of the factors that contribute to the success of implementing an innovation in the educational practice (Fullan, 1991). There are no reasons to expect that this should not also hold for the use of computers in education (see, for example, Van den Akker, Keursten and Plomp, 1992). The crucial role of staff development and training activities in the introduction of computers in the school is also stressed by Moskowitz and Birman (1985), Walker (1986), Brody (1987), the US Congress (1988) and Fullan, Miles and Anderson (1988).

Some of the Comped data also give indications for the importance of this issue. First, Pelgrum and Schipper (1992) developed a measure for computer integration in the class.

The number of subject matter topics for which a teacher indicates computer use serves as a measure of the amount of integration of the computer. The integration measure is found to be related to certain task elements the teacher is stating he or she knows or can (like evaluating usefulness of software and adapt instructional software). This result indicates that integration of computers in the lesson is partly determined by the knowledge and skills of teachers.

Second, the Comped data show that the lack of knowledge of teachers and insufficient training opportunities are considered to be two major problems in the use of the computer in the educational practice (see Chapter 4). However, teachers themselves consider these items to be a problem less frequently than principals and computer coordinators (Pelgrum and Plomp, 1991). Considering the national questionnaire (filled in by the National Project Coordinator of each country), in many countries the small number of teachers trained so far, and the lack of teacher training courses are reported as problematic.

A third indication of the relevance of training can be derived from a LISREL analysis of the Comped data by Tuijnman and ten Brummelhuis (see Chapter 7). They fitted a LISREL model for six countries, consisting of three dependent variables, namely computer use, teacher competence and readiness, and monitoring and problem coping strategy. One of the predictor variables in the models was related to internal staff development (or training activities). Tuijnman and ten Brummelhuis found that in several countries staff development is related to computer use, teacher competence and strategies to monitor computer use and to cope with problems. In summary, it can be concluded that training is clearly an important issue when dealing with the introduction of computers in the educational practice.

When looking at the findings of the Comped-project, the results indicate that schools, local educational authorities and other agencies mainly provide training in the sense of introductory courses, courses meant to use application programs and computer science courses. Involvement in these activities is not dependent on the schools' experience with computers, that is whether schools just started to work with the computer or are already working with the new technology for many years.

The training activities can be divided into general and specific training activities but no relation was found between the availability of either types of training at school and the implementation width of computers in schools.

External agencies which provide support in the area of teacher training are in general the Ministry of Education and universities and colleges in secondary education and teachers of other schools and local educational authorities in elementary education. For a number of external agencies, the support they provide the school with differs depending on whether the school can be called an early or late starter, all indicating that early starters received more support in the area of teacher training.

Besides looking at the context of training in which teachers need to operate in the sense of training activities available at school and support given to it, the results mentioned in this chapter shed some light on the teacher perspective of training in the area of computers in education. It was found that the amount of training received by existing subject teachers and the type of topics covered in training are to some extent related to the amount of computer integration in existing subjects.

As an indication of what topics could be best covered in teacher training, it was found that especially pedagogical / instructional aspects in teacher training are contributing to the integration of computers in the classroom. As the results show that these topics were rather limited in training activities up till 1989, an important implication is that teacher training institutes should take these aspects into account.

6

Administration/Policy
and Equity

This chapter addresses a number of issues related to administration, policy, and equity in regard to the use of computers in education. The focus of the section on administration and policy focuses on the school principal. Current theory and research in educational administration underscores the central role of the school principal as the educational leader of the school and his or her importance in establishing the framework and climate within which school goals are achieved (Lipham, Ranking and Hoeh, 1985, Sergiovanni, 1991, and Andrews, 1987). Furthermore, the conceptual framework for this study emphasizes the role of the principal at the meso-level of the educational system (see Chapter 1).

Policies, practices, and even the attitudes of school principals will be examined in some detail. Information on equity issues was also obtained from school principals. Here too, policies, practices, and attitudes will be examined.

The School Setting

The setting of a school can be described in a number of ways. Two have been selected for presentation here. In the first instance, schools can be described in terms of their geographic setting. Principals were asked to indicate the setting of the school in terms of urban/rural. Figure 6.1 presents this information. At the elementary level, about half the schools are located in an urban setting while at the lower and upper secondary levels, most of the participating schools are located in an urban area. Comparisons between the three educational levels cannot be made, however, because different countries participated at the different educational levels.

This chapter was written by Richard M. Wolf and Georgia Kontogiannopolou-Polydorides.

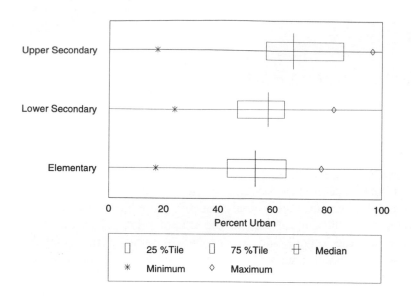

Figure 6.1 Area in which school is located.

A second way of characterizing the school setting is in terms of the educational backgrounds of the parents of the students attending the school. Information bearing on this is presented in Figure 6.2. In addition, a breakdown has been made between schools in which computers are used for instructional purposes (using schools) and schools in which computers are not used (non-using schools) for such purposes. In developing these figures, only countries with a sizable number of both using and non-using schools were included. However, in a few countries, e.g., Greece, where there was a small number of using schools, but all were included in the study, results have been reported. In general, results presented in this chapter are based on at least thirty schools unless a particular category includes virtually all schools in a country.

At the elementary level (Figure 6.2), all schools in all countries that were included show a mix of students from homes with low, medium, and high levels of parental education although the percentage of students from homes with high levels of parental education is quite small in Portugal. More important, however, is the difference in the educational backgrounds of parents of students in using versus non-using schools. At the elementary level, the proportion of students from homes with parents

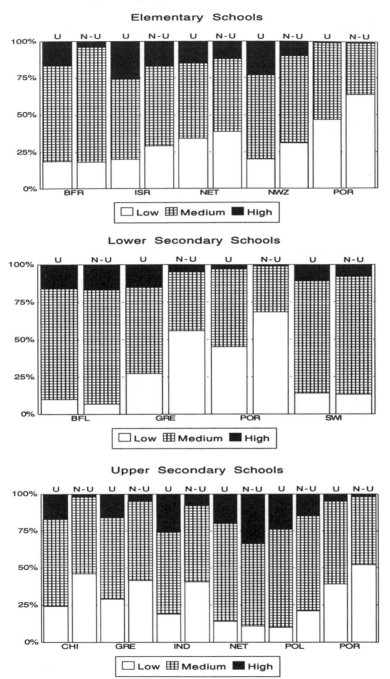

Figure 6.2 Educational background of parents in using (U) and non-using (N-U) schools.

having low levels of education is generally greater in non-using schools than in using schools. The exception to this finding is Belgium-French where the proportions are virtually identical. Furthermore, at this level, the proportion of students from homes with high levels of parental education is generally higher in using schools than in non-using schools. New Zealand and Belgium French shows the most dramatic example of this differential. Twenty three per cent of the students in using schools in New Zealand are from homes with high levels of parental education compared with ten per cent of students in non-using schools. In the Netherlands and Portugal, the differences are negligible.

At the lower secondary level, the same general results can be found but are less pronounced. Students in non-using schools generally come from homes with a larger proportion of parents with low levels of education than students in using schools. Exceptions to this general result occur in Belgium-Flemish and Switzerland. The pattern of results for students from homes with high levels of parental education is mixed. In Greece, there are higher percentages of students from homes with higher levels of parental education in using than non-using schools. However, in Belgium-Flemish, Portugal, and Switzerland the percentages are virtually identical.

At the upper secondary level, results are presented for six countries. In five of the countries (China, Greece, India, Poland and Portugal), the proportion of students from homes with lower levels of parental education is greater in non-using schools than in using schools. In the Netherlands, there is a slightly larger proportion of students from homes with lower levels of education in using than non-using schools. There is a clear tendency for students from homes with higher levels of parent education to be in using schools. In all countries except the Netherlands, the proportions for using schools are greater than for non-using schools although the differences in Portugal are negligible. The greatest difference exists in India where eight per cent of students in non-using schools come from homes with high levels of parental education compared with 26 per cent in using schools.

In summary, schools in all participating countries show a mix of students from homes with low, medium, and high levels of parent education. Countries reporting results for using and non-using schools show some social bias in the use of computers with using schools generally showing a lower proportion of student from homes with low

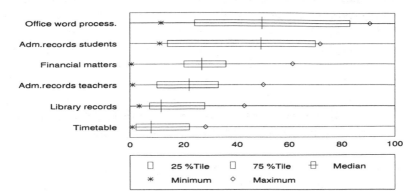

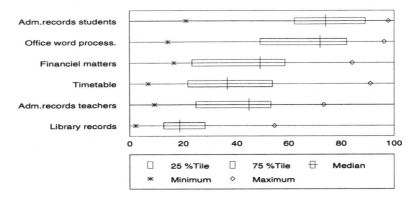

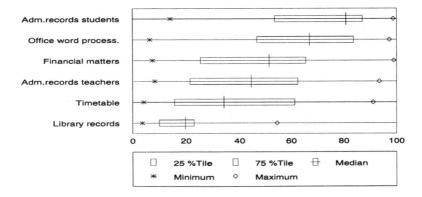

Figure 6.3 Percentages of schools using computers for various administrative tasks.

levels of parent education than in non-using schools and a higher proportion of students from homes with high levels of parent education in using schools. There are a number of notable exceptions to this general finding. However, they do not seem to be consistent across levels of schooling.

Administrative Uses of Computers

It was thought at the outset of the study that one way in which computers might work their way into the school was through administrative use and that this might lead to the use of computers in instruction. Accordingly, information was sought regarding administrative uses of computers in schools. This information is presented in summary form in Figure 6.3.

The most notable finding regarding administrative uses of computers in schools is that it is considerably lower than instructional uses of computers (See Pelgrum and Plomp, 1991, p.18). At all population levels and in all countries, the use of computers for administration only is decidedly lower than instructional uses. While highly variable, computer use for instructional purposes is far ahead of use for administration only. Within the area of administrative uses, office word processing, the maintenance of administrative records about students, and financial matters are the areas of greatest use while the maintenance of library records and construction and maintenance of the school timetable are the areas of least use. Thus, the early supposition of that the introduction of computers into schools for administrative purposes would spread to their use for instructional purposes was not supported by the data. Computers have been introduced into schools for instructional purposes and administrative use computers has lagged behind instructional use.

Principals of schools without computers were asked whether they planned to use computers for administrative purposes. Since so many schools already had computers, there were relatively few responses to this question. At the elementary level, six countries had sufficient numbers of responses to even permit a tally. The percentages of principals reporting that they planned to introduce computers into their schools for administrative purposes ranged from 33% to 81% with a median of 62%. At the lower secondary level, there were sufficient number of responses from only six countries. At this level, the percentages ranged from 10% to 95% with a median of 40%.

Table 6.1a

Percentage of elementary schools reporting changes in various aspects of organization and management as a result of using computers

Aspects of Organization	Country						
and Management	BFR	CBC	ISR	JPN	NET	NWZ	USA
Time needed for creating timetable							
Worse	-	-	20	2	-	29	-
Better	-	-	17	10	-	7	-
Quality of timetable							
Worse	-	-	14	1	-	6	-
Better	-	-	30	16	-	30	-
Allocation of students to groups							
Worse	-	-	6	1	-	3	9
Better	-	-	50	15	-	48	29
Information about student achievement							
Worse	-	0	1	2	-	0	0
Better	-	87	89	69	-	53	48
Time needed for absentee registration							
Worse	-	5	-	1	-	1	2
Better	-	86	-	13	-	10	40
Quality student administration							
Worse	-	0	3	1	1	3	2
Better	-	79	59	30	89	57	53
Quality teacher administration							
Worse	-	0	-	1	-	0	2
Better	-	90	-	27	-	64	28
Evaluation effects policies							
Worse	-	-	-	2	-	0	0
Better	-	-	-	49	-	43	15
Availability information							
Worse	-	0	-	0	-	2	-
Better	-	81	-	37	-	63	-
Efficiency school administration							
Worse	1	0	-	1	1	0	1
Better	94	91	-	57	93	80	54

Notes: - = No data collected or sample size too small for analysis.

Table 6.1b

Percentage of lower secondary schools reporting changes in various aspects of

Aspects of Organization	Country				
and Management	BFL	BFR	CBC	FRA	FRG
Time needed for creating timetable					
Worse	3	-	6	21	9
Better	73	-	82	55	80
Quality of timetable					
Worse	13	-	2	22	9
Better	41	-	78	34	59
Allocation of students to groups					
Worse	7	2	1	6	4
Better	62	64	85	57	64
Information about student achievement					
Worse	0	0	2	0	1
Better	76	79	91	87	73
Time needed for absentee registration					
Worse	-	-	7	-	-
Better	-	-	76	-	-
Quality of student administration					
Worse	1	0	1	0	1
Better	92	94	82	94	93
Quality of teacher administration					
Worse	0	1	3	2	-
Better	72	89	81	80	-
Evaluation of effects of policies					
Worse	-	0	2	2	-
Better	-	84	49	73	-
Availability of information					
Worse	1	0	2	0	-
Better	81	84	64	89	-
Efficiency of school administration					
Worse	0	2	2	0	1
Better	89	92	87	88	93

Notes: - = No data collected or sample size too small for analysis.

organization and management as a result of using computers

JPN	LUX	NET	NWZ	SWI	USA
1	-	1	2	5	-
56	-	82	62	66	-
3	-	5	2	3	-
40	-	60	64	48	-
2	0	2	0	1	41
43	49	71	74	59	45
1	-	1	0	1	0
96	-	78	65	57	59
0	-	7	9	1	15
19	-	38	53	21	43
0	-	0	0	1	18
43	-	95	87	85	61
2	-	0	1	1	7
22	-	68	71	74	33
0	-	1	0	0	0
46	-	52	30	41	22
0	-	1	0	1	-
53	-	78	70	62	-
1	-	1	0	0	0
69	-	93	84	84	64

Table 6.1c

Percentage of upper secondary schools reporting changes in various aspects of

Aspects of Organization	Country					
and Management	BFL	BFR	CBC	CHI	FRA	FRG
Time needed for creating timetable						
Worse	8	-	6	-	29	-
Better	74	-	82	-	51	-
Quality of timetable						
Worse	11	-	2	-	45	6
Better	40	-	79	-	22	57
Allocation of students to groups						
Worse	6	-	1	-	4	0
Better	45	-	85	-	66	60
Information about student achievement						
Worse	0	0	2	0	1	3
Better	79	76	91	94	75	74
Time needed for absentee registration						
Worse	-	-	7	-	6	-
Better	-	-	76	-	77	-
Quality of student administration						
Worse	0	1	1	0	1	0
Better	94	92	82	99	95	92
Quality of teacher administration						
Worse	0	1	3	-	1	-
Better	69	80	49	-	70	-
Evaluation of effects of policies						
Worse	0	0	2	-	4	0
Better	69	80	49	-	70	0
Availability of information						
Worse	1	0	2	-	3	0
Better	93	81	64	-	81	0
Efficiency of school administration						
Worse	0	2	2	0	2	0
Better	95	90	87	98	89	91

Notes: - = No data collected or sample size too small for analysis.

organization and management as a result of using computers

HUN	IND	ISR	JPN	NET	NWZ	POL	SLO	SWI	USA
2	12	-	11	4	3	-	7	4	-
36	53	-	48	84	83	-	79	79	-
4	7	-	10	1	1	-	-	8	-
22	54	-	29	64	79	-	-	66	-
2	9	10	4	1	0	3	-	1	1
27	64	65	41	74	87	46	-	66	73
1	0	3	1	4	0	1	-	0	0
76	83	80	89	65	80	64	-	71	71
0	13	-	0	6	13	-	-	0	1
47	49	-	36	53	51	-	-	45	66
0	8	2	1	0	4	-	-	1	0
49	64	84	38	94	90	-	-	92	70
1	4	3	1	1	0	3	-	0	1
35	62	64	43	54	42	56	-	52	42
1	4	4	0	0	0	2	-	2	1
35	62	64	43	54	42	56	-	52	42
1	5	0	0	0	0	5	-	1	-
44	64	76	46	65	80	29	-	72	-
1	2	1	0	0	0	3	-	0	1
72	72	94	64	96	98	55	-	91	87

At the upper secondary level, only five countries responded with sufficient numbers of replies to permit a tally. The responses here ranged from 10% to 99% with a median of 30%. Generally, little can be concluded from this information for two reasons. First, the number of schools without any computers is generally too low to permit much meaningful analysis. Second, whether computers are introduced into schools for administrative uses seems to be a matter that is not completely within the control of the principal.

In contrast to the item requesting information about intentions to introduce computers for administrative purposes, school principals who were using computers for various aspects of organization and management were asked to indicate how the introduction of computers had affected administrative operations in the school. Specifically, principals were asked whether the introduction of computers had improved the school's ability to perform certain administrative tasks or not. The results to these various questions are presented in Tables 6.1a, 6.1b, and 6.1c. For each item, the principal was asked whether the use of the computer had enabled him or her and the staff to perform a task better than before, the same as before, or worse than before. Since the percentages for the three categories add to 100%, the category "Same as before" has been omitted.

At the elementary level, the percentages in the category, "Worse", are generally negligible while the percentages in the category "Better" are generally substantial, indicating perceived benefits of the use of the computer for administrative purposes. In a number of cases, e.g., quality of teacher administration, availability of information, and efficiency of school administration, the percentage of principals reporting that the use of computers has resulted in better performance than before is fairly sizable. The only aspect of school administration in which the situation is viewed as worse than before is in the time needed to create the school timetable where two countries (Israel and New Zealand) report percentages greater than 10. It could be that initial expectations were high in this area and were not being met.

At the lower secondary level, the results were generally similar to those found at the elementary level, but more variable. Items on which principals reported the situation as worse than before involved the time needed to create the timetable and the quality of the timetable. Here, the percentages for some countries were greater than 10. For all other items, the principals, on the whole, responded that the introduction of the computer had resulted in a situation better than before. The percentage of countries reporting the situation after the introduction of computers as better than before is often quite high. The results for France are noteworthy in two respects. First, sizable percentages of principals, 21 and 22% respectively, report that the time needed to create the timetable and the quality of the timetable are worse than before. Second, sizable percentages of school principals report that other aspects of organization are better than before. In fact, the percentages for these other items are among the highest of all countries at this level.

The results for the upper secondary level are quite similar to those found for the lower secondary level. For virtually all items, the percentage of principals reporting that the introduction of computers for administrative use had resulted in a situation that was better than before is very high. The two exceptions are still the time needed for creating the timetable and the quality of the timetable where a number of countries show percentages greater than 10 for the category, "Worse than Before". In contrast, no country, with the exception of India, reports a percentage greater than 10 for any of the remaining items. In fact, the percentage of responses in the category, "Better than Before", is often strikingly high. Percentages greater than 50 are quite common for this category and many are greater than 80.

In summary, countries that use computers for administrative purposes generally report that the introduction of computers has resulted in an improvement in the administration of the school. The major exception to this general finding is in the time needed to create the school timetable and the quality of the resulting timetable. One possible explanation for this less than fully satisfactory state of affairs may be due to the software that is used to produce the timetable. High quality software for the this purpose for the types of computers used in schools may not be readily available.

Principals Attitudes Towards Computers

A series of statements seeking principals' attitudes towards computers was included in the School Principal Questionnaire. The research literature on attitude-behavior relations suggests that attitudes are an important precursor to behavior (Ajzen and Fishbein, 1977). Also, the conceptual framework of this study includes characteristics of school principals as a critical element at the meso-level of innovation (see Chapter 1). Attitudes are an important characteristic of principals. The responses of principals on the attitude items are presented in Table 6.2a-6.2c.

At the elementary school level, principals show a generally favorable disposition towards computers. The principals indicated that they try to keep themselves informed about technological changes, that the use of computers in class leads to more productivity among students, that students are generally more attentive when computers are used in class and that the principals do not mind learning about computers. These principals generally reject the idea that computers have become too dominant over us, that computers harm relations between people, and that social contacts are negatively affected by the use of computers. The major exception to these general findings is that relatively small percentages of principals in France and the Netherlands (32% and 30%, respectively) see the use of computers as leading to more productivity in students.

At the lower secondary school, the findings were highly similar to those found at the elementary level. If anything, the responses were more clear-cut. Highly similar results were found at the upper secondary level. At this level, Belgium-Flemish, the Federal Republic of Germany and Switzerland join the group of principals who do not see the use of computers as leading to greater productivity in students.

The results for the upper secondary level are generally similar to those found for the lower secondary level. There are still some anomalous findings for Greece that can not be easily explained, e.g., 93% of principals in Greece agree with the statement that computers have become too dominant over us and 45% believe that computers harm relations between people. However, since there has been relatively little experience with computers in Greece, it is questionable how much credence should be given to these results. Insofar as the use of computers leading to more productivity in students, less than half the principals in Belgium-Flemish, the Federal Republic of Germany, the Netherlands and Switzerland agree with this statement.

A few exceptions to these general findings can be noted. At the elementary level, there was an equal percentage of principals in Israel who agreed and disagreed with the statement, "Computers have become too dominant over us" (39%). At the lower secondary level, 92% of the principals in Greece agreed with this statement.

Table 6.2a

Principal's attitudes towards computers in elementary schools

Statement	Country								
	BFR	CBC	FRA	ISR	JPN	NET	NWZ	POR	USA
Computers have become too dominant over us									
Agree	19	8	16	39	7	8	14	37	15
Disagree	65	81	65	38	32	77	72	58	76
I try to keep myself informed about technological changes									
Agree	77	90	57	87	79	76	86	85	89
Disagree	7	6	19	7	3	17	9	10	4
Using computers in class leads to more productivity among students									
Agree	51	72	32	79	69	30	69	63	80
Disagree	6	3	20	2	3	8	6	1	2
Computers harm relations between people									
Agree	18	2	17	11	6	2	7	26	5
Disagree	60	81	62	69	43	72	76	61	83
Students more attentive when computers are used in class									
Agree	46	52	44	57	68	34	55	58	60
Disagree	6	12	18	12	1	17	12	1	10
Social contacts are negatively affected by use of computers									
Agree	14	8	11	6	2	4	14	22	5
Disagree	53	78	62	70	38	66	63	63	78
I don't mind learning about computers									
Agree	91	97	91	97	47	93	96	96	99
Disagree	4	1	3	1	15	5	1	4	1

Table 6.2b
Principal's attitudes towards computers in lower secondary schools

Statement	Country					
	BFL	BFR	CBC	FRA	FRG	GRE
Computers have become too dominant over us						
Agree	13	16	15	11	13	92
Disagree	76	65	76	74	66	5
I try to keep myself informed about technological changes						
Agree	92	90	90	82	87	86
Disagree	4	3	9	5	6	3
Using computers in class leads to more productivity among students						
Agree	34	60	82	43	36	71
Disagree	6	2	5	8	17	4
Computers harm relations between people						
Agree	7	12	4	15	-	41
Disagree	63	64	86	66	-	39
Students more attentive when computers are used in class						
Agree	47	68	66	66	54	51
Disagree	13	9	11	4	12	7
Social contacts are negatively affected by use of computers						
Agree	9	12	7	12	11	41
Disagree	60	55	74	69	60	43
I don't mind learning about computers						
Agree	93	92	98	94	94	92
Disagree	4	3	2	2	3	2

Notes: - = Item not administered.

JPN	LUX	NET	NWZ	POR	SWI	USA
18	23	2	24	37	35	9
31	38	89	70	54	47	74
82	100	87	95	85	86	92
5	0	6	2	8	6	6
72	65	25	67	74	34	78
3	4	4	5	2	20	2
7	8	4	12	20	29	5
46	72	76	78	67	47	81
55	42	43	66	70	35	61
2	19	12	19	1	18	11
3	16	5	18	25	25	7
49	64	74	60	61	47	68
62	100	92	91	91	95	97
15	0	7	2	8	2	0

Table 6.2c

Principal's attitudes towards computers in upper secondary schools

| Statement | Country | | | | | |
	BFL	BFR	CBC	CHI	FRA	FRG
Computers have become too dominant over us						
Agree	10	10	15	21	17	12
Disagree	83	74	76	64	68	72
I try to keep myself informed about technological changes						
Agree	94	90	90	97	91	84
Disagree	3	4	9	0	3	4
Using computers in class leads to more productivity among students						
Agree	34	60	82	76	51	27
Disagree	5	6	5	3	8	24
Computers harm relations between people						
Agree	9	12	4	8	10	14
Disagree	73	68	86	75	70	63
Students more attentive when computers are used in class						
Agree	51	68	66	71	66	46
Disagree	8	6	11	1	4	14
Social contacts are negatively affected by use of computers						
Agree	9	8	7	3	9	14
Disagree	67	64	74	76	70	60
I don't mind learning about computers						
Agree	95	90	98	90	94	97
Disagree	3	3	2	5	1	1

GRE	HUN	IND	ISR	JPN	NET	NWZ	POL	POR	SLO	SWI	USA
93	1	40	38	16	2	12	14	38	18	28	11
4	94	47	44	48	92	82	66	57	72	53	78
85	79	87	84	83	91	83	88	87	89	88	92
4	1	4	9	3	5	11	4	6	3	7	5
71	54	75	65	77	26	63	80	75	92	42	84
6	5	6	8	1	5	7	4	2	5	24	2
45	4	14	13	3	3	4	6	22	13	20	4
37	81	69	68	58	76	81	74	66	78	59	85
48	53	79	54	75	39	65	66	72	86	42	64
10	7	5	19	1	17	7	7	2	3	25	9
50	2	26	11	3	8	8	7	22	13	20	8
33	87	57	67	55	73	65	70	62	73	54	71
93	79	83	93	77	90	92	91	93	99	95	96
2	8	13	4	7	6	4	3	6	0	1	3

Since 93% of the principals in Greece at the upper secondary level agreed with this statement, one suspects that there may have been a response acquiescence, that is, a tendency to agree with statements that are presented. Similarly, 41% of the principals in Greece at the lower secondary level agreed with the statement, "Computers harm relations between people" while 45% of the principals at the upper secondary level agreed with it. Again, this result is rather out of line with all other countries.

The picture that emerges from the responses to the attitudinal items for principals is one that shows a generally favorable disposition towards computers and their potential contribution to student learning. While favorable attitudes towards computers on the part of principals does not provide any guarantee that computers will be used in schools, the existence of such attitudes can be taken as a sign of a general receptivity that indicates no barrier to their use.

An attitude scale consisting of five items was embedded in the School Principal's Questionnaire and sought to determine the principal's attitude toward the educational value of the use of computers. The items were as follows:

1. Computers are valuable tools to improve the quality of a child's education.
2. Using computers in class leads to more productivity among students.
3. Computers help to teach more effectively.
4. In-service courses about computers should be made compulsory.
5. The achievement of students can be increased when using computers for teaching.

Each statement was answered on a scale ranging from Strongly Agree (5) to Strongly Disagree (1). The results from the use of this scale for both using and non-using schools are presented in Tables 6.3a, 6.3b, and 6.3c. The means for the scale, expressed as an average of the response to the five items, range from 3.0 to 4.4. This means that the vast majority of the responses were in the favorable range. At the elementary level (Table 6.3a), eight of the means were between 3.4 and 3.9 while six of the means were between 4.0 and 4.2. In almost all cases, the mean attitude scale score for principals in using schools was above the mean for principals in non-using schools. These differences, however, were slight, ranging from 0.1 to 0.4.

Table 6.3a

Principals attitudes[1] towards educational use of computers in using and non-using elementary schools

Country/	Using			Non-using		
Educational System	Mean	St. Dev.	N	Mean	St. Dev.	N
Belgium-French	3.7	0.6	135	3.4	0.7	88
Canada-British Columbia	3.9	0.6	146	-	-	-
France	3.5	0.7	317	-	-	-
Israel	4.1	0.5	140	4.1	0.6	94
Japan	4.2	0.6	189	3.8	0.7	134
Netherlands	3.5	0.6	104	3.3	0.6	95
New Zealand	4.0	0.6	358	3.8	0.7	93
Portugal	4.1	0.5	92	3.9	0.6	131
United States of America	4.1	0.6	303	-	-	-

Notes: 1 = see page 168 for item texts. - = No non-using schools in sample or sample size too small for analysis.

Table 6.3b

Principals attitudes[1] towards educational use of computers in using and non-using lower secondary schools

Country/	Using			Non-using		
Educational System	Mean	St. Dev.	N	Mean	St. Dev.	N
Belgium-Flemish	3.6	0.5	212	3.5	0.6	55
Belgium-French	3.8	0.6	161	-		
Canada-British Columbia	4.0	0.6	126	-		
France	3.8	0.6	392	-		
Federal Republic of Germany	3.2	0.7	351	-		
Greece	4.2	0.6	58	4.1	0.7	293
Japan	3.9	0.6	223	3.7	0.6	72
Luxembourg	3.7	0.6	24 *	-		
Netherlands	3.5	0.5	229	-		
New Zealand	3.9	0.6	115	-		
Portugal	4.1	0.5	138	3.9	0.6	100
Switzerland	3.1	0.6	607	2.9	0.8	230
United States of America	4.0	0.5	303	-		

Notes: 1 = see page 168 for item texts. - = No non-using schools in sample or sample size too small for analysis.
* Total population of using schools.

Table 6.3c

Principals attitudes[1] towards educational use of computers in using and non-using schools at upper secondary level

Country/	Type of School					
	Using			Non-using		
Educational System	Mean	St. Dev.	N	Mean	St. Dev.	N
Belgium-Flemish	3.7	0.5	240	-		
Belgium-French	3.8	0.6	174	-		
Canada-British Columbia	4.0	0.6	126	-		
China	4.1	0.5	246	4.1	0.6	78
France	3.8	0.5	357	-		
Federal Republic of Germany	3.2	0.7	183	-		
Greece	4.2	0.7	29 *	4.1	0.6	399
Hungary	3.7	0.6	301	-		
India	4.4	0.6	455	4.3	0.7	385
Israel	3.9	0.7	148	-		
Japan	3.9	0.6	514	-		
Netherlands	3.5	0.4	157	3.5	0.4	54
New Zealand	3.9	0.6	105	-		
Poland	4.1	0.6	387	4.0	0.6	120
Portugal	4.1	0.5	145	4.0	0.5	57
Slovenia	4.5	0.5	70	-		
Switzerland	3.2	0.7	280	-		
United States of America	4.1	0.6	285	-		

Notes: - = No non-using schools in sample or sample size too small for analysis,
* Total population of using schools.

1. Attitudes scale scores determined from the following statements:
    Computers are valuable tools to improve the quality of a child's education.
    Using computers in class leads to more productivity among students.
    Computers help to teach more effectively.
    In-service courses about computers should be made compulsory.
    The achievement of students can be increased when using computers for teaching.

    Scale is: Strongly agree=5 to Strongly disagree=1

At the lower secondary level, all the means with the exception of non-using schools in Switzerland were above 3.0, indicating a favorable attitude toward the educational use of computers. Thirteen of the means were between 3.0 and 3.9 while four were between 4.0 and 4.2. The means for using schools were in all cases higher than the means for non-using schools.

At the upper secondary level, principals of using schools tended to have higher means than principals of non-using schools except in China and the Netherlands where the means were equal. Furthermore, the means at this level were generally higher than at the other two levels, indicating a tendency for principals at higher educational levels to see greater value in the educational use of computers. The differences between educational levels, however, is not great.

In summary, school principals at all educational levels are generally favorably disposed towards the educational use of computers. Principals at higher educational levels tend to be somewhat more positive about the educational use of computers than principals at lower educational levels, but the differences are generally small. Also, principals of using schools tended to have more favorable attitudes towards the educational use of computers than principals of non-using schools. It would seem that experience with computers inclines principals to be more favorably disposed towards their use in instruction.

Problems Experienced in the Use of Computers

Principals were presented with a lengthy list of problems that might be encountered in using computers in schools. These were classified under four major headings: hardware, software, instruction, and organization/administration. The latter category was of special interest since it represents administrative barriers to using computers. Three items from this list were of special interest since they addressed external factors that could limit utilization. These problems were:

1. Insufficient technical operational assistance.
2. Lack of administrative support.
3. Inadequate financial support.

While there is some variation between countries in the percentage of schools experiencing specific problems, there is a high degree of consistency of results across both the types of problems encountered as well as across populations. The median percentage of schools reporting problems due to a lack of technical operational assistance were 28, 29, and 35 at the elementary, lower secondary, and upper secondary levels respectively. The median percentages for lack of administrative support were 19, 19, and 35 for the three populations, respectively. Finally, the median percentages for inadequate financial support were 55, 51, and 52 for the elementary, lower secondary, and upper secondary levels, respectively. Clearly, the inadequacy of financial support stands out as the major problem area. In all populations, more than half the schools reported this as a problem area. Individual country percentages ranged from a low of 10% in Switzerland at the lower secondary level to 83% in Portugal at the same level. It would appear that many principals in many countries feel blocked in their ability to use computers for instructional purposes because of a lack of financial support.

Administrative Policies Regarding Computer Use in Schools

There were three questions on the school principal's questionnaire that sought to determine whether schools had certain formal policies regarding the use of computers. The first question asked whether the school had a written policy regarding the use of computers. The median percentage of schools reporting the existence of such a policy were 28, 28, and 39 at the elementary, lower secondary, and upper secondary levels, respectively. These are quite similar. Within each educational level, the results were fairly similar. Insofar as the assessment of how computers were used, the median percentage of schools reporting such a policy were 67, 63, and 70 at the elementary, lower secondary, and upper secondary levels, respectively. Again, the results within each population were quite similar. Principals are clearly concerned how computers are being used for educational purposes. Finally, principals were asked whether school authorities (including the principal) stimulated the use of computers in schools. The median percentages reporting such stimulation were 80, 77, and 82 at the elementary, lower secondary, and upper secondary levels, respectively. Of course, principals, especially in computer using schools, are likely to report stimulating the use of computers when responding to a questionnaire seeking information about computer use in schools. Thus, these results should be interpreted with some caution. Despite their support of the use of computers, the same principals reported a lack of financial support for computer use as noted in the above section. It may well be that the financial support that the principals seek is beyond their ability to provide.

Equity-Related Policies

The introduction of any innovation into an educational system immediately raises questions about who is to receive it. This certainly applies to computers. Accordingly, principals were asked some question about equity-related policies with regard to the use of computers. The general policies that were investigated were:

1. A policy that all students should have computer experiences before graduating.
2. A policy specifying actions to insure equity in participation, for example, with regard to gender, ability, and/or ethnicity.
3. A policy that prescribes the use of computers in a certain grade or certain subjects.

A question was included on the principal's questionnaire regarding each of the above policies. The results for these questions are presented in Tables 6.4a, 6.4b, and 6.4c. With regard to the first policy, that all students should have computer experiences before graduating, the results were generally similar for the three levels of schooling. The median percentage of principals stating that their school had such a policy were 83, 67, and 68 for the elementary, lower secondary and upper secondary levels, respectively. In general, countries that were more further along in the use of computers in schools had higher percentages of principals reporting such a policy than countries that were in the early stages of introduction of computers into schools.

Table 6.4a

Per cent of elementary schools that have specific equity-related practices

Country/ Educational System	Computer Exp[1]	Practices: Insure Equity[2]	Prescribe Use[3]
Belgium-French	29	13	28
Canada-British Columbia	84	54	64
France	82	9	56
Israel	93	67	95
Japan	46	12	10
Netherlands	85	66	61
New Zealand	71	58	60
Portugal	25	38	26
United States of America	60	18	33

Notes: 1, 2, 3 = see page 172 for item texts.

Richard M. Wolf and Georgia Kontogiannopolou-Polydorides

Table 6.4b
Per cent of lower secondary schools that have specific equity-related practices

Country/ Educational System	Computer Exp[1]	Practices: Insure Equity[2]	Prescribe Use[3]
Belgium-Flemish	84	56	84
Belgium-French	37	13	61
Canada-British Columbia	76	37	70
France	66	7	51
Federal Republic of Germany	69	17	84
Greece	80	30	59
Japan	20	6	19
Luxembourg	92	4	96
Netherlands	98	70	92
New Zealand	72	43	69
Portugal	25	21	49
Switzerland	49	18	46
United States of America	63	15	24

Table 6.4c
Per cent of upper secondary schools that have specific equity-related practices

Country/ Educational System	Computer Exp[1]	Practices: Insure Equity[2]	Prescribe Use[3]
Belgium-Flemish	92	63	92
Belgium-French	31	11	67
Canada-British Columbia	76	37	70
China	64	60	80
France	60	6	73
Federal Republic of Germany	67	10	84
Greece	49	18	60
Hungary	57	40	56
India	33	27	85
Israel	92	65	94
Japan	30	4	45
Netherlands	94	58	89
New Zealand	82	46	69
Poland	69	70	76
Portugal	26	19	49
Slovenia	92	30	84
Switzerland	88	10	50
United States of America	59	19	17

Notes: 1. A policy that all students should have computer experiences before graduating.
2. A policy specifying actions to insure equity in participation, for example, with regard to gender, ability and/or ethnicity.
3. A policy that prescribes the use of computers in a certain grade or certain subjects.

The second question dealing with policy asked whether the school specified actions to insure equity in participation, for example, with regard to gender, ability, and/or ethnicity. In most countries at each educational level, the proportion of schools having such a policy was generally small. The median percentages were 38, 20, and 27 for the elementary, lower secondary, and upper secondary levels, respectively. Four countries (Canada-British Columbia, Israel, the Netherlands, and New Zealand) had more than fifty per cent of the schools holding such a policy at the elementary level. At the lower secondary level, only two countries (Belgium-Flemish and the Netherlands) had more than fifty per cent of the schools reporting such a policy while, at the upper secondary level, only five countries (Belgium-Flemish, China, Israel, the Netherlands, and Poland) had more than fifty per cent of the schools reporting such a policy. Equity practices, in general, seem to not have emerged as an important policy issue in the use of computers at this time.

In contrast to equity, policies that prescribe the use of computers in a certain grade or certain subject appear to be more clearly formulated. The median percentages of schools reporting such a policy are 65, 56, and 73 at the elementary, lower secondary and upper secondary levels, respectively. There is, however, considerable variability among countries at each educational level. At the elementary level, the percentages range from 10 (Japan) to 95 (Israel) while at the lower secondary level, the percentages range from 19 (Japan) to 96 (Luxembourg). At the upper secondary level, the percentages range from 17 (the United States of America) to 94 (Israel). In general, there is a distinct relationship between the degree of centralization of the educational system and the percentage of schools having such a policy (See J.P. Keeves, 1991, pp.83-270).

Gender Issues in Computer Use

The issue of the differentiated use and access of technology by gender has received widespread attention in research and policy papers in recent years.

Thomas (1987), for example, is concerned about cultural differences in the acceptance of educational technology, where "cultural" means the "material culture and the patterns of thought and social interaction that typify a group of people" (including, of course, women). Others indicate that there is a difference in the frequency of use of the computers in school by gender (Collis, Hass and Kieren, 1989; Jensen and Klewe,

1989) or in the way person-to-person or person-to-machine interaction is taking place (Siann, 1990; Pozzi, 1992).

In other cases, gender differences in computer-related studies are masked by bureaucratic routine responses indicating equality where it might not exist (Whyte, 1986).

Still other studies report that gender has little or no relationship to computer experience or computer use (McCoy and Dodl, 1989); or computer literacy and achievement for student teachers (Woodrow, 1991a, 1991b).

It is clear that, overall, the educational community has expressed a legitimate concern about gender inequality in the use of computers in education and rightfully so. Clearly there has been an intensive conceptual, theoretical and political debate on the gender differences in education since the decade of the sixties. This debate has led to a good number of educational policies and practices, which one segment of the educational community views as pertaining to more equality by gender in the world's educational systems. The other part views them as inconclusive attempts which are not in a position to face the extended existing social inequalities of which educational results are a mere reflection.

Whatever the stance that educators, researchers and educational policy analysts around the world take with respect to the above general issue, they recently come to unite their concerns as to the effect that the massive introduction of computers in education might have on gender differences in education and society.

The concerns are twofold: First, it is argued that gender differences in educational practices might result in gender differences in educational and affective results. Within this concern Wu and Morgan (1989), Jones et al. (1992) and Campbell (1984) relate gender to computer experience and results at school.

Second, the concern is raised that gender differences in acquiring computer related knowledge and skills will inevitably lead to differential integration in the division of labor by gender. Cockburn (1985) bases his related analysis on Beauvoir's argument that women have been excluded from technological knowledge, "acted upon technology and not interacting with it". Apple (1992) presents the case that two out of three students in computer classes are boys, and that males dominate the top positions in the division of labor, while women occupy the lower jobs of office workers.

These concerns are more precisely expressed with respect to specific educational policies and practices and are exemplified as they are related to the wider conceptual and theoretical frameworks adopted, in terms of:

a. the curriculum structure and context regarding the introduction of computers in schools;

b. the role models that male and, especially, female teachers and administrators present to their students;

c. teaching practices and attitudes with respect to computers, which teachers and administrators employ.

It is assumed that the gender of school administrators could be related to equity policies in school computer use. It is also assumed that the gender of teachers could be related to pressure towards equity policies in school computer use.

The literature indicates that role modeling is an important element in students' active and successful participation in everyday school life. It is on the basis of this assumption that educators tend to think that, for example, gender predominance of a specific type in the teaching and administrative staff will support, or hasten, or inhibit students' further development of skills and acquisition of knowledge.

Furthermore, it is assumed that the attitudes of school administrators contribute to the overall climate and the policies regarding computers, which prevail in the school.

The IEA Computers in Education study presents an opportunity to examine some of the above issues across cultures in both computer using and non-using schools. A consistent existence of computer using schools with specific policies pertaining to gender equity would be indicative of some important or preconditions related to computer use.

This section examines gender in relation to two kinds of context characteristics: (1) the distribution of teaching staff as well as administrators in computer using and non-using schools, and (2) the opinions/attitudes about computers in education and society as well as the policies adopted to promote gender equity. Figure 6.4 presents the gender predominance in teaching staff in computer using and non-using schools.

It is apparent in elementary education, that in all participating countries there is either female dominance or no gender dominance in the teaching staff.

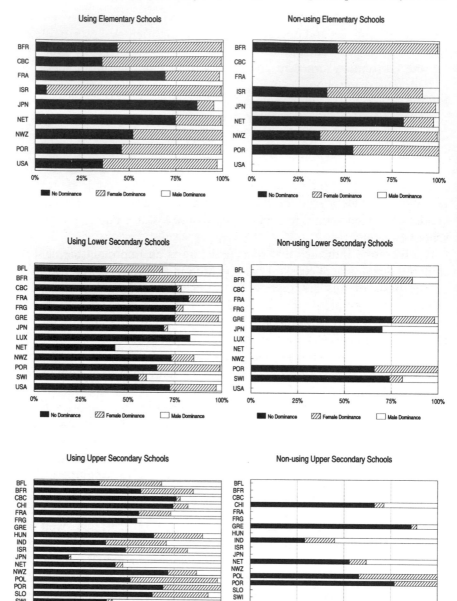

Notes: - = Sample size too small for analysis.

Figure 6.4 Gender predominance in teaching staff in using and non-using schools.

Female dominance in teaching staff is characteristic of computer using schools in Belgium-French, Canada-British Columbia, Israel, Portugal and the United States of America. All these countries, except Portugal, have also female dominance in the teaching staff of non-using schools (the sample sizes of non-using schools in Canada-British Columbia, France, and the United States of America are too small).

It is important to note that in Portugal and Israel the female dominance in the teaching staff of computer using schools is greater than in non-using schools. In Israel, there are twice as many female teachers than in non-using schools (an interesting phenomenon which might simply indicate newly founded schools or schools in urban areas, where women teachers tend to concentrate heavily).

In lower secondary education, in the schools in all participating countries there is no gender predominance in computer using schools with the exception of the Netherlands, where there is male dominance. The same holds for the five countries with sufficiently large samples of non-using schools.

Female dominance in the teaching staff is considerably lower in the computer using schools of Belgium-French than in non-using schools.

The picture appears to be quite comparable for upper secondary schools, with the exception of three countries with higher male dominance in the teaching staff of computer using schools, namely Japan, Switzerland and the Netherlands. The same holds for the non-using schools of India.

The data indicates that in India the female predominance is higher in the computer using schools than in the non-using schools and this is probably a reflection of the modernising, developing part of the educational system. Computer using schools with female predominance increase in Portugal also.

In conclusion and for all three populations, female dominance in the teaching staff differs more between populations than between using and non-using schools in the same population. In fact, it appears that female gender dominance does not hinder computer use; rather, in some countries it seems to coincide with computer use.

Table 6.5a

Percentages of elementary schools versus schools with male principals having a particular gender policy

Gender Policy	BFR	FRA	JPN	NET	NWZ
In-service training equity					
All	11	5	65	17	37
Males	11	3	65	18	40
Computer class girls					
All	2	2	14	0	2
Males	0	1	15	0	0
Information to parents					
All	23	4	34	21	16
Males	15	4	32	23	20
Supervision by females					
All	15	27	33	46	59
Males	13	21	33	43	64
Time for girls only access					
All	0	3	6	0	18
Males	0	5	6	0	16
Specific suggestions to teachers					
All	9	3	20	31	58
Males	12	3	21	32	59
Comped training female teachers					
All	43	46	49	58	77
Males	39	38	47	61	77

Notes: Countries selected with a minimum of 30 schools with gender policy and at least 25 schools with male principals and gender policy.

Table 6.5b

Percentages of lower secondary schools versus schools with male principals having a particular gender policy

Gender Policy	BFL	BFR	FRA	GRE	JPN	NET	SWI	USA
In-service training equity								
All	39	10	8	7	62	44	11	36
Males	40	6	7	0	62	44	10	48
Computer class girls								
All	0	1	1	0	9	1	4	15
Males	0	1	1	0	8	1	5	9
Information to parents								
All	47	6	1	44	31	26	11	2
Males	52	7	1	47	29	26	12	3
Supervision by females								
All	39	47	31	30	5	46	13	34
Males	43	51	31	18	5	46	12	32
Time for girls only access								
All	0	0	0	0	10	0	1	11
Males	0	1	0	0	11	0	1	6
Specific suggestions to teachers								
All	46	14	8	18	28	39	15	32
Males	44	13	8	29	29	38	14	37
Comped training female teachers								
All	39	64	67	52	30	86	46	16
Males	40	68	66	47	32	86	45	7

Notes: Countries selected with a minimum of 30 schools with gender policy and at least 25 schools with male principals and gender policy.

Table 6.5c

Percentages of upper secondary schools versus schools with male principals having a particular gender policy

Gender Policy	BFL	BFR	CHI	FRA	HUN	IND	JPN	NET	USA
In-service training equity									
All	37	3	28	8	18	45	55	60	56
Males	35	3	28	8	18	46	55	62	38
Computer class girls									
All	0	0	1	1	38	34	18	0	14
Males	0	0	1	1	40	34	18	0	16
Information to parents									
All	32	4	18	4	60	51	16	24	7
Males	34	4	20	4	55	54	16	28	4
Supervision by females									
All	47	53	30	37	33	39	16	50	63
Males	48	53	30	37	31	35	16	50	54
Time for girls only access									
All	0	0	20	1	13	57	13	2	0
Males	0	0	14	1	13	62	13	2	0
Specific suggestions to teachers									
All	27	7	29	12	26	61	9	37	50
Males	28	8	33	10	27	60	9	42	32
Comped training female teachers									
All	49	63	48	60	0	42	21	53	21
Males	47	62	51	59	0	36	21	61	23

Notes: Countries selected with a minimum of 30 schools with gender policy and at least 25 schools with male principals and gender policy.

Tables 6.5a, 6.5b, and 6.5c present the percentages of schools which have introduced special policies to promote gender equity in computer use. The data are presented both for all schools as well as for schools with male principals.

The overall picture indicates that the pattern of policy adoption, first, is quite similar across populations, and, second, does not show important changes when one moves from the total number of schools to schools with male principals.

It is important to note that elementary and lower secondary schools in a good number of countries have no policies for specific computer time or for special computer classes devoted to girls to increase their access and computer learning. In the countries where such policies exist, the proportion of schools is quite small in both populations. In New Zealand a sizeable number of schools have the policy of setting aside time for girls-only access of the computers. These policies are more common in upper secondary schools (Table 6.5c), but at this level a good number of countries have not introduced these policies at all.

A very important policy is the one dealing with computer education for female teachers. One can note that, from the countries participating in the study, New Zealand is heavily involved in the training of female teachers in elementary schools, the Netherlands in lower secondary schools, while Belgium-French and France are relatively heavily involved in providing such training in upper secondary schools.

One might wonder whether a heavy emphasis on computer related training for female teachers is a function of the female teachers' participation in the teacher force rather than an intensified policy for training female teachers in the use of computers. In the Netherlands, external information indicates that this is the result of a conscious policy decision.

Of course female predominance or no dominance in either the administrators or in the teaching staff of using and non-using schools is only suggesting a trend in the overall school structure and climate. It does not alter the fact that, as indicated in Pelgrum and Plomp (1991), computer studies teachers and computer coordinators are more likely to be men. The fact that this is true in most of the countries poses a potentially important question: Computer studies and computer related hiring processes are made despite the existing school structure and climate; and this seems to be true across cultures.

Table 6.6a

Percentage agreement with attitude items by male and female principals in elementary schools

	BFR	CBC	FRA	ISR	NWZ	POR	USA
Improve quality education							
Male	64	97	71	86	96	89	97
Female	44	100	49	64	88	86	98
Students more attentive							
Male	46	52	46	67	57	57	57
Female	48	50	42	47	45	58	64
Enhance students' creativity							
Male	48	73	41	76	69	70	73
Female	46	65	29	59	70	75	80
More productivity							
Male	54	72	32	85	70	68	81
Female	45	73	34	72	65	58	79
Teach more effectively							
Male	50	69	46	90	70	76	68
Female	30	62	35	81	61	61	68
Achievement can be increased							
Male	70	73	60	90	80	84	84
Female	51	77	47	79	76	78	82
Distorts the social climate							
Male	7	11	5	4	13	10	6
Female	9	4	7	4	9	12	3
Computers too dominant							
Male	19	9	13	41	15	36	12
Female	20	8	20	38	10	38	18
Harm relations between people							
Male	17	2	16	11	7	26	5
Female	20	0	18	11	9	26	4
Social contacts negatively affected							
Male	13	9	11	8	14	22	5
Female	16	4	12	5	13	23	6
Informed technological changes							
Male	79	88	68	91	86	84	85
Female	74	100	43	83	82	85	94
Don't mind learning about computers							
Male	89	97	91	99	95	97	98
Female	94	100	92	95	98	95	100
Like take part computer course							
Male	76	73	77	91	88	95	82
Female	84	72	82	89	80	99	81
In-service training compulsory							
Male	61	61	76	86	65	73	64
Female	54	58	80	79	46	72	70
Learn about computers as teaching aids							
Male	94	94	94	96	96	99	96
Female	97	96	91	96	91	100	96

Notes: Countries included with at least 25 male and 25 female principals.

Table 6.6b
Percentage agreement with attitude items by male and female principals in lower secondary schools

	BFL	BFR	FRA	GRE	NWZ	POR	SWI	USA
Improve quality education								
Male	88	70	68	93	94	87	29	98
Female	84	66	65	87	100	80	13	98
Students more attentive								
Male	50	68	68	54	67	71	35	62
Female	37	63	61	47	60	70	27	58
Enhance students' creativity								
Male	50	51	55	75	71	83	29	77
Female	33	42	42	71	80	74	16	68
More productivity								
Male	35	59	43	76	69	78	35	78
Female	27	62	43	62	61	69	24	78
Teach more effectively								
Male	62	71	61	82	71	79	47	73
Female	51	56	54	69	67	72	32	63
Achievement can be increased								
Male	36	70	69	82	76	90	51	80
Female	29	64	74	80	87	85	25	82
Distorts the social climate								
Male	6	3	4	81	6	10	6	3
Female	2	11	5	80	5	14	16	0
Computers too dominant								
Male	13	17	12	92	21	33	36	11
Female	10	13	10	91	36	42	34	6
Harm relations between people								
Male	8	14	15	39	15	18	29	2
Female	6	8	14	44	2	23	33	11
Social contacts negatively affected								
Male	9	11	11	39	21	23	26	8
Female	8	16	16	44	7	28	23	6
Informed technological changes								
Male	93	90	84	89	94	86	87	89
Female	87	93	76	81	95	84	76	97
Don't mind learning about comp.								
Male	93	92	93	91	90	89	95	99
Female	96	94	97	96	95	94	98	95
Like take part computer course								
Male	78	68	79	88	66	96	83	75
Female	77	87	84	93	78	91	85	79
In-service training compulsory								
Male	63	76	86	74	63	71	44	68
Female	69	63	90	77	70	65	39	65
Learn about computers as teaching aids								
Male	97	93	94	93	84	99	85	95
Female	97	100	94	96	86	100	77	97

Notes: Countries included with at least 25 male and 25 female principals.

Table 6.6c

Percentage agreement with attitude items by male and female principals in upper

	BFL	BFR	CHI	FRA	GRE
Improve quality education					
Male	95	67	79	70	97
Female	93	59	98	69	98
Students more attentive					
Male	52	72	70	66	48
Female	43	41	91	66	47
Enhance students' creativity					
Male	57	52	89	53	78
Female	42	37	95	40	69
More productivity					
Male	39	60	75	49	71
Female	11	59	94	55	66
Teach more effectively					
Male	68	71	78	66	79
Female	49	46	100	66	86
Achievement can be increased					
Male	43	69	76	65	79
Female	28	65	79	66	80
Distorts the social climate					
Male	3	5	2	2	75
Female	0	2	3	3	84
Computers too dominant					
Male	6	12	20	16	95
Female	27	0	26	22	83
Harm relations between people					
Male	9	13	7	9	46
Female	12	7	2	13	40
Social contacts negatively affected					
Male	8	8	3	9	50
Female	12	3	8	7	48
Informed technological changes					
Male	95	91	97	91	86
Female	87	82	97	91	75
Don't mind learning about computers					
Male	96	90	94	93	94
Female	91	89	100	98	86
Like take part computer course					
Male	78	65	90	79	93
Female	86	76	98	86	85
In-service training compulsory					
Male	71	80	81	84	74
Female	67	64	93	94	77
Learn about computers as teaching aids					
Male	96	94	93	90	94
Female	94	100	100	90	89

Notes: Countries included with at least 25 male and 25 female principals.

secondary schools

HUN	IND	ISR	NWZ	POL	POR	USA
82	88	68	94	92	87	97
61	84	65	100	92	83	100
52	81	57	69	66	68	61
56	77	41	53	66	77	79
78	85	65	74	84	78	85
62	80	56	55	83	76	93
55	76	67	70	79	72	83
52	69	59	36	84	77	93
72	83	78	66	78	74	76
63	72	71	64	79	72	52
64	87	80	79	85	88	89
49	79	66	76	88	86	87
0	16	10	11	5	14	2
2	27	9	8	6	20	1
2	41	39	9	13	31	10
0	41	35	26	17	45	15
3	15	11	3	4	18	3
5	12	22	9	8	27	6
2	24	10	9	7	16	8
5	36	16	6	8	30	7
81	86	82	80	88	90	92
70	94	89	91	88	84	88
80	83	92	91	91	91	97
75	82	95	98	93	95	92
68	88	81	84	66	98	78
63	94	81	74	60	92	80
46	84	81	63	74	77	68
36	94	65	67	75	72	78
74	94	89	93	85	99	94
63	94	94	79	86	100	83

Tables 6.6a, 6.6b and 6.6c present the opinions and attitudes expressed by principals of computer using schools (percentage of those who agree with each statement) broken down by gender.

It is interesting to note that there are differences in the range of the percentages in the participating countries between male and female principals. These differences appear in specific groups of variables.

Enhancement and computer[1]

Computer contribution to the quality of education and enhancement has a specific pattern.

Apparently, women's attitudes concerning the contribution of computers to education vary across countries much more than men's, indicating that they have not been developed uniformly. Such a differentiated development might indicate women-teachers status differences across countries, or computer education differences, or a different process of attitudes development in male and female teachers.

Computers effectiveness in school[2]

This set of variables follows a pattern, which is more concise for male teachers. Male teachers in all countries tend to accept the effectiveness of computers at a proportion close to or above 50% and up to 90%. Female teachers spread across countries from about 20% to 100%. This indicates a differentiation following the pattern of the variables related to enhancement (in "a" above). It is clear in this case again males express a definite, formulated ideology towards computers while females are "spread", or have ideology "in the making".

---

1 Enhancement includes the following variables:
   Computers are valuable tools to improve the quality of education
   Students are more attentive when computers are used
   Computers in school enhance student's creativity

2 Computers effectiveness includes the following variables:
   Using computers in class leads to greater productivity
   Computers help to teach more effectively
   The achievement of students can be increased by using computers

Influence of computers on human relations[3]

All variables describing the way teachers perceive the functioning of computers in the social milieu and human contacts do not indicate great difference between males and females. The percentages of the teachers adopting the specific attitudes are always (with the exception of Greece) less than 50 and the spread of countries between 0 and 50 is neither wide nor particularly differentiated by gender. This suggests that the basis for such differences in attitude is cultural more than gender defined.

Principals being informed and their training needs[4]

In this case, women's attitudes spread across countries more than any other variables. While men in all countries range above 50%, women range from less than 10 to 100%, a pattern which indicates a lack of crystallization of attitudes among women across the countries in the study.

Examining the picture presented for the three population levels, it is interesting to note that countries in general fall within a defined range of "percent agree." France is differentiated by its low proportion of principals believing that computers positively affect students' creativity in elementary schools. Greece is differentiated by the high proportion of principals being disturbed by the domination of new technology and its effects on the social environment in schools and society at large in lower and upper secondary education. China is differentiated by the very high proportion of female principals accepting the computer's positive effects on the teaching activities in upper secondary education. Finally, the principals in Switzerland are by far the least eager to accept that computers are valuable tools for the quality of education in lower secondary schools.

---

3 Influence of computers includes the following variables:
  Working with computers in class distorts the social climate
  Computers have become too dominant over us
  Computer harm relations among people
  Social contacts are negatively affected by the use of computers

4 Principals being informed and their training needs includes the following variables:
  I try to keep myself informed on technological changes
  I don't mind learning about computers
  I would like to take part in a computer course
  In-service training courses should be made compulsory
  I would like to learn more about computers as teaching aids

Summary

This chapter has presented a large amount of information regard
administrative policies and practices regarding the educational use of compute
attitudes of principals, and gender issues. Such information is not eas
summarized, especially when one considers the amount of variability that ex
both between educational levels within countries as well as between countr
There are several observations that can be offered, however.

First, there is generally restricted penetration of computers into schools in ma
countries while, in other countries, computer use is widespread.

Second, there is a slight social bias with regard to the use of computers in scho
However, this can be expected to diminish as computer use becomes m
widespread. Countries in which computer use has become widespread show little
any, social bias with regard to where computers are placed.

Third, although computer use is limited in many countries, school principals ha
generally favorable attitudes towards technology and the use of computers
education. This may be one of the most notable findings of the chapter and sugge
that even though computer use was not widespread at the time of data collectior
1989, there is a climate of receptivity towards the use of computers in schools.

Fourth, findings with regard to gender issues reveal that countries are hig
variable with regard to providing equal opportunity for males and females. So
countries have clearly developed policies while other countries have not addres
these issues yet. It will, of course, be interesting to see what changes occur betwe
the first and second stage of the Comped study.

7

Predicting Computer Use in Six Systems: Structural Models of Implementation Indicators

Previous chapters in this report present mainly descriptive results based on univariate and bivariate methods of data analysis. Those chapters focus on the main indicators identified in Chapter 1: school organization, computer hardware, computer software, teacher training and staff development, and teacher skills in using computers. It can be inferred from these analyses that the decision to introduce computers in schools and to use them not only for teaching about computers and their many applications but also as a means of facilitating classroom teaching and learning was not taken at the same time in all schools and across all educational systems. Accordingly, it can be hypothesized that certain schools and educational systems have come further than others in terms of reform initiation and actual implementation (Tuijnman and Ten Brummelhuis, 1991).

The main purpose of this chapter is to measure and compare the extent of computer use in six educational systems. A second aim is to identify the indicators that may explain why certain schools and educational systems are using computers as a means of enhancing instruction to a greater extent than others. To this end, structural equation models are developed and estimated using data collected from those countries participating in the IEA Study of Computers in Education in which the achieved sample of schools exceeds 200, a number which may be considered an absolute minimum for the multivariate data analysis carried out in the investigation reported in this chapter. Six countries meet to this criterion and hence are included in the study: France, Federal Republic of Germany, Japan, the Netherlands, Switzerland, and the United States of America.

This chapter was written by Albert C. Tuijnman and Alfons C.A. ten Brummelhuis.

A Theoretical Model

The factors underlying decisions to initiate a major change in education and the factors that influence the successful implementation of an educational innovation have been at the heart of much research. Huberman and Miles (1984), Fullan, Miles and Anderson (1988), and Fullan (1991) discusses a large number of indicators which, according to theory and previous research, influence both the decision to initiate educational change and the actual use of the innovation. Fullan (1991) identifies three clusters of indicators that seem to be associated with the decision to initiate an innovation in education: relevance, readiness, and resources.

Relevance refers to perceptions of educational practitioners concerning the usefulness of an innovation such as the introduction of computers in schools. This indicator can be measured by tapping the expectation of school leaders and teachers that the innovation will produce beneficial outcomes. Readiness involves the school's capacity to initiate and develop the innovation, and can be measured with items measuring the attitudes to reform of the principal and the prerequisite knowledge and skills of teachers. The importance of resource availability, such as financial means, computer equipment and appropriate software materials, seems rather self-evident.

Louis and Miles (1990) and Fullan (1991) suggest some additional indicators that are seen as particularly important determinants of implementation: the clarity of school policy with respect to the goals, means and ends of the innovation; the organization of staff development activities; the establishment of procedures for monitoring and evaluation; and the supply of technical support to teachers in need of practical help.

Relationships can be hypothesized among the indicators mentioned above. Figure 7.1 shows a theoretical model in which several of these implementation indicators are ordered on the basis of a sequence involving four frame factors: exogenous and endogenous preconditions, implementation conditions, and implementation outcomes.

Exogenous preconditions refer to indicators external to the school, for example the amount of logistical, financial and training support offered by central and local authorities, business, and resource centers. Certain school indicators, for example school size and area location, which are not determined by other indicators in the model, are also considered as exogenous variables. Three indicators are grouped under the heading endogenous preconditions: the previous experience of the school with respect to an educational innovation, the availability of resources, and perceptions of the school leaders concerning the relevance of the innovation. A third group of indicators is subsumed under the label implementation conditions. These are interpreted mainly in terms of the formulation of an explicit policy committing the school to introduce computers, the presence of staff development activities, the provision of technical and organizational assistance to teachers who use computers for instructional purposes, and the active use of a strategy for monitoring the implementation of the innovation. The fourth category refers to implementation outcomes. The focus is on one outcome in particular, namely the use of computers for educational purposes in central school subjects in grade 8.

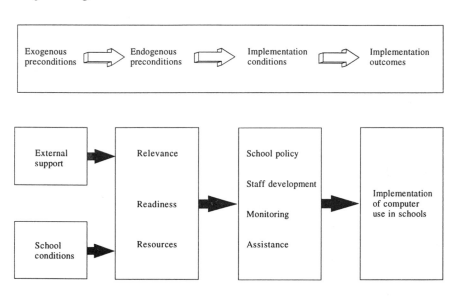

Figure 7.1 Indicators influencing the implementation of computer use in schools.

It should be noted that the design of the model shown in Figure 7.1 is to an extent also influenced by the quality of the information collected in the IEA study on computers in education. Since the aim of the data analysis is to subject the model to a rigorous empirical test, it is considered impractical to hypothesize relationships involving possibly relevant indicators that cannot be made operational because the data needed for their measurement are not available. The development of the model and the examination of the effects of additional indicators are challenges for future research.

Samples and Variables

Samples

All lower secondary schools enroling students in the grade in which the modal age is 13 years constitute the target population from which the samples of schools were drawn. For obvious reasons, the data sets examined in this chapter are restricted to schools that have computers and use them, at least to an extent, for instructional purposes. The sampling procedures and additional sample characteristics are described in Chapter 1.

For reasons of comparability, the data analyses presented in this chapter are restricted to lower secondary schools. Only six systems are studied because, in these cases, the sample size exceeds 200 schools. In the case of elementary schools (population 1), only three countries have a sample size that exceeds 200 schools. At the level of upper secondary education (population 3) the variation in school subjects between the countries is much greater than is the case in lower secondary education.

Indicators and their Measurement

The information used to measure the items employed in this investigation was taken from the questionnaires to which the school principals, different groups of teachers, and resource persons acting as computer coordinators in schools responded. A brief description of the indicators and their associated items is given below. In spite of the effort made to ensure that all of the indicators were measured on the basis of identical items, some variation has nevertheless occurred. Large variation occurs in two indicators, external financial support and external training support. Accordingly, particular care must be taken in interpreting the results based on comparisons involving these two indicators.

1. *School size.* This indicator is based on the number of students enroled in school.
2. *External financial support.* One item is used as an indicator of the financial support given by the government. Given the structure of its school system and the differences in educational finance that exist among the various States constituting the United States of America, an indicator involving several items was formed for this country by adding variables measuring whether schools received financial support from public sources at State and local

government level.

3. *External training support.* This indicator could not identically be measured across the six systems. An indicator involving 13 items is specified in the Dutch, Swiss and United States of America models. The items measure support with respect to staff development and training received from: (a) computer manufacturers; (b) software producers; and (c) other businesses. A single item measuring whether schools received external training support is employed in the French and German models, because of nonvariance in many of the items making up the indicator. Because only one item is available its 'true' reliability cannot be determined by means of a scale analysis procedure. It is therefore assumed that 15 per cent of the variance in the item is due to measurement error. Finally, in Japan, training support could not be measured because of zero variance in the items. Schools apparently do not receive such support in Japan, or principals consider the question to be inappropriate.

4. *Previous innovation experience.* Only one item is available. It is derived from the year in which computers were first introduced in the school. The item thus measures the number of years of experience schools have had with computers in education.

5. *Availability and resource needs.* Four items measuring the urgency of the need for additional hardware and software are used as indicators of availability and resource needs on the assumption that schools well supplied with, for example, computer hardware, will assign a low priority to the purchase of such new equipment. The four items used in the analysis are: (a) the need for more powerful computers; (b) need for a network for shared disk storage; (c) need for more tool software; and (d) the need for a greater variety of instructional software.

6. *Perceived innovation relevance.* This indicator is based on five items. These tap the expectations of the principal that computers will: (a) increase productivity; (b) make teaching more effective; (c) enhance student creativity; (d) increase student achievement; and (e) optimalize learning.

7. *School policy for computer use.* Four items form this indicator. These measure whether a school has determined policy with respect to the means and ends of computer education, e.g.: (a) all students should have to acquired some experience with computers before their graduation; (b) instruction with computers must be compulsory; (c) the school shall give priority to the use of

computers for instruction; and (d) the school prescribes which hardware and software should be used by teachers and students.

8. *Internal staff development.* Four items are employed. These measure whether the teachers can attend: (a) an introductory course on how to use computers; (b) a course on the use of application programs; (c) a course on how to use computers for teaching in specific subjects; and (d) a course in computer programming.

9. *Internal innovation assistance.* Subject teachers in schools were asked whether internal support was available at school level to solve problems arising from: (a) the use of hardware; (b) the use of software; (c) the use of computers in instruction; and (d) the organization of the teaching and learning process. This information, which gives an indication of the assistance available to teachers who use computers for instruction, is aggregated to school level.

10. *Teacher competence and readiness.* Subject teachers were sampled for the subject matter areas computer education, mother tongue, mathematics and science in each sampled school with computer use. The teachers, whether user or non-user, were asked to indicate by checking 'yes' or 'no' whether they had the knowledge or could perform the task mentioned in three groups of statements, which are explained elsewhere in this report: (a) knowledge of computers and applications [I know ..., 9 items]; (b) the ability to write or adapt software [I can write a program for ..., 5 items]; and (c) the capacity to actually use computers as an aid in instruction [I am capable of ..., 8 items]. A total score was computed per teacher. As this factor indicates the knowledge and skill level available at school, the teacher with the highest score was selected to represent the school.

11. *Monitoring and problem coping strategy.* Three items are employed. Two items serving as indicators whether monitoring procedures are used in the school are based on responses to questions asking whether the schools exchange information and experience on how computers can and are used as an aid in teaching. A third item, which concerns the use of internal evaluation procedures, is used in the cases of the Federal Republic of Germany and the Netherlands.

12. *Implementation outcome: computer use in grade 8.* This criterion variable is based on information provided by the school principals and the computer coordinators. Since only one item is used for this

indicator, and in order to facilitate the interpretation of results, this dependent variable warrants special consideration.

The indicator has rank scale scores from 4 to 0 from the highest to the lowest categories. It is based on the use of computers for educational purposes in four subjects, namely computer education, mother tongue, mathematics and science. A value of 0 indicates that, in a given school, computers are not used for educational purposes in any of these subjects in grade 8. In contrast, a value of 4 indicates that computers are used for educational purposes in all four subjects. The accuracy of the information provided by the principal or the computer coordinator could be checked because information was also collected from the teachers.

It must be noted that only information with respect to the target grade 8 is used in measuring the indicator, although similar information was collected on computer use in the adjacent grades. There are three reasons for this decision. First, the items measuring computer use in grades 7, 8 and 9 showed very high correlations in all of the countries. An exception is the United States of America where, possibly due to the sampling strategy taken, the correlation between computer use in grade 8 and grade 9 was less substantial compared with the other countries. Second, the items involving grade 8 were shown in one-factor models to have the highest reliability. Third, by specifying only one item as an indicator of the outcome, the results of the regression analysis can readily be interpreted.

Methodology

Computation of Correlation Matrices

The following strategy was taken in developing the correlation matrices. The bi- and multivariate distributions and standard deviations of the items were examined prior to an analysis of principal components, which aimed at finding out whether certain items were consistently associated with the same indicators across the six systems. Tests of one-factor models were also carried out.

The next step involved the computation of optimal correlations among the retained items. Polychoric and polyserial correlation coefficients for items classified as ordinal, censored and continuous were computed using a preprocessor to the LISREL computer program (Jöreskog and Sörbom, 1988). However, chi-square tests showed that this approach was not admissible for certain variable pairs; product moment correlations were computed in these cases.

Determination of Reliability

The third major step involved the estimation of item and indicator reliability. The reliability of certain indicators such as external training support and teacher competence (see Table 7.1) could be determined using a scale analysis procedure. These estimates were directly built into the model. Only one item was available for measuring a few indicators such as school size and previous innovation experience (see Table 7.1). Since in these cases reliability could not be determined from the data, measurement errors with assumed values of 0.15 were assigned to these indicators. Larger measurement errors were only allowed if these could be shown on the basis of the corresponding modification indices to result in a substantial decrease in the value of chi-square associated with model fit.

Identification of Indicators

Table 7.1 shows which items are associated with which indicators in the six measurement models. It can be seen that the measurement models are not fully consistent, although comparability was, of course, the intention from the outset. In order to reduce the number of degrees of freedom in the measurement models while safeguarding the stability of the indicators, which is necessary in order to reduce the number of residuals, not more than three items are specified per indicator. Because not all items performed equally well in all six models in terms of, for example, reliability, only the three items that most appropriately measured a given indicator were specified. However, there is good reason to assume that the indicators can nevertheless be considered comparable, not only because three out of the possible four items are similar, but also because identical items are used in assigning a scale to each indicator in the six models. The factor loadings and unique variances of the items used to measure the indicators are shown in Tables A 7.1 through A 7.6 in the statistical annex to this chapter. Whereas Table 7.1 presents information that makes it possible to compare the measurement models in terms of their overall structure, detailed information on the differences and similarities is provided in the annex.

Table 7.1

Comparison of measurement models

Indicator Y$_i$ Item	FRA λ_i	FRG λ_i	JPN λ_i	NET λ_i	SWI λ_i	USA λ_i
η_1 School size	X	X	X	X	X	X
η_2 External financial support	X	X	X	X	X	X
η_3 External training support	X	X	O	X	X	X
η_4 Previous innovation experience	X	X	X	X	X	X
η_5 Availability and resource needs						
Y$_1$ need more powerful computers	X	X	X	X	X	X
Y$_2$ need network for disk storage	X	X	X	X	O	X
Y$_3$ need greater variety of software	O	O	O	O	X	X
Y$_4$ need more tool software	X	X	X	X	X	O
η_6 Perceived innovation relevance						
Y$_1$ computers increase productivity	X	X	X	X	X	X
Y$_2$ computers enhance teaching	O	X	O	O	O	X
Y$_3$ computers increase achievement	X	X	X	X	X	X
Y$_4$ computers enhance creativity	X	O	X	O	X	O
Y$_5$ computers improve learning	O	O	O	X	O	O
η_7 School policy for computer use						
Y$_1$ computer experience	X	X	X	O	O	X
Y$_2$ compulsory instruction	X	X	X	X	X	X
Y$_3$ priorities for instructional use	X	O	O	X	X	X
Y$_4$ prescribe soft- and hardware	O	X	X	X	X	O
η_8 Internal staff development						
Y$_1$ introductory course on computers	X	X	X	O	X	X
Y$_2$ course in application programs	X	X	X	X	X	X
Y$_3$ course in computer programming	X	X	O	X	X	O
Y$_4$ subject-specific course	O	O	X	X	O	X
η_9 Internal innovation assistance						
Y$_1$ hardware support to teacher	O	O	X	O	X	X
Y$_2$ software support to teacher	X	X	X	X	X	X
Y$_3$ instructional support to teacher	X	X	X	X	X	O
Y$_4$ organizational support to teacher	X	X	O	X	O	X
η_{10} Teacher competence and readiness	X	X	X	X	X	X
η_{11} Monitoring and problem coping strategy						
Y$_1$ internal information exchange	X	X	X	X	X	X
Y$_2$ external information exchange	X	X	X	X	X	X
Y$_3$ internal evaluation of computer use	O	X	O	X	O	O
η_{12} Implementation of computer use						
Y$_1$ computer use in grade 8	X	X	X	X	X	X

Notes: X = fitted parameter, O = not included, λ_i denotes the association of an item with an indicator.

Estimation of Structural Models

Linear structural equation models were developed in the last step. Useful summaries of the theories and principles guiding the development of such models is given in Lohnes (1988), Keeves (1988), and Jöreskog and Sörbom (1990). The maximum likelihood method was used in the fitting of the models to the data. The models are presented in Figures 7.4a through 7.4f. The overidentified structural models shown in these Figures were only estimated after the measurement models had been modified and were shown to have achieved an adequate fit.

Determination of Goodness of Fit

Table 7.2 presents estimates of the goodness of fit of the models to the data. The following criteria are used in the assessment of overall model fit: the value of chi-square relative to the degrees of freedom; the probability that the true chi-square value is larger than the obtained value; the adjusted goodness of fit index; the root mean square residual; the number of fitted residuals; and the number of unconstrained residuals.

The following guidelines may be used in interpreting the goodness of fit estimates given in Table 7.2. The adequacy of a model is determined, first, on the interpretability of the parameter estimates and, second, on the basis of the consistency of the values compared with those estimated in comparison models. The fit of a model may be judged acceptable if the chi-square ratios are below two, the probability value P exceeds the 0.10 level commonly used as a threshold for statistical significance, the goodness of fit index exceeds the value of 0.90, and the value of the root mean square residual lies below 0.05 (Reynolds and Walberg, 1991). Furthermore, the fewer the number of unconstrained residuals with standardized values outside the range from -2.0 to 2.0, the better the fit of the model. It can be seen from the values recorded in Table 7.2 that, judged by these criteria, the fit of the models is adequate in all six cases.

Table 7.2

Estimates of the goodness of fit of models and data

	LISREL model fitted against data from:					
	FRA	FRG	JPN	NET	SWI	USA
Number of cases	265	268	230	247	402	305
Chi-square	206.30	240.11	190.04	261.68	215.73	218.71
Degrees of freedom	188	216	173	241	196	201
Probability	0.171	0.125	0.178	0.172	0.159	0.186
Goodness-of-fit index	0.938	0.931	0.931	0.929	0.957	0.943
Root mean square residual	0.047	0.055	0.048	0.056	0.041	0.050
Number of fitted residuals	27	24	15	25	21	13
Unfitted residuals with standardized values ≥ 2.0 or ≤ -2.0	2	5	4	2	2	2

Model Stability and Cross-validation

The present study provides a stringent test of the model of implementation indicators shown in Figure 7.1. Its strength lies in the fact that similar models are estimated using data derived from national probability samples of schools in six countries while taking advantage of structural modeling procedures that facilitate the specification of multiple indicators of implementation indicators, allow for the estimation and control of measurement error, and make it possible to adjust correlations of variables for the lack of equal interval scales. It is common to test the stability of parameters estimated in structural equation models by cross-validating the results on a split-half independent sample (Reynolds and Walberg, 1991). Instead of employing an artificially created split-half sample, a more elaborate and rigorous approach to cross-validation could be taken in the present study because six truly independent samples are available for data scrutiny.

Results

Cross-System Variation in Computer Use

Figure 7.2 presents for each of the six systems a curve indicating computer use in the four subjects in 1989. The indices are derived as follows. The percentage of lower secondary schools in a system that have access to computers are shown on the horizontal axis. It can be seen, for example, that 66 per cent of the Japanese lower secondary schools did not use computers in 1989, whereas nearly all of the schools at this level in the United States of America did. The percentage of schools using computers for educational purposes in each of the four subjects is indicated on the vertical axis. Thus the larger the shaded area on the right-hand side of the curve, the higher the proportion of schools that have computers and that actually use these for educational purposes in the four major subjects. A limitation is that the indicator cannot be interpreted as showing the actual amount of instruction with computers to which the students are exposed in the different school systems.

Based on the data in Figure 7.2 a yield score of computer implementation is calculated for each system. This score represents the shaded area for each of the countries in Figure 7.2. The application of such yield scores is explained in Keeves (1992).

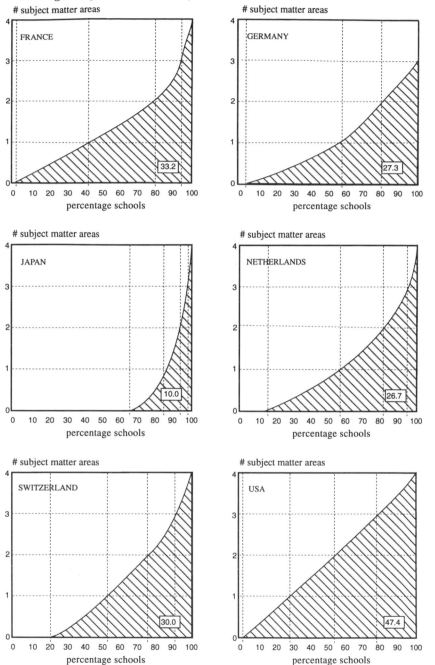

Figure 7.2 Degree of implementation of computer use in four subjects of lower secondary schools.

The six systems investigated in this chapter are ranked on their yield score in Figure 7.3. It can be seen that from the six examined countries, the United States of America (47.4) has the highest degree of computer use for educational purposes, whereas the lowest degree is found in Japan (10.0). The European countries -- France, the Federal Republic of Germany, the Netherlands and Switzerland -- are at an intermediate level.

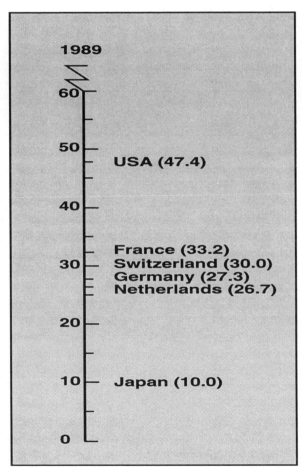

Figure 7.3 Degree of computer use for educational purposes based on a yield score for four subjects.

Associations Among the Indicators

The purpose of the data analysis was not only to find out how well the antecedents served as predictors of computer use in grade 8, but also to establish the extent of interrelatedness of these indicators. It is important in investigations such as the present one, which involves highly theoretical variables such as 'teacher competence and readiness', 'school policy for computer use' and 'perceived innovation relevance', to minimize the biasing influences of measurement error. The LISREL method used in this chapter presents an effective means of estimating 'true' or disattenuated correlations among the indicators by estimating and controlling for measurement error. These disattenuated correlations can be considered optimal or 'true' because the influences of measurement error components such as item specific error, design and sampling error, and response error are 'partialled out' of the correlation coefficients.

Full matrices of disattenuated correlations are presented in Tables B 7.1 through B 7.6 in the statistical annex. These matrices are of interest for theoretical as well as practical reasons, and they can appropriately be used for secondary data analysis. In this study, disattenuated correlations with values of 0.20 or larger are considered meaningful.

Table 7.3 presents disattenuated correlation coefficients estimated among four indicators influencing the dependent variable, computer use in four subjects in grade 8. The data in Table 7.3 can only be interpreted as showing that there are substantial differences between the school systems in the extent to which the indicators are associated with the outcome variable. The correlations are generally the highest in Japan and the lowest in Switzerland and the Netherlands. France, and the United States of America show much similarity.

Table 7.3
Disattenuated correlations, estimated in full LISREL models

Antecedent Indicators	Dependent Indicator: Computer Use in Grade 8					
	FRA	FRG	JPN	NET	SWI	USA
η_8 Internal staff development	-.013	.114	.430	.254	-.021	.009
η_9 Internal innovation assistance	.107	.223	.344	.054	.077	.248
η_{10} Teacher competence and readiness	.225	.170	.326	-.039	.051	.201
η_{11} Monitoring and problem coping strategy	.201	.071	.546	-.043	-.063	.203

For obvious reasons, the coefficients in Table 7.3 cannot and should not be interpreted in causal terms. They only give some indication of the degree of association existing among the indicators in each of the six systems. Effect relationships are examined in the next section, in which structural equation models are examined. As Jöreskog and Sörbom (1988, p. 1) observe:

"Because the equation represents a causal link rather than a mere empirical association, the structural parameters do not, in general, coincide with coefficients of regressions among observed variables. Instead, the structural parameters represent relatively unmixed, invariant and autonomous features of the mechanism under study".

Whereas unstandardized coefficients are commonly used in comparing regression models that involve different samples, the putative cause-and-effect variables were standardized in the data analysis reported below. This seems justified because, as the above quotation indicates, LISREL parameters can be considered relatively unmixed and autonomous. Another aspect is that the items specified in the models are conceptually identical and measured on similar scales.

Structural Equation Models of Implementation Indicators

Six overidentified LISREL models -- e.g., models estimated after all paths which are not statistically significant have been removed -- which predict computer use in four subjects in lower secondary schools are presented in Figures 7.4a through 7.4f. Significant effect relationships are denoted by the unidirectional arrows. For each path, two values are shown. The first estimate concerns the size of the standardized regression coefficient. The second one, which is presented in brackets, denotes the size of the standard error.

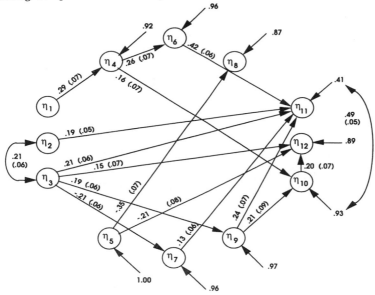

Figure 7.4a Standardized effects on computer use in France.

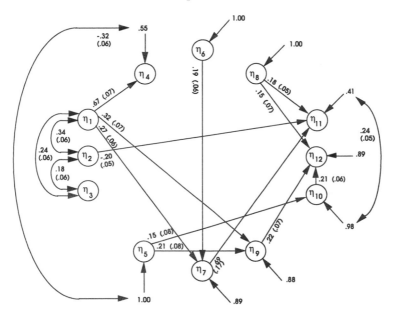

Figure 7.4b Standardized effects on computer use in Germany.

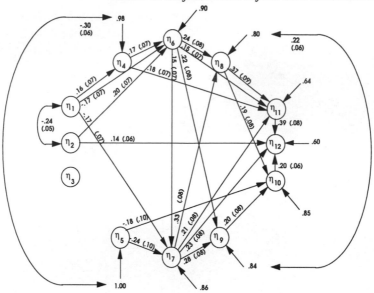

Figure 7.4c Standardized effects on computer use in Japan.

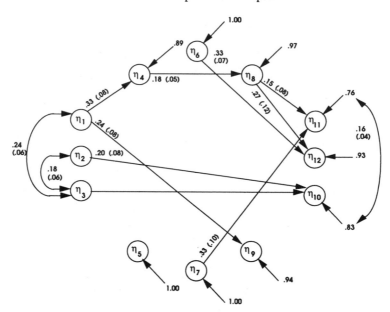

Figure 7.4d Standardized effects on computer use in the Netherlands.

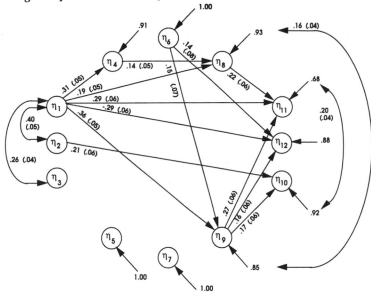

Figure 7.4e Standardized effects on computer use in Switzerland.

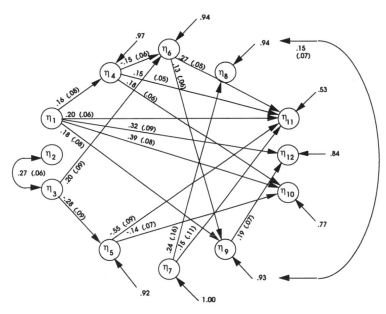

Figure 7.4f Standardized effects on computer use in the United States of America.

The model for France shows that external training support has a significant but weak effect on computer use (0.15), even if all other indicators are held constant in the model. Teacher competence also had a direct influence (0.20). It can be inferred from the results that the model explains 11 percent of the 'true' variance in computer use. The indicator monitoring and problem coping strategy is well predicted compared to computer use. Five antecedents seem to exert an influence, accounting for 59 percent of the variation in the dependent variable.

Although the structure of the German model differs in many respects from that of the French model, the capacity of the models to predict computer use seems to be identical. External training support does not play a significant role in the Federal Republic of Germany, where school-based staff development (0.15) and innovation assistance (0.22) play a modest role. Teacher competence also exerts an influence (0.21). As in France, these indicators account for 11 percent of the variance in computer use. Three indicators exert an influence on monitoring and problem coping strategy, explaining, as in France, 59 percent of the variation in this dependent variable.

The model estimated on the basis of data from Japan corresponds very well to the conceptual model that was hypothesized at the outset. Perceived innovation relevance, school policy for computers in education, and internal staff development, are major structural factors. The Japanese model explains 40 per cent of the variation in the dependent variable, computer use in grade 8, and 36 per cent of the variance in monitoring and problem coping strategy is accounted for. Teacher competence, which also in this case plays a role in explaining variation in implementation outcomes, is influenced by internal staff development and innovation assistance. As was the case in the Federal Republic of Germany, external training support does not seem to play an important role.

The Dutch model shows fewer significant relationships compared with the other models. It is of interest to note that internal staff development and perceived relevance influence computer use, whereas teacher competence and readiness is influenced by external financial and training support. General school policy and internal innovation assistance play only a marginal role compared with other systems, such as the Federal Republic of Germany and Japan, where little emphasis is put on external factors.

The model estimated using data collected in Switzerland is of interest because it seems to fit in with some of the patterns so far discerned. As in Japan and the Federal Republic of Germany, external training support plays no structural role. The effect of external financial support on teacher competence is similar (0.21) to that found in the Dutch model (0.20). The fit of previous innovation experience and availability is also the same. About 12 per cent of the variance in the dependent variable, computer use, is accounted for in the Swiss model. The main determinants are school size, perceived innovation relevance and internal innovation support. Three indicators predict monitoring and problem coping strategy, explaining 32 per cent of the variance. Also interesting is the result that school size has moderate positive effects on several of the mediating indicators in the model but, surprisingly, negatively influences computer use.

School size seems to be a major structural determinant in the case of the United States of America. However, a note of caution should be made. Although school size was used as a stratifier in all sampling plans, the effect of this procedure is particularly influential in the United States of America, mainly because of the large number of schools in this country compared to the other countries. Some of the influence of school size may therefore be due to a design effect. External financial support is not a factor of importance in the United States of America. Two antecedents, school size and internal innovation assistance, account for 16 per cent of the variance in computer use, whereas five indicators explain 47 per cent in monitoring and problem coping strategy. Compared with the previous five models, more of the variation in teacher competence and readiness is accounted for. School size and previous innovation history are the main determinants in this case.

Further Comparisons

Table 7.4 presents a comparison of the indicators influencing teacher competence and readiness across the six systems. Total effect coefficients are indicated. These represent the sum of the direct and the indirect effects of the antecedents on the outcome variable. If there are few structural relationships in a model, as is the case in the Dutch model, then there will also be few mediated effects. The total effect coefficients will therefore be rather similar to the estimates of structural parameters in path models. But if there are many structural relationships, as in the case of Japan and the United States of America then there can be significant indirect influences. Comparisons of total effect coefficients are therefore appropriate.

Albert C. Tuijnman and Alfons C.A. ten Brummelhuis

Table 7.4

Indicators influencing the variable "Teacher competence and readiness" (cumulative and standardized effects; standard errors in brackets)

	Dependent Variable					
Antecedent Indicators	FRA	FRG	JPN	NET	SWI	USA
η_1 School size	.05 (.02)	-.04 (.02)	-.04 (.02)	.00 (.00)	.07 (.02)	.50 (.08)
η_2 External financial support	.00 (.00)	.00 (.00)	.02 (.01)	.22 (.08)	.22 (.06)	.00 (.00)
η_3 External training support	.04 (.02)	.00 (.00)	n.i.	.36 (.10)	.00 (.00)	.05 (.03)
η_4 Previous innovation experience	.17 (.07)	-.05 (.03)	.02 (.01)	.00 (.00)	.00 (.00)	.19 (.06)
η_5 Availability and resource needs	.00 (.00)	.20 (.09)	-.30 (.10)	.00 (.00)	.00 (.00)	-.18 (.08)
η_6 Perceived innovation relevance	.00 (.00)	.00 (.00)	.13 (.04)	.00 (.00)	.03 (.02)	.00 (.00)
η_7 School policy for computer use	.00 (.00)	.00 (.00)	.13 (.04)	.00 (.00)	.00 (.00)	.00 (.00)
η_8 Internal staff development	.00 (.00)	.00 (.00)	.21 (.09)	.00 (.00)	.00 (.00)	.00 (.00)
η_9 Internal innovation assistance	.27 (.09)	.00 (.00)	.20 (.08)	.00 (.00)	.18 (.06)	.00 (.00)
Explained variance (R^2)	.07	.02	.15	17	.08	.23

Notes: n.i. = not included.

It can be seen from the coefficients in Table 7.4 that school size only has a major impact on teacher competence in the United States of America. External financial support has a significant effect in only two systems: Switzerland and the Netherlands. The Netherlands is the only country where external training support is a factor of importance in raising teacher competence. In contrast, 'internal' indicators such as staff development and internal innovation assistance play a more important role in France, Japan and Switzerland.

Table 7.5 shows whether and how much the indicators influence monitoring and problem coping strategy. The results show that there is considerable variation amongst the six systems. School size plays a positive role in the Federal Republic of Germany, Switzerland and the United States of America. External training support is implicated in only two models, namely in those of France and the United States of America. If significant effects of resource (non-)availability are recorded, then these are mainly negative as in Japan and the United States of America. Especially in the latter country, where computers are generally available, this is a strong determinant, as can be expected. Innovation relevance has moderate effects in all of the models except that of Switzerland. School policy is also an important factor, especially in the Federal Republic of Germany and the Netherlands. The effects of staff development and internal innovation support come through in all of the models -- the United States of America excepted.

Table 7.5

Indicators influencing the variable "Monitoring and problem coping strategy" (cumulative and standardized effects; standard errors in brackets)

	Dependent Variable					
Antecedent Indicators	FRA	GER	JPN	NET	SWI	USA
η_1 School size	.03 (.01)	.15 (.05)	-.06 (.04)	.01 (.01)	.38 (.05)	.18 (.06)
η_2 External financial support	.16 (.05)	-.15 (.05)	.05 (.03)	.00 (.00)	.00 (.00)	.00 (.00)
η_3 External training support	.21 (.06)	.00 (.00)	n.i.	.00 (.00)	.00 (.00)	.18 (.05)
η_4 Previous innovation experience	.12 (.04)	-.01 (.01)	.21 (.07)	.02 (.02)	.03 (.01)	.07 (.04)
η_5 Availability and resource needs	.00 (.00)	.04 (.02)	-.10 (.04)	.00 (.00)	.00 (.00)	-.46 (.09)
η_6 Perceived innovation relevance	.39 (.06)	.11 (.05)	.29 (.08)	.31 (.07)	.04 (.02)	.20 (.05)
η_7 School policy for computer use	.13 (.06)	.69 (.17)	.30 (.08)	.33 (.10)	.00 (.00)	.27 (.13)
η_8 Internal staff development	.00 (.00)	.14 (.05)	.21 (.08)	.19 (.09)	.21 (.06)	.00 (.00)
η_9 Internal innovation assistance	.34 (.07)	.00 (.00)	.20 (.00)	.00 (.00)	.24 (.06)	.00 (.00)
Explained variance (R^2)	.59	.59	.36	.24	.32	.47

Notes: n.i. = not included.

Table 7.6 shows the total effects on the criterion variable, computer use in four subjects in grade 8. Whether the strong effect observed in the United States of America is real or due to the design of the sample cannot be determined from the data. The coefficients presented in Table 7.6 show that computer use, which varies across systems, cannot be systematically and consistently predicted by the indicators specified in the path models. Not only are different variables involved but also the amount of explained variance is generally low.

Table 7.6

Indicators influencing the variable "Computer use" (cumulative and standardized effects; standard errors in brackets)

	Dependent Variable					
Antecedent Indicators	FRA	GER	JPN	NET	SWI	USA
η_1 School size	.01 (.01)	.06 (.03)	-.08 (.04)	.02 (.01)	-.23 (.06)	.42 (.09)
η_2 External financial support	.00 (.00)	.00 (.00)	.17 (.06)	.00 (.00)	.00 (.00)	.00 (.00)
η_3 External training support	.16 (.07)	.00 (.00)	n.i.	.00 (.00)	.00 (.00)	.01 (.00)
η_4 Previous innovation experience	.03 (.02)	-.03 (.01)	.10 (.03)	.05 (.03)	.00 (.00)	.00 (.00)
η_5 Availability and resource needs	-.26 (.08)	.10 (.04)	-.18 (.05)	.00 (.00)	.00 (.00)	.00 (.00)
η_6 Perceived innovation relevance	.00 (.00)	.00 (.00)	.20 (.05)	.00 (.00)	.22 (.08)	.03 (.02)
η_7 School policy for computer use	.00 (.00)	.00 (.00)	.39 (.08)	.00 (.00)	-.15 (.07)	.02 (.01)
η_8 Internal staff development	.00 (.00)	.15 (.07)	.20 (.05)	.42 (.12)	.00 (.00)	.03 (.02)
η_9 Internal innovation assistance	.05 (.03)	.25 (.07)	.04 (.02)	.00 (.00)	.16 (.06)	.21 (.07)
Explained variance (R^2)	.11	.11	.40	.07	.12	.16

Notes: n.i. = not included.

Discussion

A general observation is that there is much variation among the six systems in terms of the indicators that influence computer use in lower secondary education. Computer use in the four subjects also varies substantially. There can be no doubt that the United States of America has come a long way on the road to full implementation, especially in comparison with Japan, where the process has begun more recently. The four European systems that are examined in this chapter find themselves in an intermediate position.

In the cases of France, the Federal Republic of Germany and the United States of America, the results show that a sizeable amount of variance in one or more of the key indicators related to the frame factor implementation conditions (see the theoretical model in Figure 7.1) is explained. The variable monitoring and problem coping strategy could be especially well predicted in these countries. However, a significant effect of this indicator on the outcome, computer implementation, was not found in any of the countries.

The highest degree of confirmation for the influence of indicators on computer use among countries was found for internal innovation assistance and teacher competence and readiness. Both directly influenced the outcome variable in three of the six countries.

In none of the examined countries could a direct influence be found of the number of years of computer experience at school on the degree of computer use.

The variation among the six countries in terms of the indicators that influence computer use can be explained by differences in the stage of the innovation process and country-specific policies for the introduction of computers. It can be hypothesized that certain indicators are more or less related to specific stages of the innovation process, such as initiation, implementation and institutionalization. As the results obtained for the two countries that occupy the high and low ends of the computer implementation scale, the United States of America and Japan, illustrate, there is some support for this hypothesis.

As previously shown in Figure 7.3, the schools in the United States of America have come further than the schools in the other five systems in terms of the actual use of computers for educational purposes. The results of the data analysis show that a school system such as that of Japan, where computers were recently introduced compared with the United States of America, has more variation in the indicators predicting reform initiation and implementation. In the United States of America, on the other hand, where many schools have had a decade or more of experience with computers, less variation is found among the antecedents that are used in the data analysis. Hence, the fact that the model seems to function better in predicting the situation in Japan compared with the United States of America cannot be interpreted as suggesting that the Japanese students receive more instruction with computers than their peers in the United States of America. The result that there is less variation among the indicators in the United States of America compared with Japan may arise because many schools in Japan are still working on the introduction of the innovation, whereas schools in the United States of America have gone beyond the initiation and implementation process and have reached a stage of institutionalization.

The central conclusion is thus that the key indicators specified in the models are relevant more to an explanation of reform initiation and implementation than to the continuation or institutionalization of an already implemented reform.

Statistical Annex

Table A 7.1

Measurement model, France, lower secondary schools, N = 265

Indicator Y_i Item		Factor Loading λ_i^y	t	Unique Variance θ_{ii}^ε	t	No. items	Notes
η_1	School size	.87	n.a.	.25	n.a.	1	Ass. α
η_2	External financial support	.87	n.a.	.25	n.a.	1	Ass. α
η_3	External training support	.90	n.a.	.20	n.a.	1	Ass. α
η_4	Previous innovation experience	.89	n.a.	.20	n.a.	1	Ass. α
η_5	Availability and resource needs					3	Est. R
	Y_2 more powerful computers	.75	n.a.	.17	5.54		
	Y_3 network for disk storage	.82	8.72	.56	3.94		
	Y_4 more tool software	.42	7.49	.77	11.14		
η_6	Perceived innovation relevance					3	Est. R
	Y_5 increase productivity	.82	n.a.	.07	6.80		
	Y_6 enhance creativity	.72	11.79	.60	9.46		
	Y_7 increase achievement	.79	12.61	.60	7.63		
η_7	School policy for computer use					3	Est. R
	Y_8 instruction with computers	.79	n.a.	.05	6.71		
	Y_9 priorities for instructional use	.78	10.62	.56	6.77		
	Y_{10} computer experience	.68	10.18	.62	8.85		
η_8	Internal staff development					3	Est. R
	Y_{11} course on application programs	.82	n.a.	.10	5.90		
	Y_{12} introductory course	.81	10.94	.52	5.62		
	Y_{13} computer programming course	.62	9.69	.64	10.59		
η_9	Internal innovation assistance					3	Est. R
	Y_{14} software support	.74	n.a.	.11	7.67		
	Y_{15} instructional support	.63	10.34	.63	10.10		
	Y_{16} organizational support	.79	10.97	.53	6.02		
η_{10}	Teacher competence and readiness	.96	n.a.	.08	n.a.	1	Est. α
η_{11}	Monitoring and problem coping					2	Est. R
	Y_{18} internal information exchange	.76	n.a.	.08	3.74		
	Y_{19} external information exchange	.36	4.29	.86	10.69		
η_{12}	Implementation of computer use					1	Ass. R
	Y_{20} computer use in grade 8	.92	n.a.	.15	n.a.		

Notes: n.a. = not applicable, Ass. = Assumed, Est. = Estimated.

Table A 7.2

Measurement model, Federal Republic of Germany, lower secondary schools, N = 268

Indicator Y_i Item	Factor Loading λ^y_i	t	Unique Variance θ^ε_{ii}	t	No. items	Notes
η_1 School size	.85	n.a.	.25	n.a.	1	Ass. α
η_2 External financial support	.92	n.a.	.15	n.a.	1	Ass. α
η_3 External training support	.92	n.a.	.15	n.a.	1	Ass. α
η_4 Previous innovation experience	.92	n.a.	.15	n.a.	1	Ass. α
η_5 Availability and resource needs					3	Est. *R*
Y_2 more powerful computers	.73	n.a.	.44	5.30		
Y_3 more tool software	.63	6.38	.59	7.60		
Y_4 network for disk storage	.50	6.15	.76	10.12		
η_6 Perceived innovation relevance					3	Est. *R*
Y_5 enhance teaching	.83	n.a.	.34	5.52		
Y_6 increase achievement	.74	10.30	.46	7.85		
Y_7 increase productivity	.70	10.15	.52	8.81		
η_7 School policy for computer use					3	Est. *R*
Y_8 instruction with computers	.54	n.a.	.70	8.29		
Y_9 computer experience	.34	4.42	.86	10.29		
Y_{10} prescribe soft- and hardware	.59	4.92	.65	7.39		
η_8 Internal staff development					3	Est. *R*
Y_{11} course on application programs	.92	n.a.	.16	1.60		
Y_{12} introductory course	.71	7.82	.48	6.87		
Y_{13} computer programming course	.46	6.26	.79	10.87		
η_9 Internal innovation assistance					3	Est. *R*
Y_{14} software support	.82	n.a.	.29	9.90		
Y_{15} organizational support	.84	19.37	.29	9.76		
Y_{16} instructional support	.95	23.65	.11	4.36		
η_{10} Teacher competence and readiness	.97	n.a.	.09	n.a.	14	Est. α
η_{11} Monitoring and problem coping					3	Est. *R*
Y_{18} internal evaluation	.69	n.a.	.52	8.30		
Y_{19} internal information exchange	.74	9.21	.50	7.75		
Y_{20} external information exchange	.84	6.45	.60	8.01		
η_{12} Implementation of computer use					1	Ass. α
Y_{21} computer use in grade 8	.93	n.a.	.15	n.a.		

Notes: n.a. = not applicable, Ass. = Assumed, Est. = Estimated.

Table A 7.3

Measurement model, Japan, lower secondary schools, N = 230

Indicator Y_i Item	λ^y_i	t	θ^ε_{ii}	t	No. items	Notes
	Factor Loading		Unique Variance			
η_1 School size	.92	n.a.	.15	n.a.	1	Ass. α
η_2 External financial support	.92	n.a.	.15	n.a.	1	Ass. α
η_3 External training support	.71	n.a.	.50	n.a.	13	n.i.
η_4 Previous innovation experience	.92	n.a.	.15	n.a.	1	Ass. α
η_5 Availability and resource needs					3	Est. R
$\quad Y_2$ more powerful computers	.69	n.a.	.53	8.85		
$\quad Y_3$ network for disk storage	.65	9.78	.27	4.17		
$\quad Y_4$ more tool software	.88	9.00	.58	9.30		
η_6 Perceived innovation relevance					3	Est. R
$\quad Y_5$ increase achievement	.85	n.a.	.22	6.40		
$\quad Y_6$ enhance creativity	.82	13.20	.41	7.18		
$\quad Y_7$ increase productivity	.77	12.63	.44	8.31		
η_7 School policy for computer use					3	Est. R
$\quad Y_8$ computer experience	.90	n.a.	.35	1.81		
$\quad Y_9$ instruction with computers	.62	6.77	.52	8.34		
$\quad Y_{10}$ prescribe soft- and hardware	.53	6.15	.64	9.37		
η_8 Internal staff development					3	Est. R
$\quad Y_{11}$ course on application programs	.86	n.a.	.24	4.17		
$\quad Y_{12}$ introductory course	.79	10.63	.38	6.46		
$\quad Y_{13}$ subject specific computer use	.47	6.69	.78	10.13		
η_9 Internal innovation assistance					3	Est. R
$\quad Y_{14}$ hardware support	.95	n.a.	.12	2.01		
$\quad Y_{15}$ software support	.80	12.55	.41	6.42		
$\quad Y_{16}$ instructional support	.44	6.91	.61	10.23		
η_{10} Teacher competence and readiness	.97	n.a.	.06	n.a.	22	Est. α
η_{11} Monitoring and problem coping					2	Est. R
$\quad Y_{18}$ internal information exchange	.84	n.a.	.17	4.60		
$\quad Y_{19}$ external information exchange	.78	10.07	.46	6.23		
η_{12} Implementation of computer use					1	Ass. α
$\quad Y_{20}$ computer use in grade 8	.92	n.a.	.15	n.a.		

Notes: n.i. = not included, Ass. = Assumed, Est. = Estimated.

Table A 7.4

Measurement model, the Netherlands, lower secondary schools, N = 253

Indicator Y_i Item	Factor Loading λ^y_i	t	Unique Variance θ^ε_{ii}	t	No. items	Notes
η_1 School size	.85	n.a.	.26	n.a.	1	Ass. α
η_2 External financial support	.85	n.a.	.26	n.a.	1	Ass. α
η_3 External training support	.78	n.a.	.40	n.a.	13	Est. α
η_4 Previous innovation experience	.85	n.a.	.26	n.a.	1	Ass. α
η_5 Availability and resource needs					3	Est. α
Y_2 more powerful computers	.78	n.a.	.39	2.85		
Y_3 network for disk storage	.73	4.41	.46	3.72		
Y_4 more tool software	.33	4.04	.87	10.55		
η_6 Perceived innovation relevance					3	Est. *R*
Y_5 increase productivity	.76	n.a.	.42	6.89		
Y_6 increase achievement	.89	10.13	.19	2.80		
Y_7 improve learning	.54	8.64	.74	10.48		
η_7 School policy for computer use					3	Est. *R*
Y_8 priorities for instructional use	.72	n.a.	.50	4.53		
Y_9 prescribe soft- and hardware	.54	4.86	.71	8.31		
Y_{10} instruction with computers	.47	4.69	.78	9.35		
η_8 Internal staff development					3	Est. *R*
Y_{11} course on application programs	.58	n.a.	.64	9.55		
Y_{12} computer programming course	.85	7.93	.28	3.71		
Y_{13} subject specific computer use	.66	7.87	.56	8.25		
η_9 Internal innovation assistance					3	Est. *R*
Y_{14} software support	.83	n.a.	.33	7.97		
Y_{15} instructional support	.95	16.12	.09	2.17		
Y_{16} organizational support	.73	14.24	.46	9.87		
η_{10} Teacher competence and readiness	.94	n.a.	.12	n.a.	22	Est. α
η_{11} Monitoring and problem coping					3	Est. *R*
Y_{18} internal information exchange	.72	n.a.	.48	5.78		
Y_{19} external information exchange	.59	5.51	.64	7.25		
Y_{20} internal evaluation	.79	6.50	.36	3.68		
η_{12} Implementation of computer use					1	Inf. *P*
Y_{21} computer use in grade 8	.91	n.a.	.15[a]	n.a.		

Notes: n.a. = not applicable, Ass. = Assumed, Est. = Estimated, Inf. = Inferred.
[a] Reliability coefficient approximated on the basis of information on use of computers in grade 7 and grade 9.

Table A 7.5

Measurement model, Switzerland, lower secondary schools, N = 402

Indicator Y$_i$ Item	Factor Loading λ^y_i	t	Unique Variance θ^ε_{ii}	t	No. items	Notes
η_1 School size	.92	n.a.	.15	n.a.	1	Ass. α
η_2 External financial support	.92	n.a.	.15	n.a.	1	Ass. α
η_3 External training support	.68	n.a.	.54	n.a.	13	Est. α
η_4 Previous innovation experience	.92	n.a.	.15	n.a.	1	Ass. α
η_5 Availability and resource needs					3	Est. R
$\quad$ Y$_2$ more powerful computers	.47	n.a.	.79	12.14		
$\quad$ Y$_3$ greater variety of software	.58	7.15	.65	9.60		
$\quad$ Y$_4$ more tool software	.81	6.05	.38	3.72		
η_6 Perceived innovation relevance					3	Est. R
$\quad$ Y$_5$ increase achievement	.75	n.a.	.43	6.60		
$\quad$ Y$_6$ enhance creativity	.62	8.58	.61	10.37		
$\quad$ Y$_7$ increase productivity	.63	8.61	.60	10.15		
η_7 School policy for computer use					3	Est. R
$\quad$ Y$_8$ instruction with computers	.80	n.a.	.36	8.62		
$\quad$ Y$_9$ prescribe soft- and hardware	.76	14.28	.43	10.04		
$\quad$ Y$_{10}$ priorities for instructional use	.80	14.60	.36	8.54		
η_8 Internal staff development					3	Est. R
$\quad$ Y$_{11}$ introductory course	.83	n.a.	.31	7.33		
$\quad$ Y$_{12}$ course on application programs	.89	15.40	.19	4.14		
$\quad$ Y$_{13}$ computer programming course	.57	11.74	.68	13.18		
η_9 Internal innovation assistance					3	Est. R
$\quad$ Y$_{14}$ hardware support	.89	n.a.	.21	7.59		
$\quad$ Y$_{15}$ instructional support	.74	17.79	.45	12.51		
$\quad$ Y$_{16}$ software support	.92	23.38	.16	6.00		
η_{10} Teacher competence and readiness	.97	n.a.	.07	n.a.	22	Est. α
η_{11} Monitoring and problem coping					2	Est. R
$\quad$ Y$_{18}$ internal information exchange	.80	n.a.	.34	4.39		
$\quad$ Y$_{19}$ external information exchange	.63	7.88	.58	9.50		
η_{12} Implementation of computer use					1	Ass. α
$\quad$ Y$_{20}$ computer use in grade 8	.92	n.a.	.15	n.a.		

Notes: n.a. = not applicable, Ass. = Assumed, Est. = Estimated.

Table A 7.6

Measurement model, the United States of America, lower secondary schools, N = 305

Indicator Y_i Item	Factor Loading λ_i^y	t	Unique Variance θ_{ii}^ε	t	No. items	Notes
η_1 School size	.79	n.a.	.35	n.a.	1	Ass. α
η_2 External financial support	.84	n.a.	.30	n.a.	12	Est. R
η_3 External training support	.77	n.a.	.41	n.a.	13	Est. α
η_4 Previous innovation experience	.92	n.a.	.15	n.a.	1	Ass. α
η_5 Availability and resource needs					3	Est. R
$\quad Y_2$ more powerful computers	.79	n.a.	.38	4.84		
$\quad Y_3$ network for disk storage	.60	7.18	.59	9.20		
$\quad Y_4$ greater variety of software	.45	6.09	.82	11.12		
η_6 Perceived innovation relevance					3	Est. R
$\quad Y_5$ increase productivity	.75	15.98	.48	10.46		
$\quad Y_6$ enhance teaching	.88	18.98	.21	6.56		
$\quad Y_7$ increase achievement	.90	n.a.	.19	5.92		
η_7 School policy for computer use					3	Est. R
$\quad Y_8$ instruction with computers	.36	n.a.	.53	9.81		
$\quad Y_9$ priorities for instructional use	.88	2.58	.78	0.71		
$\quad Y_{10}$ computer experience	.19	2.82	.98	12.04		
η_8 Internal staff development					3	Est. R
$\quad Y_{11}$ course on application programs	.87	15.88	.25	6.65		
$\quad Y_{12}$ introductory course	.84	15.64	.30	7.82		
$\quad Y_{13}$ subject specific course	.80	n.a.	.34	9.24		
η_9 Internal innovation assistance					3	Est. R
$\quad Y_{14}$ hardware support	.85	n.a.	.20	6.15		
$\quad Y_{15}$ software support	.86	15.74	.32	6.58		
$\quad Y_{16}$ organizational support	.69	13.53	.52	10.77		
η_{10} Teacher competence and readiness	.96	n.a.	.07	n.a.	22	Est. α
η_{11} Monitoring and problem coping					2	Est. R
$\quad Y_{18}$ internal information exchange	.67	n.a.	.45	7.03		
$\quad Y_{19}$ external information exchange	.95	4.87	.47	2.82		
η_{12} Implementation of computer use					1	Est. α
$\quad Y_{20}$ computer use in grade 8	.94	n.a.	.12	n.a.		

Notes: n.a. = not applicable, Ass. = Assumed, Est. = Estimated.

Table B 7.1

Matrix of disattenuated correlation coefficients, France, N = 265

Indicators	1	2	3	4	5	6	7	8	9	10	11	12
1. School size	1.000											
2. External financial support	-.072	1.000										
3. External training support	-.015	.192	1.000									
4. Previous innovation experience	.273	-.008	.001	1.000								
5. Availability and resource needs	.005	-.070	.061	-.025	1.00							
6. Perceived innovation relevance	-.016	-.004	-.143	.173	-.165	1.000						
7. School policy for computer use	.052	-.100	-.207	.024	-.096	.094	1.000					
8. Internal staff development	.061	-.038	-.105	-.023	-.351	.013	-.029	1.000				
9. Internal innovation assistance	.094	.063	.179	.036	-.093	.106	.062	-.038	1.000			
10. Teacher competence and readiness	.092	-.057	.060	.144	-.150	.026	.021	.009	.195	1.000		
11. Monitoring and problem coping	.043	.219	.246	.166	-.146	.369	.172	.031	.446	.493	1.000	
12. Implementation of computer use	-.116	.014	.148	.078	-.242	.021	-.015	-.013	.107	.225	.201	1.000

Table B 7.2

Matrix of disattenuated correlation coefficients, Federal Republic of Germany, N = 268

Indicators	1	2	3	4	5	6	7	8	9	10	11	12
1. School size	1.000											
2. External financial support	.299	1.000										
3. External training support	.210	.178	1.000									
4. Previous innovation experience	.632	.295	.203	1.000								
5. Availability and resource needs	-.240	-.111	-.010	-.327	1.000							
6. Perceived innovation relevance	-.052	-.099	.069	-.173	-.140	1.000						
7. School policy for computer use	.217	.127	.196	.164	-.228	.187	1.000					
8. Internal staff development	.062	.003	.038	.025	.005	.069	-.010	1.000				
9. Internal innovation assistance	.246	.126	.141	.183	.154	-.018	.135	.017	1.000			
10. Teacher competence and readiness	-.106	.123	-.011	-.045	.162	.003	-.090	.002	-.059	1.000		
11. Monitoring and problem coping	.042	-.103	.119	-.056	-.045	.107	.569	.182	.070	.218	1.000	
12. Implementation of computer use	.045	.118	.091	.129	.066	.002	.004	.144	.223	.170	.071	1.000

Table B 7.3

Matrix of disattenuated correlation coefficients, Japan, N = 230

Indicators	1	2	3	4	5	6	7	8	9	10	11	12
1. School size	1.000											
2. External financial support	-.234	1.000										
3. External training support	n.i.	n.i.	n.i.									
4. Previous innovation experience	.149	-.074	n.i.	1.000								
5. Availability and resource needs	.040	.024	n.i.	-.262	1.000							
6. Perceived innovation relevance	-.194	.222	n.i.	.133	-.075	1.000						
7. School policy for computer use	-.205	.076	n.i.	.105	-.238	.242	1.000					
8. Internal staff development	-.174	.171	n.i.	.065	-.119	.307	.379	1.000				
9. Internal innovation assistance	-.078	.154	n.i.	.147	-.201	.288	.335	.412	1.000			
10. Teacher competence and readiness	-.035	.025	n.i.	.059	-.248	.162	.105	.282	.310	1.000		
11. Monitoring and problem coping	-.136	.114	n.i.	.300	-.114	.330	.387	.486	.289	.257	1.000	
12. Implementation of computer use	-.195	.210	n.i.	.059	-.234	.402	.402	.430	.344	.326	.546	1.000

Notes: n.i. = not included.

Albert C. Tuijnman and Alfons C.A. ten Brummelhuis

Table B 7.4
Matrix of disattenuated correlation coefficients, the Netherlands, N = 247

Indicators	1	2	3	4	5	6	7	8	9	10	11	12
1. School size	1.000											
2. External financial support	-.134	1.000										
3. External training support	.235	.285	1.000									
4. Previous innovation experience	.334	.044	.210	1.000								
5. Availability and resource needs	.057	-.114	-.114	.146	1.000							
6. Perceived innovation relevance	.044	-.034	-.019	.036	-.135	1.000						
7. School policy for computer use	.132	-.022	.092	.165	-.062	.106	1.000					
8. Internal staff development	.114	.095	-.049	.194	-.130	-.013	.017	1.000				
9. Internal innovation assistance	.241	-.077	.005	.115	.027	.005	-.126	-.107	1.000			
10. Teacher competence and readiness	-.046	.293	.402	.165	-.058	-.006	-.008	-.068	.024	1.000		
11. Monitoring and problem coping	.057	.045	.181	.045	.023	.336	.352	.148	.069	.212	1.000	
12. Implementation use of computers	.164	-.026	-.012	.149	-.089	-.089	.063	.254	.054	-.039	.043	1.000

Table B 7.5
Matrix of disattenuated correlation coefficients, Switzerland, N = 402

Indicators	1	2	3	4	5	6	7	8	9	10	11	12
1. School size	1.000											
2. External financial support	.389	1.000										
3. External training support	.302	.086	1.000									
4. Previous innovation experience	.298	.207	.079	1.000								
5. Availability and resource needs	.011	-.028	-.255	.070	1.000							
6. Perceived innovation relevance	-.041	-.003	.030	-.005	-.142	1.000						
7. School policy for computer use	-.087	-.039	-.128	.052	.050	.043	1.000					
8. Internal staff development	.223	.156	.075	.196	.073	-.009	.068	1.000				
9. Internal innovation assistance	.358	.136	.167	.113	-.018	.126	-.057	.239	1.000			
10. Teacher competence and readiness	.239	.234	.015	.061	-.129	.072	.003	.134	.191	1.000		
11. Monitoring and problem coping	.437	.239	.210	.194	-.017	.049	-.084	.356	.418	.347	1.000	
12. Implementation of computer use	-.217	-.195	-.037	-.089	-.061	.183	-.112	-.021	.077	.051	-.063	1.000

Table B 7.6

Matrix of disattenuated correlation coefficients, the United States of America, N = 305

Indicators	1	2	3	4	5	6	7	8	9	10	11	12
1. School size	1.000											
2. External financial support	.103	1.000										
3. External training support	.106	.298	1.000									
4. Previous innovation experience	.174	.053	.070	1.000								
5. Availability and resource needs	-.123	-.103	-.254	-.142	1.000							
6. Perceived innovation relevance	.050	-.103	.183	-.148	-.107	1.000						
7. School policy for computer use	-.018	-.084	-.005	-.090	-.062	.056	1.000					
8. Internal staff development	-.004	-.009	.053	.025	-.102	.069	.218	1.000				
9. Internal innovation assistance	.156	.049	.068	.047	.086	.141	.035	.174	1.000			
10. Teacher competence and readiness	.400	-.009	.104	.254	-.187	-.063	.094	.027	.156	1.000		
11. Monitoring and problem coping	.212	.060	.236	.200	-.442	.264	.178	.190	.123	.217	1.000	
12. Implementation of computer use	.336	.119	.064	-.010	-.097	.017	.019	.009	.248	.201	.203	1.000

8

Summary and Conclusions

The 1980s can be characterized as the decade of technology revolution in education. Although in the decades before a number of new technologies were introduced in schools (educational television, educational radio, audio-visual media, language labs, etc.), the introduction of computers was unprecedented in terms of expectations and hopes for really innovating education. In many countries the technology fever rose quickly in the beginning of the 1980s: many teachers invested their own money in this innovation, and in many countries governmental stimulation programs (quite often based on the fear to lose the technology race) were started. Gradually, in most developed countries, computers were introduced into schools (starting at the higher educational levels, but quite quickly penetrating the lower secondary and elementary level), and even in developing countries (where frequently basic materials, like chalk, paper and pencil are lacking in many schools) projects were started to introduce computers in education (Hawkridge, 1990; Makau, 1990) with the not uncommon argument that this technology might constitute a catalytic factor in the developmental process. Even without governmental stimulation, the basis for adopting the new computer technology was so broad that considerable numbers of schools acquired computers on their own or with local support (for example, before the start of a governmental program for introducing computers in elementary schools in the Netherlands, already 50% of the schools acquired equipment on their own). Although, from a superficial point of view, these developments seem to indicate that we are dealing with an innovation that is non-controversial in terms of its goals and implementation, educational practice (as presented in the previous chapters) shows a different picture: the application and integration of computers in education is a very complicated process, expensive and beset with problems, asking for lots of time-investments from educational practitioners and above all: it is unclear what the goals of this innovation are.

This chapter aims at summarizing the findings resulting from our study so far.

This chapter was written by Willem J. Pelgrum, Tjeerd Plomp and
Ingeborg A.M. Janssen Reinen.

227

Therefore, we will draw upon the conclusions from the previous chapters. However, as the authors of the chapters deliberately tried to avoid overlap with earlier publications from our study, we will also refer to these publications which are all based on the Comped data (see also Janssen Reinen and Pelgrum, 1992). The selection of these results is inspired by the idea of providing policy makers and educational practitioners with some help in interpreting the many results of this study. The final section presents some possibilities for future action.

Summary of main findings

The start of computer use

In Chapter 2, the process of getting involved in the use of computers is discussed. It was concluded that schools seemed to stress the social rationale for using computers, namely preparing students through computer literacy for their place in society.

Furthermore it was found that those schools which emphasized the use of the computer for the teaching and learning process (the pedagogical rationale), use the computer in more different subject matter areas and for applications directed towards the improvement of the teaching and learning process.

Hardware and software availability

Chapter 3 showed that during the 1980s an increasing number of schools gained access to computers and that typically a period of about 4 years is needed to equip all schools in a system with computers. In most countries, computers were first introduced at upper and lower secondary levels, but ultimately elementary schools in many countries also acquired hardware. It was shown that in 1989, in most countries, a majority of lower and upper secondary schools used computers for instructional purposes, while this was the case to a lesser extent in elementary schools.

Not only are increasing numbers of schools equipped with computers, but also the average number of computers in schools already possessing computers changed gradually during the 1980s. In some countries, sudden jumps can be observed as a result of (governmental) stimulation programs (Pelgrum and Plomp, 1991). In Chapter 3, it was concluded that the quantity of hardware in computer using schools tends to increase with the number of years of using computers, which was reflected in the decreasing median student:computer ratio as a function of time. Although it seems that, in general, getting more computers is a matter of time, in some countries (for instance, elementary schools in Japan, and lower secondary schools in Switzerland) this development went relatively fast, while the progress in other countries (for instance lower secondary schools in Luxembourg and upper secondary schools in the Federal Republic of Germany), went relatively slow.

Chapter 3 also showed that in the majority of lower and upper secondary schools in almost all countries computers were mainly located in special computer rooms. There is a clear trend that elementary schools were more inclined to locate computers in classrooms than secondary schools. France and New Zealand are examples of countries where a considerable number of elementary schools (between 40-50%) located computers almost exclusively in classrooms. There are clear indications that the availability of computers in classrooms tends to be associated with more integration of computer activities into the existing curriculum.

Typically, teachers organize the use of computers in such a way that 2-3 students share the available equipment and, if necessary, the class is split up allowing one group of students to work with computers, while the others perform other activities (Pelgrum and Plomp, 1991).

As shown in Chapter 3, there was a considerable variation between countries with respect to the availability in schools of particular types of software. Educational tool software (drill/practice, tutorial and educational games) as well as general purpose programs (word processing and database programs) were quite consistently at the top of available types of software at all educational levels (see also Pelgrum and Plomp, 1991). However, it was also shown that large differences existed with regard to the access of schools to software. Noteworthy is that a positive association was observed between the availability of educational tool software and the integration of computers in existing subjects (see Chapter 3).

Despite the developments during the 1980s with regard to access to computers, in 1989, most educational practitioners still perceived a shortage of hardware and software as the two main problems for introducing computers into the school curriculum. Computer coordinators saw a greater variety of software as the highest priority item for spending money. Apparently (as was concluded in Chapter 4) the critical mass of computers and software needed for orderly integration of computers into the curriculum was not yet reached, which means that there was still a lack of basic infrastructure for using computers.

Type of use

It seems that, as indicated in Chapter 4, in secondary education, computers are used mostly as an add-on to the already existing curriculum in the form of teaching students how to use computers. Most secondary schools in many countries created a new subject (often called Informatics) in which students learn about computers, computer applications etc. By the end of the 1980s the use of computers as a tool in existing subjects was still not very widespread in secondary schools: Chapter 3 showed that in most countries only a minority of teachers of mathematics, science and mother tongue were using computers frequently in their lessons, while about 3/4 of this group used computers very infrequently. Becker (1992) concludes, based on the USA-Comped data, that *'the proportion of exemplary teachers* (that is, teachers who integrate computers to a substantial extent) *among all teachers of the studied subjects* (that is mathematics, science and mother tongue) *and grade levels is only 3%'*. The two subjects with the highest frequency of computer use across countries were mathematics and commercial studies (Chapter 4). In elementary schools, the situation is somewhat different. Not only do a majority of teachers in computer using schools actually use computers, the type of use tends to be more integrated in the existing curriculum, which shows up in the finding that the predominant subjects in which computers are used in elementary school are mathematics and mother tongue rather than computer education courses (see Chapter 4).

The place of computer education in the school curriculum has been an issue for debate in many countries. As shown in Chapter 4, the most common practice in lower and upper secondary education is to offer computer education instruction as a separate course. If such a separate course does not exist, the subject matter most used for providing computer education is mathematics.

As shown in Chapter 4, students in elementary schools used computers most frequently for drill and practice, while in secondary schools word processing and programming were most popular. The topics for which computers are used in *mathematics* are most often arithmetic in elementary and lower secondary schools and algebra in upper secondary schools. *Science* topics are hardly mentioned in elementary schools (relatively popular is earth science), while in secondary education the computer is most frequently used for covering topics from physics such as electricity, time and movement, and wave phenomena. In elementary education, reading is frequently mentioned as a topic from *mother tongue* for which computers are used, while writing is most often mentioned by mother tongue teachers in secondary schools.

Integration of the computer in the school curriculum

As indicated above, looking only at some rough indicators, the integration of computers into the existing subjects of secondary schools was, in 1989, still in an initial stage. Therefore, it is important to search for empirical indications which may give guidance in improving this situation.

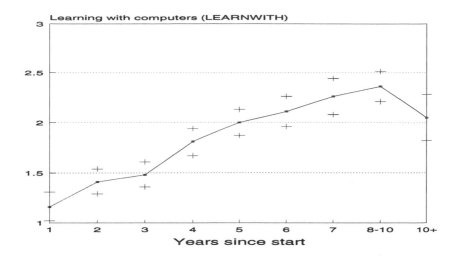

Figure 8.1 Plot for lower secondary schools of school means across countries (solid lines) for integrative use of computers versus number of years experience in using computers. + = 95% confidence interval. Source: Pelgrum and Schipper (1992).

The findings reported by Pelgrum and Schipper (1992) indicate that the extent to which schools integrate computers tends to increase slowly as a function of the number of years schools gained experience in using computers (see Figure 8.1). Moreover, the more emphasis school authorities placed on using computers for improving education, the more the computer is integrated into the curriculum. Chapter 3 showed that the integration of computers covaries with the amount of educational tool software which is available in schools.

These kinds of covariation leave the question about causal relations between variables unanswered.

Chapter 7 was especially aimed at finding causal relations between constructs. It was shown, on the basis of statistical modelling, that computer integration is most consistently associated with the knowledge and skills of teachers.

Attitudes

As shown in Chapter 6 (and in more detail in Pelgrum and Plomp, 1991), in general, educational practitioners have very positive attitudes about the use of computers in education. School principals at all educational levels are generally favorably disposed towards the educational use of computers, but principals of computer using schools tend to have more favorable attitudes than principals of non-using schools.

Pelgrum (1993) found that principals with more positive attitudes tend to stimulate the use of computers in their school more frequently.

Teachers with positive attitudes behave differently than their colleagues who are less positive, in terms of using the computer for more subject matter topics and those teachers are inclined to use more drill and practice programs, tutorial programs and CAI programs. One way of influencing the attitudes of teachers might be to include pedagogical/instructional aspects in training courses. As Pelgrum (1993) reports, the amount of information teachers received in training courses about these aspects is strongly associated with their attitudes about the educational impact of computers (see Figure 8.2). At the same time, Janssen Reinen and Plomp (1993a) found that these aspects are least covered in teacher training.

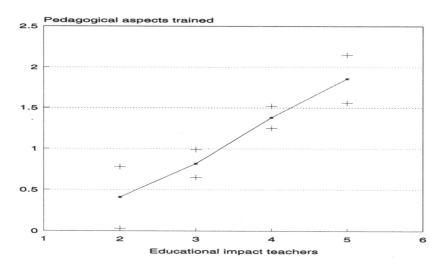

Figure 8.2 Plots for lower secondary schools teachers of attitudes on educational impact versus amount of training in pedagogical/instructional aspect of computer use. + = 95% confidence interval. Source: Pelgrum (1993).

Staff Development

Pelgrum and Plomp (1991) reported that there is a large need among school principals and teachers for training with regard to computers, but integration of the computer is also clearly a matter of time (Janssen Reinen and Plomp, 1993a).

Chapter 5 shows that teacher's knowledge and skills are significantly related to the amount of training received. Furthermore, the amount of training received and the type of topics covered in training are related to the amount of computer integration by existing subject teachers. It was shown that the amount of training received with regard to pedagogical/instructional aspects covaries with the extent to which teachers integrate computers in their lessons. This seems to suggest that, whereas at the same time these aspects were least covered in the training activities up till 1989, much could be gained when teacher training institutes would take these aspects into account.

Administration and Policy

Most schools also use computers for administrative purposes, mainly (as shown in Chapter 6) in the areas of office word processing, student administration and financial matters. Maintenance of library records and construction and maintenance of the school timetable were less frequently mentioned administrative applications. School principals have, in general, positive experiences with administrative applications, as sizeable groups indicate that various aspects of organization and management have improved as a result of using computers. Some (relatively small) groups saw the time needed for making the school timetable and the quality of the timetable as worse than before computers were used.

School principals seem to be clearly concerned about how computers are being used for educational purposes and a majority of schools have policies to assess how computers were used. However, it should also be noted (as reported by Pelgrum and Plomp, 1991) that most of these policies are not formalized, because, in most cases, there is no written documentation with regard to this policy available in the school.

Gender

In many countries, equity is an important issue at various levels of policy making. In quite a number of countries gender equity is explicitly addressed as special issue in the strategy for introducing computers in schools. As shown in Chapter 6 (and by Janssen Reinen and Plomp, 1993, as well as Pelgrum and Plomp, 1991) most schools do not seem to bother about this issue (except for the French speaking European countries), as a majority of schools does not have a special policy for promoting gender equity with regard to computers.

There is a broad range of possible policies schools might adopt in order to promote gender equity (or rather to prevent inequity), which may be aimed at teachers (information via in-service sessions, specific suggestions, or training for female teachers), parents (information provision for promoting awareness), and organizational measures (like computer classes for girls only and supervision by females). In practice, however, there is a large variation across countries in the extent to which these policies are actually followed by schools. The most popular measures are supervision by and special computer training for female teachers, and, hence it seems that schools aim to prevent inequity by promoting policies directed at offering more female role models to girls. However, there is reason for concern, because a number of studies report findings pointing to gender inequity with regard to computers (see citations in Chapter 6).

Chapter 6 shows that these concerns need to be taken seriously, as the number of potential female role models for girls (being female teachers who use the computer or female computer coordinators) is found to be relatively low, indicating in general that computer use in schools is dominated by males (except for a few countries like Israel and Portugal). This finding confirms (as feared by many policy makers, educators and those engaged in the emancipation of girls), that the daily practice too strongly suggests to students that the use of computers is predominantly a matter for males and not for females.

When female teachers are involved in using computers, they seem to feel less confident than their male colleagues, as they rate their knowledge and skills towards computers lower than male teachers (Pelgrum and Plomp, 1991, Janssen Reinen and Plomp, 1993b). The largest differences are found in the field of programming. Asked for problems in using computers, female teachers in general indicate less problems with computer use, but do have more organizational problems and view their lack of knowledge and skills more often as a problem than male teachers.

Although Janssen Reinen and Plomp (1993b) could not detect significant differences in attitudes between male and female principals, a closer inspection at the item level in Chapter 6 shows that across countries there is much more variation between females than between males. These differences appear in attitudes dealing with enhancement and computers, computer effectiveness in school, influence of computers on human relations, teachers' being informed and learning.

Possible future actions

The summary of results from stage 1 of the IEA-Comped study, as given above, show that regarding the future of computers in education there is reason for optimism as well as pessimism.

The optimistic side of the story is that new technologies in the form of computers are nowadays available for many schools in most developed countries, and that in spite of the complexity of this innovation, educational practitioners and students are still very enthusiastic about this new technology. Although many school administrators and teachers feel they are overburdened due to budget cuts, it is remarkable that they are willing to invest additional time to get acquainted with this new technology or as one of the teachers worded it "*It costs so much time. If students were not so enthusiastic we already would have given up*".

On the other hand, one should note that there is still quite a lot of inequity in access to computers. Some developed as well as developing countries are lagging far behind in terms of the availability of computers in schools.

As pointed out in a number of places above, there are several perspectives or models regarding the goals of computer use. A main distinction is between learning about computers (sometimes called the technical model) and learning with computers (sometimes referred to as the integration model or the functionality perspective).

At present computers are used mainly as an add-on to the existing curriculum, rather than as productivity tools which may enhance the quality of education. It is probably this lack of integration of computers into existing curricula, which is most challenging in determining our agenda for the future, or as Anderson and Collis (1992) stated: "*....we believe that the 'functionality' perspective will prove to be the most useful for policy and planning in the future*".

The evolution of these models can be seen as a typical product of the 1980s. In the early 1980s computer hardware and software characteristics were such that "*..one often had to write a program in Basic, Fortran or Pascal to accomplish a computer related task*" (Anderson and Collis, 1992). Later, in North America and many Western European countries, the concern for integration grew (which also may be interpreted as a consequence of the increased hardware and software capabilities).

The distinction between these main models is clearly also reflected in the data, that is in the results of the principal component analyses of the answers of school principals which showed a main distinction between learning about computers and learning with computers. The data show that in many countries there is an emphasis on learning about computers, but some countries have come relatively far with integrating computers in the curriculum.

The question arises why some schools and teachers integrate computers to a greater extent than others. As shown in Chapter 7, *"The highest degree of confirmation for the influence of indicators on computer use among countries was found for internal innovation assistance and teacher competence and readiness"*. Becker (1992), using a different analysis technique, confirms this finding for the United States of America: *"Exemplary teachers teach in an environment that helps them to be better computer using teachers, they are themselves better prepared to use computers well in their teaching"*.

Reflecting on the results of the stage 1 data of the Comped study, the situation in most participating educational systems can be characterized as follows: the implementation of computers in education has been successfully accomplished at school level, but not yet at teacher level. The successful implementation of computers at school level can be concluded from data such as: almost all schools in most participating countries do already have computers or intend to acquire them soon; in secondary education in a vast majority of schools teaching about computers is taking place either as a separate course or as part of existing subjects, and the attitude of school leaders and teachers towards this new technology is positive. However, at the level of the individual teachers, or at the level of the use of computers in the classroom, we have to conclude that in many countries only a relatively small number of teachers is actively using this new technology as an integral part of his of her teaching. A further illustration of the lack of computer implementation on teacher level is given by Brummelhuis and Plomp (1992). They show that, although over the period 1989-1992 an increase in the use of computers in existing subjects (mathematics, science and mother tongue) in lower secondary education can be observed, this increase is almost completely caused by schools where, until then the computer was not used at all in these subjects, hardly any increase in the number of computer using teachers was found in schools where computers were already used in 1989. It seems that in Dutch lower secondary schools the low implementation of computer use on teacher level has not improved, only the number of schools with low implementation has increased.

We saw (in Chapter 6) that both at school level and at teacher level the same problems were mentioned as the most important ones, namely lack of: hardware, high quality software, knowledge in using computers, and time to get acquainted with the new technology and to prepare 'computer assisted' lessons. All these major problems experienced on the school and teacher level refer to the infrastructure for the use of computers (or more general, new technologies) on the school level.

If one starts to reflect on possible actions for policy makers (on whatever level), it is tempting to suggest that they should strive to resolve those infrastructural problems at the school level. We think that this is an unrealistic expectation, for at least two reasons. First, from an economic and logistical perspective it is not reasonable to expect that these problems can be resolved completely. Second, from a innovation strategic perspective it would be too optimistic to treat these four problem areas independently; a coherent strategy needs to be applied to broaden the implementation of new technology on teacher level. We will briefly discuss both reasons.

Economic and logistical perspective

It would not be realistic from a *hardware perspective* to expect, on a short term, that schools can afford buying and renewing computers to the extent that every student or pair of students has unlimited access to computers. Rather one needs to think within the constraints of limited availability of hardware. From the data about how computers are currently used, one may derive the suggestion that the available equipment might be used more optimally, for example more integrated into whole class activities. Another interesting possibility, as suggested by Kontogiannopoulou-Polydorides (1992) might be to take advantage of the fact that increasing numbers of computers have become available in homes, and to pursue the idea of schools as resource centers to promote out of school learning. This, of course, raises the issue of equity and one has to consider the idea of compensatory measures for allowing priority access at school to students not having access to home computers.

Taking a *software perspective*, one has to be careful with the suggestion that more instructional software needs to be developed. Our results show that some teachers exploit the available software to a much smaller extent than colleagues who manage to integrate computers to a substantial extent in their instruction. In this respect, a finding of Pelgrum, Brummelhuis, and Plomp (1990) is interesting: educational practitioners are often not very well informed about the availability of software, even if present at their own school. On the other side the argument makes sense to the extent that it is known from software evaluations that the amount of high quality software is quite limited. For instance, reviews of High Scope in the United States of America indicate that about 10% of all software available for young students is qualitatively acceptable.

Relating software development to the expectations about the hardware infrastructure of schools, one may suggest that the development of educational software suitable for whole class use should be stimulated.

Taking a *training need perspective*, our results indicate that (school-based) in-service teacher training definitely should be intensified. However, more trained teachers also will result in heavier demands on hardware and software and, hence, such an action cannot be taken without careful estimates as to its side-effects. Training courses should pay particular attention to pedagogical / instructional aspects of using computers, by showing teachers how to use computers in their lessons.

From the *teachers' time perspective*, one often hears the suggestion to provide teachers with extra time to get better acquainted with new technologies. This might be a good suggestion for teachers starting to work with computers, but this kind of measure seems unrealistic as a structural one because of its high costs. Moreover, teachers neither get extra time to get familiar with other curricular materials such as text books and laboratory kits. Rather, one should think about developing courseware and/or tools that do not require unreasonable time investments by teachers, OR -what may be an even more realistic option- about tools that are time-efficient, that is that they ultimately lead to saving time.

Innovation strategical perspective

Looking back on the 1980s, we see that most countries followed quite 'simplistic' introduction strategies, based upon the assumption that the provision of hardware and software might result almost automatically in fundamental changes in instructional practices. For real changes, more sophisticated strategies need to be developed, taking into account that ultimately it is the teacher who determines changes in classroom practice (see for example, Fullan, Miles, and Anderson, 1988). Probably, one of the most compelling perspectives for the future should be multi-disciplinary approaches with input from curriculum developers, textbook writers, teacher trainers, media experts, etc. with a main focus on the role of the teacher as one of the most important factors in promoting change.

Such an option requires a careful look at teacher time investments for lesson preparation and must be devised in a way that investments are perceived as relevant and rewarding because it reduces time investments to an extent that teachers would feel foolish if they would not use these tools. Computer use should not be too complex and fit in the didactical approach of the teacher.

References

Ajzen I., Fishbein M. (1977). Attitude-behavior Relations: A Theoretical Analysis and Review of Empirical Research. *Psychological Bulletin*, 84, 888-910.

Akker, van den, J.J.H., Keursten, P., Plomp, Tj. (1992). The integration of computer use in education. *International Journal of Educational Research*, 17 (1), 65-75.

Anderson, R.E., Collis, B. (1993). International Assessment of Functional Computer Abilities. *Studies in Educational Evaluation*, 19 (2), 213-228.

Andrews R. (1987). On Leadership and Student Achievement. *Educational Leadership*, 45, 1.

Apple, M. (1992). New Technology Part of the Solution or Part of the Problem in Education. In: Beynon, J., Mackay, H. (Eds.) *Technological Literacy and the Curriculum*. London: Falmer.

Becker, H.J. (1986). *Instructional uses of school computers: reports from the 1985 national survey*, 1. Baltimore: Center for Social Organization of Schools, The John Hopkins University.

Becker, H.J., (1990). *An initial Report of U.S. Participation in the IEA Computers in Education Survey*. Baltimore: John Hopkins University.

Becker, H.J. (1992). *How our best computer-using teachers differ from other teachers: implications for realizing the potential of computers in schools*. Paper presented at the AERA Conference, San Francisco, April 20-24.

Becker, H.J. (1993). Computer Experience, Patterns of Computer Use, and Effectiveness - An Inevitable Sequence or Divergent National Cultures? *Studies in Educational Evaluation*, 19 (2), 127-148.

Brody, P.J. (1987). Computers in the classroom, infusing computers into the curriculum: teacher preparation. *Educational Technology*, XXVII (1), 34-35.

Brummelhuis, ten, A.C.A., Plomp, Tj. (1992). *De groei van computergebruik binnen het basisonderwijs en het voortgezet onderwijs. [The increase in computer use in elementary and secondary education]*. Paper presented at the NIOC Conference, Maastricht (the Netherlands).

Campbell, P. (1984). The computer revolution: "guess who's left out". *Interracial Books for Children Bulletin*, 15 (3), p. 3.

Cerych, L. (1982). *Computeronderwijs in zes landen [Computer Education in Six Countries]*. Europees Instituut voor Onderwijs en Sociale Politiek van de Europese Culturele Stichting.

Cockburn, C. (1985). *Machinery of Dominance: Women, Men and Technical Know-How*. Pluto Press.

Collis, B.A. (1988). *Computers, curriculum and whole-class instruction*. Belmont (CA, USA): Wadsworth.

Collis, B.A., Hass, H., Kieren, T.E. (1989). National Trends in Computer Use among Canadian Secondary School Students. *Journal of Research on Computing in Education*, 22 (1), 77-89.

Davis, D., Vinner, S., Finkelstein, T., Regev, C. (1985). *Observations in School Computer Rooms*. The NCJW Research Institute for Innovation in Education, School of Education, in cooperation with the Amos Deshalit Science Teaching Centre, The Hebrew University of Jerusalem.

Fullan, M.G. (1991). *The New Meaning of Educational Change*. London: Cassell Educational Limited.

Fullan, M.G., Miles, M.B., Anderson, S.E. (1988). *Strategies for implementing microcomputers in schools: the Ontario case*. Ontario: Ministry of Education, Queen's printer.

Hannafin, M.J. (1989). Interaction strategies and emerging instructional technologies: psychological perspectives. *Canadian Journal of Educational Communication*, 18 (3), 167-179.

Hawkridge, D. (1990). Computers in third world schools: the example of China. *British Journal of Educational Technology*, 21 (1), 4-20.

Huberman, M., Miles, M.B. (1984). *Innovation Up Close*. New York: Plenum.

Hunter, B. (1984). *My students use computers*. Reston (VA, USA): Reston Publishing Company.

Inspectorate, (1986). *Een beschrijving van de stand van zaken in het schooljaar 1985/1986 [A description of the status in the school year 1985/1986]*. Inspectierapport 7, deel 1 en 2. Ministerie van Onderwijs en Wetenschappen, Onderwijs en Informatietechnolgie.

Janssen Reinen, I.A.M., Pelgrum, W.J. (1992). *Main results from the IEA-Computers in Education project stage 1*. Enschede (The Netherlands): University of Twente (internal report).

Janssen Reinen, I.A.M., Plomp, Tj. (1993). Some gender issues in educational computer use: results of an international comparative survey. *Computers in Education* (accepted for publication).

Janssen Reinen, I.A.M., Plomp, Tj. (1993a). Staff development as condition for computer integration. *Studies in Educational Evaluation*, 19 (2), 149-166.

Jensen P.E., Klewe, L. (1989). *Gender Differences and Computer Use in Education*. Copenhagen: The Danish Institute for Educational Research.

Jones A., Kirkup, G., Kirkwood, A., Mason, R. (1992). Providing computing for distance learners: a strategy for home use. *Computers and Education*, 18 (1-3), 183-192.

Jöreskog, K.G., Sörbom, D. (1988). *LISREL 7. A Guide to the Program and Applications.* Gorinchem, The Netherlands: SPSS International B.V.

Jöreskog, K.G., Sörbom, D. (1990). Linear Structural Relations Analysis. In: Husén, T., Postlethwaite, T.N. (Eds.) *The International Encyclopedia of Education, Supplementary Volume II.* Oxford: Pergamon Press.

Keeves, J.P. (1988). Path analysis. In: Keeves, J.P. (Ed.) *Educational Research, Methodology, and Measurement: An International Handbook.* Oxford: Pergamon Press.

Keeves, J.P. (1991). *The IEA Study of Science I: Science Educaton and Curricula in Twenty-Three Countries.* Oxford: Pergamon Press.

Keeves, J.P. (1992). *Learning Science in a Changing World. Cross-national Studies of Science Achievement: 1970 to 1984.* The Hague: International Association for the Evaluation of Educational Achievement.

Kontogiannopoulou-Polydorides, G. (1992). *The model of computer use in Greek education - A European perspective introduction.* Paper presented at the AERA conference San Francisco, April 1992.

Lipham, J.M., Rankin, R.E., Hoeh, J.A. (1985). *The Principalship: Concepts, Competencies, and Cases.* New York: Longman.

Lohnes, P.R. (1988). Factorial Modeling. In: Keeves, J.P. (Ed.) *Educational Research, Methodology, and Measurement: An International Handbook.* Oxford: Pergamon Press.

Louis, K., Miles, M.B. (1990). *Improving the Urban High School: What Works and Why.* New York: Teachers College Press.

Makau, B.M. (1990). *Computers in Kenya's secondary schools: case study of an innovation in education.* Ottawa: IDRC.

Makrakis, V. (1988). *Computers in school education: the cases of Sweden and Greece.* Stockholm: Institute of International Education, University of Stockholm.

McCoy, L.P., Dodl, N.R. (1989). Computer Programming Experience and Mathematical Problem Solving. *Journal of Research on Computing in Education*, 22 (1), 14-25.

Moskowitz, J.H., Birman, F. (1985). Computers in the schools: implications of change. *Educational Technology*, XXV (1), 7-14.

Niederer, R., Frey, K. (1992). *What factors influence the rate of use of computers in secondary education?* Paper presented at the European Conference for Educational Research. Enschede (the Netherlands), June 22-25.

Orlich, D.C. (1989). *Staff development: enhancing Human Potential.* Boston: Washington State University.

Pelgrum, W.J., Brummelhuis, ten, A.C.A., Plomp, Tj. (1990). *The availability and use of instructional computer materials by teachers: Results from the Dutch participation in the IEA Computers in Education Study.* Paper presented at the AERA conference Boston, April.

Pelgrum, W.J., Plomp, Tj. (1991). *The use of Computers in Education worldwide: results from the IEA 'Computers in Education' survey in 19 education systems.* Oxford: Pergamon Press.

Pelgrum, W.J., Schipper, A.T. (1992). *Indicators of technology integration in education.* Paper presented at the European Conference for Educational Research. Enschede (the Netherlands), June 22-25.

Pelgrum, W.J. (1993). Attitudes of school principals and teachers towards computers: does it matter what they think? *Studies in Educational Evaluation,* 19 (2), 199-213.

Pelgrum, W.J., Plomp, Tj. (1993). The Use of Computers in Education in 18 Countries. *Studies in Educational Evaluation,* 19 (2), 101-127.

Plomp, Tj. (1989). *Introductory computer education: developments in a time perspective.* Paper presented at the IEA General Assembly. Seoul, Republic of Korea.

Plomp, Tj., Janssen Reinen, I.A.M. (in press). *Computer Literacy.* Contribution to the 2nd edition of the International Encyclopedia of Education.

Pozzi, S., Hoyles, C., Healy, L. (1992). Towards a Methodology for Analysing Collaboration and Learning in Computer-based Groupwork. *Computers and Education,* 18 (1-3), 223-229.

Reynolds, A.J., Walberg, H.J. (1991). *A Process Model of Mathematics Achievement and Attitude.* Research report prepared for the U.S. National Science Foundation. Chicago: Northern Illinois University.

Sergiovanni, T. (1991). *The Principalship: A Reflective Practice Perspective.* Needham Heights, MA: Allyn and Bacon.

Siann, G., Macleod, H., Glissov, P., Durndell, A. (1990). The Effect of Computer Use on Gender Differences in Attitudes to Computers. *Computers and Education,* 14 (2), 183-191.

Stasz, C., Shavelson, R.J. (1985). Staff development for Instructional Uses of Microcomputers. *AEDA Journal,* 19 (1), 1-19.

Thomas, R.M. (1987). The Nature of Educational Technology. In: Thomas, R.M. Kobayashi, V.N. *Educational Technology.* Oxford: Pergamon Press.

Tobin, J. (1988). Teacher Training. In: Beishuizen, J. et al. (Eds.) *The use of the Microcomputer in Teaching and Learning.* Amsterdam: Swets en Zeitlinger.

Tuijnman, A.C., Brummelhuis, ten, A.C.A. (1991). Measuring and Predicting Computer Implementation in Dutch and United States Schools: A Structural Model. In: Pelgrum, W.J., Plomp, T. *The Uses of Computers in Education Worldwide.* Oxford: Pergamon Press.

United States Congres (1988). *Power on! New tools for teaching and learning.* Washington: U.S. Government Printing Office.

Walker, D.F. (1986). Computers in the curriculum. In: Culbertson, J.A., Cunningham, L.L. (Eds.) *Microcomputers and education, eighty-fifth yearbook of the National Society for the Study of Education.* Chicago: Chicago Press.

Watson, J. (1991). Cooperative learning and computers: one way to address student differences. *Computing Teacher*, 18, 9-15.

Whyte J. (1986). *Girls into Science and Technology.* London: Routledge and Kegan.

Wolf, R., Plomp, Tj., Pelgrum, W. J. (1986). *IEA Computers in education: design and planning.* Enschede (the Netherlands): University of Twente, Department of Education.

Woodrow, J.E.J. (1991a). Locus of Control and Computer Attitudes as Determinants of the Computer Literacy of Student Teachers. *Computers and Education*, 16 (3), 237-245.

Woodrow, J.E.J. (1991b). Determinants of Student Teacher Computer Literacy Achievement. *Computers and Education*, 16 (3), 247-256.

Wu, Y.K., Morgan, M. (1989). Computer Use, Computer Attitudes and Gender: Differential Implications of Micro and Mainframe Usage Among College Students. *Journal of Research on Computing Education*, 22 (2) 214-228.

Appendix A

Sampling Information

The sampling information consists of a section with population definitions and for each population a sampling table and an annex with more elaborated stratum names.

Austria

Population 2 (lower secondary education).

All schools of general education till grade 9. Special schools for handicapped children are excluded.

Population 3 (upper secondary education).

Included are only general secondary and vocational schools which qualify for university. Excluded are lower vocational schools (48% of all schools), and some special schooltypes (7% of all schools).

Belgium-Flemish

Population 2 (lower secondary education) and Population 3 (upper secondary education).

All (state, province/community and catholic) schools offering comprehensive general or comprehensive technical/arts education.

Belgium-French

Population 1 (elementary education).

All (state, province/community and catholic) schools, except special education (3,7% of all students).

Population 2 (lower secondary education).

All (state, province/community and catholic) schools offering comprehensive general or comprehensive vocational education (technical and arts). Excluded is vocational education (22,8% of all students) and special education (3,9% of all students).

Population 3 (upper secondary education).

All general secondary and vocational schools, except special education (3,9%).

Canada-British Columbia

Population 1 (elementary education), Population 2 (lower secondary education) and Population 3 (upper secondary education).

All schools.
For the Principal and Computer Coordinator questionnaires no distinction was made between Population 2 and Population 3.

China

Population 3 (upper secondary education).

All schools in the cities/provinces Beijing, Shanghai, Xingxiang city (Henon province), Neimong, Guangxi Zhuang autonomous region, Jiling, Anhui, Sichuan, Guangdong provinces.

France

Population 1 (elementary education).

All schools except private education (15% of students) and special education (less than 0,5% of students).

Population 2 (lower secondary education).

All schools except private education (students in "Collèges": 20% of all students) and special education.

Population 3 (upper secondary education).

All schools except private education (3% of students).

Federal Republic of Germany

Population 2 (lower secondary education) & Population 3 (upper secondary education).

All schools in 9 Bundesländer (58% of all students).

Greece

Population 2 (lower secondary education) & Population 3 (upper secondary education).

All schools except private and evening schools (altogether 4% of all students).

Hungary

Population 3 (upper secondary education).

All schools.

India

Population 3 (upper secondary education).

All schools in some districts of Delhi and Utter Pradesh, Maharashtra, West Bengal and Tamil Madu (which are the states with the maximum number of computer using schools (in respectively the regions NORTH, WEST, EAST AND SOUTH). These districts (about 30%) have been choosen at random within the states.

Israel

Population 1 (elementary education).

All schools except special education (7% of all students).

Population 3 (upper secondary education).

All academic schools and technological schools with courses leading to certification. This excludes vocational education as well as independent schools (about 4% of all students).

Italy

Population 1 (elementary education).

All schools except private schools (8.3% of the schools and 7.8% of the students).

Population 2 (lower secondary education).

All schools except private schools (9.3% of the schools and 4.6% of the students).

Population 3 (upper secondary education).

All schools except private schools (25.8% of the schools and 12.3% of the students).

Japan

Population 1 (elementary education) and Population 2 (lower secondary education).

All schools except special education.

Population 3 (upper secondary education).

All general and vocational schools.

Luxembourg

Population 2 (lower secondary education).

All general and technical secondary schools.

The Netherlands

Population 1 (elementary education).

All schools except special education.

Population 2 (lower secondary education).

All schools except (5% of all students) international transition year, English stream, individual agricultural education, agricultural education and nautical education.

Population 3 (upper secondary education).

All general secondary, social nursery, economical/administrative and technical schools. Excluded are all other vocational schools (about 6.4 % of all students). Teachers were only sampled from general secondary schools.

New Zealand

Population 1 (elementary education).

All schools with students in standard 4 except the Correspondence School and special education.

Population 2 (lower secondary education).

All schools with students in <u>form 3</u>, except the Correspondence School and special education.

Population 3 (upper secondary education).

All schools with students in <u>form 7</u>, except the Correspondence School and special education.

Poland

Population 3 (upper secondary education).
All schools.

Portugal

Population 1 (elementary education).

All schools in the public school system of the continental territory, except distance education.

Population 2 (lower secondary education) & Population 3 (upper secondary education).

All schools in the public schools system of the continental territory.

Slovenia

Population 3 (upper secondary education).
All schools.

Switzerland

Population 2 (lower secondary education).
All schools except schools in canton Argau, Genève, Vaud.

Population 3 (upper secondary education).
All schools except schools in canton Genève.

USA

The sampling frame included all U.S. schools, public and private, that contained a 4th grade or higher, plus vocational and "alternative" high schools. The frame excluded separate schools for the special education population and also excluded schools that only exist to provide part-day or part-year pull-out classes for students from other schools.

Each school was allocated to one or more of three sub-frames, "primary", "lower-secondary", or "upper-secondary", depending on whether it contained a 5th grade, 7th or 8th grade, or 10th, 11th, or 12th grade.

Sixth-grade-only schools were allocated to the primary sub-frame and 9th-grade-only schools to the lower-secondary sub-frame.

General remarks regarding sampling information tables:

'Selected' = Schools selected for the screening survey, which was intended to invite schools for participation and to collect data regarding use/non-use, teacher names, etc.

'Sent' = To these schools all questionnaires have been sent. Usually these are the same schools as 'use/non-use' from selected, but for some systems questionnaires have been sent to a part of these schools.

'Received' = At least one questionnaire has been received from that school.

Categories within 'selected' and 'sent' are based on the screening survey.

Categories within 'received' are based on the data, which explains shifts from non-using to using or visa versa.

Formulas used to compute rates:

Participation rate = (selected using schools + selected non-using schools) / total selected (use + non-use + non respons) schools.

Return rate = total received / total sent.

Respons rate = participation rate * return rate.

The data contain a few errors which in some strata lead to rates > 1.00.

Dots mean missing information, which may be due to

- Unknown stratumcode for returned questionnaires.
- Missing or unreliable information (e.g. number of students).
- Unknown rates due to missing information.
- Undefined rates if the numbers 'Selected' and/ or 'Sent' are 0.

Sampling methods:

EP = Equal Probability;

PPS = Probability Proportional to Size.

School weights are based on the information in these tables, unless stated otherwise.

| **Population 1** | | | Number of | | Ep (0) | Selected | |
| | Stratum | | | | Or | Using | Non-use |
Country	Number	Stratum Name	Schools	Students	Pps (1)	Schools	Schools
Belgium-French							
	.	.	.	.	.	.	.
	1	State educ	229	42692	1	32	26
	2	Cathol educ	735	137198	1	85	88
	3	Local boards	1151	146119	1	105	75
Canada-British Columbia							
	1	All schools	1068	36290	1	326	0
France							
	1	Rural Outside	10747	.	0	109	15
	2	Rural Inside	12877	.	0	129	13
	3	Urban	14230	.	0	151	15
	4	Paris	2381	.	0	15	4
Israel							
	.	.	.	.	.	.	.
	10	Jerusal newp	62	.	0	7	8
	11	Jerusal ewp	35	.	0	8	1
	20	North notewp	125	.	0	27	5
	21	North ewp	49	.	0	10	2
	30	Haifa notewp	101	.	0	14	7
	31	Haifa ewp	33	.	0	6	1
	40	Central newp	156	.	0	22	19
	41	Central ewp	44	.	0	19	2
	50	Tel Aviv newp	168	.	0	28	10
	51	Tel Aviv ewp	83	.	0	11	0
	60	South notewp	88	.	0	18	4
	61	South ewp	91	.	0	16	6
	70	Arabic lang	254	.	0	10	53
Italy							
	1	All schools	26342	809748	0	.	.

	Sent		Received					
Non-respons Schools	Using Schools	Non-use Schools	Using Schools	Non-use Schools	Unclear Schools	Partic. Rate	Return Rate	Response Rate
.	.	.	4	2	0	.	.	.
6	32	26	26	13	1	.91	.69	.63
20	85	88	55	46	1	.90	.59	.53
18	105	75	65	44	0	.91	.61	.55
0	326	0	207	2	0	1.00	.64	.64
9	118	15	90	6	5	.93	.76	.71
18	147	13	119	13	3	.89	.84	.75
11	162	15	134	14	4	.94	.86	.81
11	26	4	21	2	0	.63	.77	.49
.	.	.	8	0	0	.	.	.
0	7	8	6	8	0	1.00	.93	.93
0	8	1	7	1	0	1.00	.89	.89
0	27	5	24	4	0	1.00	.88	.88
0	10	2	7	2	0	1.00	.75	.75
5	14	7	11	7	0	.81	.86	.69
0	6	1	6	1	0	1.00	1.00	1.00
3	22	19	16	15	0	.93	.76	.70
0	19	2	13	1	0	1.00	.67	.67
1	28	10	22	10	0	.97	.84	.82
0	11	0	8	0	0	1.00	.73	.73
0	18	4	17	4	0	1.00	.95	.95
0	16	6	15	3	0	1.00	.82	.82
0	10	53	7	45	0	1.00	.83	.83
.	.	.	212	281	0	.	.	.

Population 1			Number of		Ep (0)	Selected	
Country	Stratum Number	Stratum Name	Schools	Students	Or Pps (1)	Using Schools	Non-use Schools
Japan							
	.	.	.	.	.	.	.
	11	Big_cit_smal	1445	96349	1	8	93
	12	Big_cit_midd	1026	124998	1	6	125
	13	Big_cit_larg	503	89828	1	6	89
	21	City_small	5662	270670	1	16	289
	22	City_middle	2967	365863	1	25	384
	23	City_large	2207	404848	1	39	409
	31	Village_smal	9128	274056	1	17	290
	32	Village_midd	772	93138	1	6	98
	33	Village_larg	314	55452	1	5	57
Netherlands							
	1	Small	4723	55015	0	74	80
	2	Medium	2323	55705	0	84	68
	3	Large	1373	52952	0	75	71
New Zealand							
	1	Small_urb_fp	43	144	1	1	1
	2	Small_urb_co	14	86	1	1	1
	3	Small_urb_ac	2	8	1	0	0
	4	Small_sur_fp	10	34	1	0	0
	5	Small_sur_co	12	46	1	1	1
	7	Small_mur_fp	26	90	1	1	1
	8	Small_mur_co	5	17	1	0	0
	9	Small_mur_ac	1	1	1	0	0
	10	Small_rur_fp	416	1405	1	13	4
	11	Small_rur_co	135	617	1	4	2
	12	Small_rur_ac	1	7	1	0	0
	13	Med_urb_fp	152	2552	1	21	10
	14	Med_urb_co	232	5782	1	48	22
	15	Med_urb_ac	16	284	1	3	0
	16	Med_sur_fp	16	270	1	2	1
	17	Med_sur_co	35	915	1	7	4
	19	Med_mur_fp	69	1135	1	9	4

	Sent		Received					
Non-respons Schools	Using Schools	Non-use Schools	Using Schools	Non-use Schools	Unclear Schools	Partic. Rate	Return Rate	Response Rate
.	.	.	4	4	0	.	.	.
8	27	4	17	6	1	.93	.77	.72
10	23	13	19	14	0	.93	.92	.85
6	9	8	7	8	2	.94	1.00	.94
0	41	23	28	25	2	1.00	.86	.86
3	38	31	26	28	8	.99	.90	.89
8	55	21	35	25	10	.98	.92	.90
2	59	21	52	23	1	.99	.95	.94
1	8	9	5	10	1	.99	.94	.93
0	7	3	7	2	1	1.00	1.00	1.00
15	49	52	42	35	5	.91	.81	.74
18	46	41	42	31	5	.89	.90	.80
15	50	47	48	36	2	.91	.89	.80
0	0	0	0	0	0	1.00	.	.
0	1	0	1	0	0	1.00	1.00	1.00
0	0	0	0	0	0	.	.	.
0	0	0	0	0	0	.	.	.
0	1	1	1	1	0	1.00	1.00	1.00
0	1	1	1	1	0	1.00	1.00	1.00
0	0	0	0	0	0	.	.	.
0	0	0	0	0	0	.	.	.
0	11	2	11	1	0	1.00	.92	.92
0	4	2	3	2	0	1.00	.83	.83
0	0	0	0	0	0	.	.	.
0	20	10	20	9	0	1.00	.97	.97
0	40	17	37	14	1	1.00	.91	.91
0	3	0	3	0	0	1.00	1.00	1.00
0	2	1	3	0	0	1.00	1.00	1.00
0	5	3	5	3	0	1.00	1.00	1.00
0	8	3	9	2	0	1.00	1.00	1.00

Population 1	Stratum Number	Stratum Name	Number of		Ep (0) Or Pps (1)	Selected	
Country			Schools	Students		Using Schools	Non-use Schools
New Zealand							
	20	Med_mur_co	32	816	1	8	3
	21	Med_mur_ac	3	54	1	0	0
	22	Med_rur_fp	275	3072	1	30	7
	23	Med_rur_co	118	1993	1	16	8
	24	Med_rur_ac	29	445	1	5	0
	25	Large_urb_fp	109	4847	1	45	13
	26	Large_urb_co	349	18617	1	160	61
	27	Large_urb_ac	6	253	1	2	1
	28	Large_sur_fp	10	383	1	4	1
	29	Large_sur_co	35	1782	1	18	3
	31	Large_mur_fp	48	1937	1	23	0
	32	Large_mur_co	34	1766	1	20	1
	33	Large_mur_ac	3	120	1	2	0
	34	Large_rur_fp	11	415	1	5	0
	35	Large_rur_co	11	523	1	4	2
	36	Large_rur_ac	2	67	1	2	0
Portugal							
	.	.	.	.	.	.	.
	1	Small use	31	6442	1	18	11
	2	Medium use	33	14617	1	25	6
	3	Large use	11	8393	1	11	0
	4	Small non-use	259	50135	1	19	74
	5	Medium non-use	142	64641	1	45	85
	6	Large non-use	20	15586	1	8	10
United States of America							
	1	All schools	62077	19028000	1	443	17

Notes: Remarks for specific countries:
CBC: No complete sampling information available. Weights have not been computed.
ITA: No complete sampling information available. Weights have not been computed.
JPN: After the first selection, additional using schools have been selected, which is the reason that 'sent using schools' is greater than 'selected using schools'.
USA: Extended sampling information about all 81 strata is available in the 'Final Sampling Report for the USA'. Computation of weights took place in the USA.

	Sent		Received					
Non-respons Schools	Using Schools	Non-use Schools	Using Schools	Non-use Schools	Unclear Schools	Partic. Rate	Return Rate	Response Rate
0	6	3	6	3	0	1.00	1.00	1.00
0	0	0	0	0	0	.	.	.
0	22	6	26	1	0	1.00	.96	.96
0	15	8	13	7	1	1.00	.91	.91
0	5	0	5	0	0	1.00	1.00	1.00
0	41	12	38	12	0	1.00	.94	.94
0	141	51	143	39	4	1.00	.97	.97
0	1	1	1	0	1	1.00	1.00	1.00
0	4	1	4	1	0	1.00	1.00	1.00
0	13	3	14	2	0	1.00	1.00	1.00
0	19	0	18	0	0	1.00	.95	.95
0	20	1	19	1	0	1.00	.95	.95
0	2	0	2	0	0	1.00	1.00	1.00
0	4	0	4	0	0	1.00	1.00	1.00
0	4	2	4	2	0	1.00	1.00	1.00
0	2	0	1	0	0	1.00	.50	.50
.	.	.	1	2	4	.	.	.
2	18	11	22	5	2	.94	1.00	.94
2	25	6	20	2	5	.94	.87	.82
0	11	0	11	0	0	1.00	1.00	1.00
7	19	74	9	59	7	.93	.81	.75
12	45	85	36	68	6	.92	.85	.77
2	8	10	6	11	0	.90	.94	.85
21	443	17	378	0	52	.96	.94	.89

Population 1

Stratum Extended
Country Number Stratum Name

Belgium-French
.

1	State education
2	Catholic education
3	Local boards

Canada-British
Columbia

1	All schools

France

1	Rural, outside urban areas
2	Rural, inside urban areas
3	Urban
4	Paris and its region

Israel
.

10	Jerusalem, not educational welfare program
11	Jerusalem, educational welfare program
20	North, not educational welfare program
21	North, educational welfare program
30	Haifa, not educational welfare program
31	Haifa, educational welfare program
40	Central, not educational welfare program
41	Central, educational welfare program
50	Tel Aviv, not educational welfare program
51	Tel Aviv, educational welfare program
60	South, not educational welfare program
61	South, educational welfare program
70	Arabic Language

Italy

1	All schools

Population 1

Stratum Extended
Country Number Stratum Name

Japan

.

11	Big city, small schools (<100)
12	Big city, middle size schools (100-150)
13	Big city, large schools (>=150)
21	City, small schools (<100)
22	City, middle size schools (100-150)
23	City, large schools (>=150)
31	Village, small schools (<100)
32	Village, middle size schools (100-150)
33	Village, large schools (>=150)

Netherlands

1	Small schools (<20 grade 5 students)
2	Medium size schools (20-30 grade 5 students)
3	Large schools (>=30 grade 5 students)

New
Zealand

1	Small (<51), urban, full primary schools
2	Small (<51), urban, contributing schools
3	Small (<51), urban, area/composite schools
4	Small (<51), second urban, full primary schools
5	Small (<51), second urban, contributing schools
7	Small (<51), minor urban, full primary schools
8	Small (<51), minor urban, contributing schools
9	Small (<51), minor urban, area/composite schools
10	Small (<51), rural, full primary schools
11	Small (<51), rural, contributing schools
12	Small (<51), rural, area/composite schools
13	Medium (51-230), urban, full primary schools
14	Medium (51-230), urban, contributing schools
15	Medium (51-230), urban, area/composite schools
16	Medium (51-230), second urban, full primary schools
17	Medium (51-230), second urban, contributing schools
19	Medium (51-230), minor urban, full primary schools
20	Medium (51-230), minor urban, contributing schools
21	Medium (51-230), minor urban, area/composite schools

Population 1

Stratum Extended
Country Number Stratum Name

New
Zealand

22	Medium (51-230), rural, full primary schools
23	Medium (51-230), rural, contributing schools
24	Medium (51-230), rural, area/composite schools
25	Large (>=230), urban, full primary schools
26	Large (>=230), urban, contributing schools
27	Large (>=230), urban, area/composite schools
28	Large (>=230), second urban, full primary schools
29	Large (>=230), second urban, contributing schools
31	Large (>=230), minor urban, full primary schools
32	Large (>=230), minor urban, contributing schools
33	Large (>=230), minor urban, area/composite schools
34	Large (>=230), rural, full primary schools
35	Large (>=230), rural, contributing schools
36	Large (>=230), rural, area/composite schools

Portugal

1	Small, using schools (grade 5)
2	Medium size, using schools (grade 5)
3	Large, using schools (grade 5)
4	Small, non-using schools (grade 5)
5	Medium size, non-using schools (grade 5)
6	Large, non-using schools (grade 5)

United States
of America

1	All schools

Country	Stratum Number	Stratum Name	Number of		Ep (0) Or Pps (1)	Selected	
			Schools	Students		Using Schools	Non-use Schools
Austria							
	.	.	.	.	.	.	.
	11	Burgenl_huse	22	.	0	22	0
	12	Karnten_huse	40	.	0	40	0
	13	Niedero_huse	131	.	0	131	0
	14	Oberost_huse	129	.	0	129	0
	15	Salzbur_huse	42	.	0	42	0
	16	Steierm_huse	108	.	0	108	0
	17	Tirol_huse	21	.	0	21	0
	18	Vorarlb_huse	3	.	0	3	0
	19	Wien_huse	22	.	0	22	0
	21	Burgenl_ahs	6	.	0	2	0
	22	Karnten_ahs	14	.	0	6	0
	23	Niedero_ahs	38	.	0	22	0
	24	Oberost_ahs	35	.	0	20	0
	25	Salzbur_ahs	16	.	0	8	0
	26	Steierm_ahs	34	.	0	17	0
	27	Tirol_ahs	15	.	0	6	0
	28	Vorarlb_ahs	8	.	0	3	0
	29	Wien_ahs	71	.	0	39	0
	51	Burgenl_hnus	22	.	0	0	12
	52	Karnten_hnus	56	.	0	0	30
	53	Niedero_hnus	135	.	0	0	71
	54	Oberost_hnus	107	.	0	0	66
	55	Salzbur_hnus	29	.	0	0	23
	56	Steierm_hnus	89	.	0	0	28
	57	Tirol_hnus	88	.	0	0	39
	58	Vorarlb_hnus	49	.	0	0	21
	59	Wien_hnus	104	.	0	0	43
Belgium-Flemish							
	1	State 1 aso/tso	176	9389	0	73	18
	3	Loc/prov 1 aso/tso	71	3382	0	11	14
	5	Loc/prov 2 aso/tso	6	423	0	2	1
	6	Cath 1 aso/tso	273	20458	0	71	63

| Non-respons Schools | Sent | | Received | | | Partic. Rate | Return Rate | Response Rate |
	Using Schools	Non-use Schools	Using Schools	Non-use Schools	Unclear Schools			
.	.	.	1	2	0	.	.	.
0	22	0	17	0	0	1.00	.77	.77
0	40	0	28	2	0	1.00	.75	.75
0	131	0	84	1	0	1.00	.65	.65
0	129	0	91	1	0	1.00	.71	.71
0	42	0	27	1	1	1.00	.69	.69
0	108	0	83	0	0	1.00	.77	.77
0	21	0	15	0	0	1.00	.71	.71
0	3	0	1	0	0	1.00	.33	.33
0	22	0	7	0	0	1.00	.32	.32
0	2	0	2	0	0	1.00	1.00	1.00
0	6	0	4	0	0	1.00	.67	.67
0	22	0	13	0	0	1.00	.59	.59
0	20	0	15	0	0	1.00	.75	.75
0	8	0	3	0	0	1.00	.38	.38
0	17	0	8	0	0	1.00	.47	.47
0	6	0	3	0	0	1.00	.50	.50
0	3	0	1	0	0	1.00	.33	.33
0	39	0	12	2	0	1.00	.36	.36
0	0	12	0	8	0	1.00	.67	.67
0	0	30	0	23	0	1.00	.77	.77
0	0	71	0	37	0	1.00	.52	.52
0	0	66	0	52	0	1.00	.79	.79
0	0	23	0	19	0	1.00	.83	.83
0	0	28	0	18	0	1.00	.64	.64
0	0	39	0	25	0	1.00	.64	.64
0	0	21	0	16	0	1.00	.76	.76
0	0	43	0	23	0	1.00	.53	.53
85	68	15	64	12	3	.52	.95	.49
46	10	11	15	2	0	.35	.81	.29
3	2	1	3	0	0	.50	1.00	.50
139	65	53	74	19	3	.49	.81	.40

Population 2			Number of		Ep (0)	Selected	
Country	Stratum Number	Stratum Name	Schools	Students	Or Pps (1)	Using Schools	Non-use Schools
Belgium-Flemish							
	8	Cath 2 aso	154	14693	0	6	69
	9	Cath 2 tso	147	9138	0	25	56
Belgium-French							
	.	.	.	.	.	.	.
	1	State educ	209	95227	1	110	30
	2	Cathol educ	414	174040	1	153	67
	3	Local boards	136	73223	1	59	33
Canada-British Columbia							
	1	All schools	299	37634	0	299	0
France							
	1	Rural Outside	352	.	0	34	2
	2	Rural Inside	546	.	0	54	0
	3	Urban	3284	.	0	312	8
	4	Paris	643	.	0	58	1
Federal Republic of Germany							
	1	Hauptschule	5000	1356000	.	117	103
	2	Realschule	2593	915000	.	76	41
	3	Gymnasium SI	2455	1596000	.	142	116
	4	Gesamtschule SI	292	190000	.	14	5
Greece							
	1	N-U Athens(CofC)	158	18501	1	0	49
	2	N-U Athens(E&N)	42	4439	1	0	12
	3	N-U Athens(west)	75	7947	1	0	21
	4	N-U Attika	37	2871	1	0	8
	5	N-U Thessa(city)	36	5329	1	0	14
	6	N-U Thessa(pref)	17	1252	1	0	3
	7	N-U Patras	21	1886	1	0	5
	8	N-U Ur12 501-800	36	4590	1	0	12

	Sent			Received				
Non-respons Schools	Using Schools	Non-use Schools	Using Schools	Non-use Schools	Unclear Schools	Partic. Rate	Return Rate	Response Rate
79	6	56	26	21	1	.49	.77	.38
66	17	51	47	7	1	.55	.81	.45
.	.	.	2	1	0	.	.	.
7	106	27	73	8	0	.95	.61	.58
12	144	65	81	21	0	.95	.49	.46
4	57	31	34	10	0	.96	.50	.48
0	299	0	177	21	0	1.00	.66	.66
0	34	2	27	2	0	1.00	.81	.81
3	57	0	53	3	0	.95	.98	.93
20	332	8	307	0	2	.94	.91	.86
8	66	1	52	1	1	.88	.81	.71
36	148	48	142	17	0	.86	.81	.70
73	43	3	33	5	0	.62	.83	.51
.	190	65	230	5	2	.	.93	.
.	9	0	10	0	0	.	1.11	.
0	0	49	0	35	2	1.00	.76	.76
0	0	12	0	10	0	1.00	.83	.83
0	0	21	0	17	0	1.00	.81	.81
0	0	8	0	6	0	1.00	.75	.75
0	0	14	0	13	0	1.00	.93	.93
0	0	3	0	3	0	1.00	1.00	1.00
0	0	5	0	5	0	1.00	1.00	1.00
0	0	12	0	9	0	1.00	.75	.75

Country	Stratum Number	Stratum Name	Schools	Students	Ep (0) Or Pps (1)	Using Schools	Non-use Schools
Population 2			Number of			Selected	

Country	Stratum Number	Stratum Name	Schools	Students	Ep (0) Or Pps (1)	Using Schools	Non-use Schools
Greece							
	9	N-U Ur12 301-500	43	4634	1	0	12
	10	N-U Ur12 201-300	31	3438	1	0	9
	11	N-U SU12 101-200	25	2328	1	0	6
	12	N-U SU12 <=100	13	990	1	0	3
	13	N-U Rural areas	826	36710	1	0	97
	101	Use Athens(CofC)	29	.	0	29	0
	102	Use Athens(E&N)	9	.	0	9	0
	103	Use Athens(west)	21	.	0	21	0
	104	Use Attika	5	.	0	5	0
	105	Use Thessa(city)	10	.	0	10	0
	106	Use Thessa(pref)	3	.	0	3	0
	107	Use Patras	3	.	0	3	0
	108	Use Ur12 501-800	15	.	0	15	0
	109	Use Ur12 301-500	33	.	0	33	0
	110	Use Ur12 201-300	34	.	0	34	0
	111	Use SU12 101-200	29	.	0	29	0
	112	Use SU12 <=100	9	.	0	9	0
	113	Use Rural areas	48	.	0	48	0
Italy							
	1	All schools	9119	822399	0	.	.
Japan							
	.	.	.	.	.	.	.
	11	Big_cit_smal	592	70021	1	3	26
	12	Big_cit_midd	539	134474	1	7	55
	13	Big_cit_larg	460	175662	1	14	64
	21	City_small	2256	212819	1	8	96
	22	City_middle	1389	346850	1	21	147
	23	City_large	1694	640818	1	58	252
	31	Village_smal	3459	255175	1	22	102
	32	Village_midd	504	123544	1	4	56
	33	Village_larg	238	84881	1	8	33

	Sent		Received					
Non-respons Schools	Using Schools	Non-use Schools	Using Schools	Non-use Schools	Unclear Schools	Partic. Rate	Return Rate	Response Rate
0	0	12	0	11	0	1.00	.92	.92
0	0	9	0	7	0	1.00	.78	.78
0	0	6	0	6	0	1.00	1.00	1.00
0	0	3	0	3	0	1.00	1.00	1.00
0	0	97	0	78	0	1.00	.80	.80
0	29	0	16	7	4	1.00	.93	.93
0	9	0	1	3	5	1.00	1.00	1.00
0	21	0	10	5	2	1.00	.81	.81
0	5	0	2	2	1	1.00	1.00	1.00
0	10	0	0	7	3	1.00	1.00	1.00
0	3	0	0	3	0	1.00	1.00	1.00
0	3	0	2	1	0	1.00	1.00	1.00
0	15	0	1	8	5	1.00	.93	.93
0	33	0	5	18	8	1.00	.94	.94
0	34	0	12	13	7	1.00	.94	.94
0	29	0	11	9	8	1.00	.97	.97
0	9	0	1	5	2	1.00	.89	.89
0	48	0	8	33	5	1.00	.96	.96
.	.	.	242	173	0	.	.	.
.	.	.	8	5	1	.	.	.
5	15	6	14	4	0	.85	.86	.73
4	26	10	17	4	6	.94	.75	.70
8	24	5	17	6	3	.91	.90	.81
0	32	21	31	12	3	1.00	.87	.87
1	33	21	32	19	2	.99	.98	.98
5	78	22	64	19	10	.98	.93	.92
0	55	6	42	8	6	1.00	.92	.92
0	20	13	20	8	3	1.00	.94	.94
0	10	3	9	2	2	1.00	1.00	1.00

Population 2			Number of		Ep (0) Or Pps (1)	Selected	
Country	Stratum Number	Stratum Name	Schools	Students		Using Schools	Non-use Schools
Luxembourg							
	3	General Sch	14	1110	0	14	0
	4	Technical Sch	18	2059	0	18	0
Netherlands							
	11	Sec/voc small	35	2180	0	12	1
	12	Sec/voc medium	37	4515	0	28	0
	13	Sec/voc large	16	2600	0	16	0
	21	Sec small	598	34450	0	50	12
	22	Sec medium	269	29077	0	44	8
	23	Sec large	379	73401	0	108	7
	31	Voc small	301	13244	0	27	6
	32	Voc medium	259	22188	0	49	6
	33	Voc large	85	9584	0	22	3
	41	Ind/voc small	118	2926	0	11	8
	42	Ind/voc medium	185	6771	0	48	4
	43	Ind/voc large	55	3017	0	17	5
New Zealand							
	1	Small_sta_co	81	3439	1	10	1
	3	Small_sta_bo	2	163	1	0	0
	4	Sm_in_pr_co	28	1021	1	4	0
	5	Sm_in_pr_gi	27	1566	1	5	0
	6	Sm_in_pr_bo	16	1083	1	3	0
	10	Med_sta_co	77	11541	1	36	1
	11	Med_sta_gi	7	1212	1	4	0
	12	Med_sta_bo	8	1469	1	5	0
	13	Med_in_pr_co	7	855	1	2	0
	14	Med_in_pr_gi	11	1465	1	5	0
	15	Med_in_pr_bo	14	1825	1	5	1
	19	Large_sta_co	83	22236	1	69	2
	20	Large_sta_gi	18	4065	1	13	0
	21	Large_sta_bo	17	4291	1	14	0

	Sent			Received				
Non-respons Schools	Using Schools	Non-use Schools	Using Schools	Non-use Schools	Unclear Schools	Partic. Rate	Return Rate	Response Rate
0	14	0	12	0	0	1.00	.86	.86
0	18	0	15	0	0	1.00	.83	.83
3	5	0	5	0	0	.81	1.00	.81
1	15	0	15	0	0	.97	1.00	.97
0	13	0	12	1	0	1.00	1.00	1.00
5	37	8	29	9	0	.93	.84	.78
3	30	4	24	2	1	.95	.79	.75
7	82	2	79	1	2	.94	.98	.92
7	18	2	15	2	0	.83	.85	.70
8	35	3	29	3	0	.87	.84	.74
0	15	1	13	0	0	1.00	.81	.81
4	9	4	9	2	1	.83	.92	.76
4	37	1	35	0	1	.93	.95	.88
2	14	3	15	2	0	.92	1.00	.92
0	7	1	8	0	0	1.00	1.00	1.00
0	0	0	0	0	0	.	.	.
0	3	0	3	0	0	1.00	1.00	1.00
0	5	0	5	0	0	1.00	1.00	1.00
0	2	0	2	0	0	1.00	1.00	1.00
0	30	1	27	0	0	1.00	.87	.87
0	4	0	4	0	0	1.00	1.00	1.00
0	4	0	4	0	0	1.00	1.00	1.00
0	2	0	2	0	0	1.00	1.00	1.00
0	3	0	2	0	0	1.00	.67	.67
0	4	1	4	0	0	1.00	.80	.80
0	53	2	51	2	0	1.00	.96	.96
0	11	0	11	0	0	1.00	1.00	1.00
0	12	0	12	0	0	1.00	1.00	1.00

			Number of		Ep (0) Or Pps (1)	Selected	
Country	Stratum Number	Stratum Name	Schools	Students		Using Schools	Non-use Schools
Portugal							
	.	.	.	.	.	.	.
	7	Small use	53	7015	1	3	12
	8	Medium use	115	30710	1	26	38
	9	Large use	142	57408	1	71	50
	10	Small non-use	135	12583	1	15	69
	11	Medium non-use	62	13545	1	16	43
	12	Large non-use	24	8115	1	13	8
Switzerland							
	3	Kanton Bern	584	24469	0	77	478
	33	All except Bern	1084	130764	0	493	542
United States of America							
	1	All schools	38329	10286000	1	433	14

Notes: Remarks for specific countries:

CBC: No complete sampling information available. Weights have not been computed.

FRG: No complete sampling information available. Weights have not been computed.

ITA: No complete sampling information available. Weights have not been computed.

JPN: After the first selection, additional using schools have been selected, which is the reason that 'sent using schools' is greater than 'selected using schools'.

SWI: Stratum 3: Based on the screening survey 'sent non-use schools' have been selected PPS from the 'selected non-use schools'.

USA: Extended sampling information about all 81 strata is available in the 'Final Sampling Report for the USA'. Computation of weights took place in the USA.

	Sent		Received					
Non-respons Schools	Using Schools	Non-use Schools	Using Schools	Non-use Schools	Unclear Schools	Partic. Rate	Return Rate	Response Rate
.	.	.	1	3	0	.	.	.
2	3	12	4	6	1	.88	.73	.65
7	26	38	39	12	6	.90	.89	.80
21	71	50	88	6	1	.85	.79	.67
8	15	69	7	49	6	.91	.74	.67
3	16	43	14	26	4	.95	.75	.71
3	13	8	7	9	2	.88	.86	.75
29	77	85	83	47	3	.95	.82	.78
49	493	591	614	232	35	.95	.81	.78
27	433	14	382	3	40	.96	.95	.92

Population 2

Country	Stratum Number	Extended Stratum Name
Austria		

	11	Burgenland, Hauptschulen user
	12	Kärnten, Hauptschulen user
	13	Niederösterreich, Hauptschulen user
	14	Oberösterreich, Hauptschulen user
	15	Salzburg, Hauptschulen user
	16	Steiermark, Hauptschulen user
	17	Tirol, Hauptschulen user
	18	Vorarlberg, Hauptschulen user
	19	Wien, Hauptschulen user
	21	Burgenland, AHS-Unterstufe
	22	Kärnten, AHS-Unterstufe
	23	Niederösterreich, AHS-Unterstufe
	24	Oberösterreich, AHS-Unterstufe
	25	Salzburg, AHS-Unterstufe
	26	Steiermark, AHS-Unterstufe
	27	Tirol, AHS-Unterstufe
	28	Vorarlberg, AHS-Unterstufe
	29	Wien, AHS-Unterstufe
	51	Burgenland, Hauptschulen non-user
	52	Kärnten, Hauptschulen non-user
	53	Niederösterreich, Hauptschulen non-user
	54	Oberösterreich, Hauptschulen non-user
	55	Salzburg, Hauptschulen non-user
	56	Steiermark, Hauptschulen non-user
	57	Tirol, Hauptschulen non-user
	58	Vorarlberg, Hauptschulen non-user
	59	Wien, Hauptschulen non-user

Belgium-Flemish

	1	State education, type I, ASO+TSO
	3	Local and provincial education, type I, ASO+TSO
	5	Local and provincial education, type II, ASO+TSO
	6	Catholic education, type I, ASO+TSO
	8	Catholic education, type II, ASO
	9	Catholic education, type II, TSO

Belgium-French

	1	State education
	2	Catholic education
	3	Local boards

Population 2

Stratum Extended

Country Number Stratum Name

Canada-British Columbia		
	1	All schools
France		
	1	Rural, outside urban areas
	2	Rural, inside urban areas
	3	Urban
	4	Paris and its region
Federal Republic of Germany		
	1	Hauptschule
	2	Realschule
	3	Gymnasium SI
	4	Gesamtschule SI
Greece		
	1	N-Users; Athens, center of city
	2	N-Users; Athens, eastern and northern regions
	3	N-Users; Athens, western region
	4	N-Users; Attika, except the Athens region
	5	N-Users; Thessaloniki city
	6	N-Users; Thessaloniki Prefecture (except city)
	7	N-Users; Patras
	8	N-Users; Urban areas (501-800 st. grade 12)
	9	N-Users; Urban areas (301-500 st. grade 12)
	10	N-Users; Urban areas (201-300 st. grade 12)
	11	N-Users; Semi-urban areas (101-200 st. grade 12)
	12	N-Users; Semi-urban areas (<100 st. grade 12)
	13	N-Users; Rural areas (<100 st. grade 12)
	101	Users; Athens, center of city
	102	Users; Athens, eastern and northern regions
	103	Users; Athens, western region
	104	Users; Attika, except the Athens region
	105	Users; Thessaloniki city
	106	Users; Thessaloniki Prefecture (except city)
	107	Users; Patras
	108	Users; Urban areas (501-800 st. grade 12)
	109	Users; Urban areas (301-500 st. grade 12)
	110	Users; Urban areas (201-300 st. grade 12)
	111	Users; Semi-urban areas (101-200 st. grade 12)
	112	Users; Semi-urban areas (<100 st. grade 12)
	113	Users; Rural areas (<100 st. grade 12)

Population 2

Stratum Extended

Country Number Stratum Name

Italy

	1	All schools

Japan

	11	Big city, small schools (<200)
	12	Big city, middle size schools (200-300)
	13	Big city, large schools (>=300)
	21	City, small schools (<200)
	22	City, middle size schools (200-300)
	23	City, large schools (>=300)
	31	Village, small schools (<200)
	32	Village, middle size schools (200-300)
	33	Village, large schools (>=300)

Luxembourg

	3	General secondary schools
	4	Technical secondary schools

Netherlands

	11	General secondary/vocational schools, small (<400)
	12	General secondary/vocational schools, medium (400-800)
	13	General secondary/vocational schools, large (>=800)
	21	General secondary schools, small (<400)
	22	General secondary schools, medium (400-800)
	23	General secondary schools, large (>=800)
	31	Vocational schools, small (<400)
	32	Vocational schools, medium (400-800)
	33	Vocational schools, large (>=800)
	41	Individual vocational schools, small (<400)
	42	Individual vocational schools, medium (400-800)
	43	Individual vocational schools, large (>=800)

New Zealand

	1	Small, state, co-educational schools
	3	Small, state, single sex boys schools
	4	Small, integrated or private, co-educational schools
	5	Small, integrated or private, single sex girls schools
	6	Small, integrated or private, single sex boys schools
	10	Medium size, state, co-educational schools
	11	Medium size, state, single sex girls schools
	12	Medium size, state, single sex boys schools
	13	Medium size, integrated or private, co-educational schools
	14	Medium size, integrated or private, single sex girls schools
	15	Medium size, integrated or private, single sex boys schools

Population 2

Stratum Extended
Country Number Stratum Name

New Zealand		
	19	Large, state, co-educational schools
	20	Large, state, single sex girls schools
	21	Large, state, single sex boys schools

Portugal		
	7	Small, using schools (grade 8)
	8	Medium size, using schools (grade 8)
	9	Large, using schools (grade 8)
	10	Small, non-using schools (grade 8)
	11	Medium size, non-using schools (grade 8)
	12	Large, non-using schools (grade 8)

Switzerland		
	3	Kanton Bern
	33	All except Kanton Bern

United States of America		
	1	All schools

	Stratum		Number of		Ep (0)	Selected	
Country	Number	Stratum Name	Schools	Students	Or Pps (1)	Using Schools	Non-use Schools

Population 3

Austria

	2	Karnte_hbla	1	317	1	0	0
	3	Nieder_hbla	4	1136	1	2	0
	4	Oberos_hbla	2	468	1	1	0
	5	Salzbu_hbla	1	255	1	0	0
	6	Steier_hbla	2	721	1	1	0
	7	Tirol_hbla	1	148	1	0	0
	9	Wien_hbla	1	157	1	1	0
	11	Burgenl_ahs	10	4710	1	5	0
	12	Karnten_ahs	21	11934	1	9	0
	13	Niedero_ahs	44	24961	1	19	0
	14	Oberost_ahs	44	22395	1	21	0
	15	Salzbur_ahs	22	10252	1	11	0
	16	Steierm_ahs	45	23533	1	20	0
	17	Tirol_ahs	23	11446	1	11	0
	18	Vorarlb_ahs	12	6039	1	5	0
	19	Wien_ahs	80	43089	1	39	0
	71	Burgenl_htl	2	1619	1	1	0
	72	Karnten_htl	7	3322	1	4	0
	73	Niedero_htl	11	7908	1	6	0
	74	Oberost_htl	12	6770	1	5	0
	75	Salzbur_htl	6	2468	1	3	0
	76	Steierm_htl	9	4541	1	4	0
	77	Tirol_htl	7	2589	1	4	0
	78	Vorarlb_htl	3	1179	1	1	0
	79	Wien_htl	14	7729	1	9	0
	81	Burgenl_hak	6	1609	1	3	0
	82	Karnten_hak	8	3051	1	4	0
	83	Niedero_hak	21	6091	1	9	0
	84	Oberost_hak	18	5585	1	8	0
	85	Salzbur_hak	7	2205	1	3	0
	86	Steierm_hak	12	4456	1	5	0
	87	Tirol_hak	8	2713	1	4	0
	88	Vorarlb_hak	4	1328	1	2	0
	89	Wien_hak	12	4435	1	6	0

	Sent		Received					
Non-respons Schools	Using Schools	Non-use Schools	Using Schools	Non-use Schools	Unclear Schools	Partic. Rate	Return Rate	Response Rate
0	0	0	0	0	0	.	.	.
0	2	0	2	0	0	1.00	1.00	1.00
0	1	0	1	0	0	1.00	1.00	1.00
0	0	0	0	0	0	.	.	.
0	1	0	1	0	0	1.00	1.00	1.00
0	0	0	0	0	0	.	.	.
0	1	0	0	0	0	1.00	0.00	0.00
0	5	0	2	0	0	1.00	.40	.40
0	9	0	7	0	0	1.00	.78	.78
0	19	0	13	0	0	1.00	.68	.68
0	21	0	15	0	0	1.00	.71	.71
0	11	0	8	0	0	1.00	.73	.73
0	20	0	14	0	0	1.00	.70	.70
0	11	0	5	0	1	1.00	.55	.55
0	5	0	3	0	0	1.00	.60	.60
0	39	0	15	1	0	1.00	.41	.41
0	1	0	1	0	0	1.00	1.00	1.00
0	4	0	2	0	0	1.00	.50	.50
0	6	0	4	0	0	1.00	.67	.67
0	5	0	4	0	0	1.00	.80	.80
0	3	0	3	0	0	1.00	1.00	1.00
0	4	0	4	0	0	1.00	1.00	1.00
0	4	0	2	0	0	1.00	.50	.50
0	1	0	0	0	0	1.00	0.00	0.00
0	9	0	5	0	0	1.00	.56	.56
0	3	0	3	0	0	1.00	1.00	1.00
0	4	0	4	0	0	1.00	1.00	1.00
0	9	0	7	0	0	1.00	.78	.78
0	8	0	6	0	0	1.00	.75	.75
0	3	0	3	0	0	1.00	1.00	1.00
0	5	0	4	0	0	1.00	.80	.80
0	4	0	3	0	0	1.00	.75	.75
0	2	0	2	0	0	1.00	1.00	1.00
0	6	0	3	0	0	1.00	.50	.50

Population 3			Number of		Ep (0) Or Pps (1)	Selected	
Country	Stratum Number	Stratum Name	Schools	Students		Using Schools	Non-use Schools
Austria							
	91	Burgen_hbla	4	777	1	2	0
	92	Karnte_hbla	5	1751	1	2	0
	93	Nieder_hbla	10	2538	1	5	0
	94	Oberos_hbla	11	2456	1	4	0
	95	Salzbu_hbla	4	977	1	2	0
	96	Steier_hbla	7	1676	1	3	0
	97	Tirol_hbla	3	1093	1	1	0
	98	Vorarl_hbla	3	684	1	2	0
	99	Wien_hbla	4	2019	1	2	0
Belgium-Flemish							
	.	.	.	.	.	.	.
	1	State 1 doorstr	101	4556	1	45	0
	2	State 1 techn	69	1652	1	12	0
	4	Loc/prov 1 doorstr	37	886	1	10	1
	5	Loc/prov 1 techn	60	1784	1	14	3
	8	Loc/prov 2 TSO	6	318	1	2	0
	10	Cath 1 doorstr	217	11282	1	79	1
	11	Cath 1 techn	132	4398	1	33	2
	13	Cath 2 ASO	167	11167	1	54	18
	14	Cath 2 TSO	185	9032	1	66	3
Belgium-French							
	.	.	.	.	.	.	.
	1	State educ	209	95227	1	112	20
	2	Cathol educ	414	174040	1	174	25
	3	Local boards	136	73223	1	73	15
Canada-British Columbia							
	1	All schools	197	35512	0	197	0

| Non-respons Schools | Sent | | Received | | | Partic. Rate | Return Rate | Response Rate |
	Using Schools	Non-use Schools	Using Schools	Non-use Schools	Unclear Schools			
0	2	0	2	0	0	1.00	1.00	1.00
0	2	0	2	0	0	1.00	1.00	1.00
0	5	0	4	0	0	1.00	.80	.80
0	4	0	4	0	0	1.00	1.00	1.00
0	2	0	1	0	0	1.00	.50	.50
0	3	0	2	0	0	1.00	.67	.67
0	1	0	0	0	0	1.00	0.00	0.00
0	2	0	1	0	0	1.00	.50	.50
0	2	0	1	0	0	1.00	.50	.50
.	.	.	1	0	0	.	.	.
15	38	0	39	0	0	.75	1.03	.77
8	12	0	11	0	0	.60	.92	.55
0	9	1	10	0	0	1.00	1.00	1.00
6	10	3	11	0	0	.74	.85	.63
4	1	0	1	0	0	.33	1.00	.33
39	61	1	59	0	0	.67	.95	.64
10	26	2	27	1	0	.78	1.00	.78
45	48	18	51	4	0	.62	.83	.51
26	54	2	54	1	0	.73	.98	.71
.	.	.	8	0	0	.	.	.
7	112	20	70	3	0	.95	.55	.53
12	174	26	101	8	0	.94	.55	.51
3	73	15	40	0	0	.97	.45	.44
0	197	0	175	7	1	1.00	.93	.93

Country	Stratum Number	Stratum Name	Number of Schools	Number of Students	Ep (0) Or Pps (1)	Selected Using Schools	Selected Non-use Schools
China							
	11	S1_Beijing	58	11200	0	26	0
	12	S2_Beijing	89	9000	0	24	0
	13	S3_Beijing	4	1000	0	1	0
	14	S4_Beijing	25	4700	0	6	0
	15	S5_Beijing	34	2400	0	0	11
	16	S6_Beijing	55	6300	0	0	17
	21	S1_Neimong	11	3188	0	11	0
	22	S2_Neimong	18	3436	0	18	0
	25	S5_Neimong	26	3909	0	0	11
	26	S6_Neimong	17	2929	0	0	3
	31	S1_Jiling	4	852	0	4	0
	32	S2_Jiling	14	3348	0	14	0
	34	S4_Jiling	13	2787	0	13	0
	35	S5_Jiling	71	13540	0	0	10
	36	S6_Jiling	123	22685	0	0	2
	41	S1_Shanghai	116	21390	0	38	0
	42	S2_Shanghai	52	6085	0	9	0
	43	S3_Shanghai	27	5622	0	12	0
	44	S4_Shanghai	52	5439	0	11	0
	45	S5_Shanghai	12	1038	0	0	4
	46	S6_Shanghai	27	1897	0	0	6
	51	S1_Anhui	10	2023	0	10	0
	52	S2_Anhui	9	1430	0	9	0
	53	S3_Anhui	3	680	0	3	0
	55	S5_Anhui	50	8477	0	0	9
	56	S6_Anhui	6	657	0	0	1
	61	S1_Xinxiang	6	1705	0	6	0
	62	S2_Xinxiang	2	729	0	2	0
	64	S4_Xinxiang	2	613	0	2	0
	65	S5_Xinxiang	8	481	0	0	8
	66	S6_Xinxiang	2	350	0	0	2
	71	S1_Shichuan	38	8661	0	16	0
	72	S2_Shichuan	35	4487	0	8	0
	73	S3_Shichuan	46	8006	0	14	0
	74	S4_Shichuan	39	3968	0	7	0

	Sent		Received					
Non-respons Schools	Using Schools	Non-use Schools	Using Schools	Non-use Schools	Unclear Schools	Partic. Rate	Return Rate	Response Rate
0	26	0	25	0	0	1.00	.96	.96
0	24	0	22	0	0	1.00	.92	.92
0	1	0	1	0	0	1.00	1.00	1.00
0	6	0	3	0	1	1.00	.67	.67
0	0	11	0	9	0	1.00	.82	.82
0	0	17	0	8	0	1.00	.47	.47
0	11	0	11	0	0	1.00	1.00	1.00
0	18	0	18	0	0	1.00	1.00	1.00
0	0	11	1	8	2	1.00	1.00	1.00
0	0	3	0	3	0	1.00	1.00	1.00
0	4	0	4	0	0	1.00	1.00	1.00
0	14	0	10	0	0	1.00	.71	.71
0	13	0	8	0	0	1.00	.62	.62
0	0	10	6	3	0	1.00	.90	.90
0	0	2	0	2	0	1.00	1.00	1.00
0	38	0	38	0	0	1.00	1.00	1.00
0	9	0	8	0	0	1.00	.89	.89
0	12	0	12	0	0	1.00	1.00	1.00
0	11	0	9	0	0	1.00	.82	.82
0	0	4	2	3	0	1.00	1.25	1.25
0	0	6	0	5	0	1.00	.83	.83
0	10	0	8	0	0	1.00	.80	.80
0	9	0	9	0	0	1.00	1.00	1.00
0	3	0	3	0	0	1.00	1.00	1.00
0	0	9	0	9	0	1.00	1.00	1.00
0	0	1	0	1	0	1.00	1.00	1.00
0	6	0	2	0	0	1.00	.33	.33
0	2	0	3	0	0	1.00	1.50	1.50
0	2	0	2	0	0	1.00	1.00	1.00
0	0	8	2	5	0	1.00	.88	.88
0	0	2	0	2	0	1.00	1.00	1.00
0	16	0	11	0	0	1.00	.69	.69
0	8	0	4	0	0	1.00	.50	.50
0	14	0	10	0	0	1.00	.71	.71
0	7	0	2	0	0	1.00	.29	.29

| | | | Number of | | Ep (0) | Selected | |
| | Stratum | | | | Or | Using | Non-use |
Country	Number	Stratum Name	Schools	Students	Pps (1)	Schools	Schools
Population 3							
China							
	75	S5_Shichuan	99	11705	0	0	15
	76	S6_Shichuan	101	12230	0	0	16
	81	S1_Guangxi	14	4576	0	12	0
	82	S2_Guangxi	19	3454	0	16	0
	83	S3_Guangxi	4	2205	0	4	0
	84	S4_Guangxi	15	4741	0	13	0
	85	S5_Guangxi	18	3872	0	0	4
	86	S6_Guangxi	91	14282	0	0	23
	91	S1_Guangdong	33	7724	0	31	0
	92	S2_Guangdong	24	5206	0	17	0
	93	S3_Guangdong	17	4895	0	5	0
	94	S4_Guangdong	39	10168	0	26	0
	95	S5_Guangdong	13	2759	0	0	11
	96	S6_Guangdong	9	1524	0	0	8
France							
	.	.	.	.	.	.	.
	1	Rural Lycee	4	.	0	3	0
	2	Rural LT	2	.	0	2	0
	3	Rural Lep	28	.	0	5	0
	4	Urbal Lycee	766	.	0	137	2
	5	Urban LT	193	.	0	33	3
	6	Urban Lep	1073	.	0	195	1
	7	Paris Lycee	151	.	0	20	1
	8	Paris LT	52	.	0	7	0
	9	Paris Lep	248	.	0	44	0
Federal Republic of Germany							
	3	Gymnasium SII	2455	1596113	0	289	38
	4	Gesamtschule SII	292	190253	0	35	3
	5	Vocational	997	203445	0	28	9

	Sent			Received				
Non-respons Schools	Using Schools	Non-use Schools	Using Schools	Non-use Schools	Unclear Schools	Partic. Rate	Return Rate	Response Rate
0	0	15	0	8	0	1.00	.53	.53
0	0	16	3	1	0	1.00	.25	.25
0	12	0	12	0	0	1.00	1.00	1.00
0	16	0	17	0	0	1.00	1.06	1.06
0	4	0	3	0	0	1.00	.75	.75
0	13	0	14	0	0	1.00	1.08	1.08
0	0	4	1	3	0	1.00	1.00	1.00
0	0	23	0	17	0	1.00	.74	.74
0	31	0	8	0	0	1.00	.26	.26
0	17	0	12	0	0	1.00	.71	.71
0	5	0	0	0	0	1.00	0.00	0.00
0	26	0	9	0	0	1.00	.35	.35
0	0	11	0	1	0	1.00	.09	.09
0	0	8	0	1	0	1.00	.13	.13
.	.	.	1	0	0	.	.	.
0	3	0	3	0	0	1.00	1.00	1.00
0	2	0	2	0	0	1.00	1.00	1.00
1	6	0	6	0	0	.83	1.00	.83
13	150	2	132	4	0	.91	.89	.82
2	35	3	31	0	0	.95	.82	.77
17	212	1	181	0	1	.92	.85	.79
9	29	1	22	0	1	.70	.77	.54
3	10	0	8	0	0	.70	.80	.56
5	49	0	31	0	2	.90	.67	.60
.	.	.	207	7	2	.	.	.
.	.	.	4	0	0	.	.	.
29	.	.	8	0	0	.56	.	.

Population 3			Number of		Ep (0) Or Pps (1)	Selected	
Country	Stratum Number	Stratum Name	Schools	Students		Using Schools	Non-use Schools
Greece							
	.	.	.	.	.	.	.
	1	N-U Athens(CofC)	136	14582	1	0	54
	2	N-U Athens(E&N)	34	4230	1	0	16
	3	N-U Athens(west)	42	4565	1	0	17
	4	N-U Attika	25	1767	1	0	7
	5	N-U Thessa(city)	44	4826	1	0	18
	6	N-U Thessa(pref)	15	853	1	0	3
	7	N-U Patras	13	1307	1	0	5
	8	N-U Ur12 501-800	34	4100	1	0	15
	9	N-U Ur12 301-500	44	4540	1	0	17
	10	N-U Ur12 201-300	42	4809	1	0	18
	11	N-U SU12 101-200	40	3790	1	0	14
	12	N-U SU12 <=100	16	1058	1	0	4
	13	N-U Rural areas	362	17139	1	0	63
	23	N-U Tel	190	.	1	0	190
	24	N-U Tes	82	.	1	0	82
	26	U Tel	17	.	1	17	0
	27	U Tes	3	.	1	3	0
	28	U Epl	22	4111	1	22	0
Hungary							
	1	All schools	500	.	0	500	0
India							
	1	Using; R/G/B	4	.	0	4	0
	2	Using; R/G/G	4	.	0	4	0
	3	Using; R/G/C	19	.	0	19	0
	4	Using; R/LB/B	1	.	0	1	0
	6	Using; R/LB/C	9	.	0	9	0
	7	Using; R/PA/B	10	.	0	10	0
	8	Using; R/PA/G	3	.	0	3	0
	9	Using; R/PA/C	37	.	0	37	0
	10	Using; R/PUA/B	1	.	0	1	0
	12	Using; R/PUA/C	5	.	0	5	0
	13	Using; U/G/B	28	.	0	28	0

	Sent		Received					
Non-respons Schools	Using Schools	Non-use Schools	Using Schools	Non-use Schools	Unclear Schools	Partic. Rate	Return Rate	Response Rate
.	.	.	1	0	0	.	.	.
0	0	54	0	47	0	1.00	.87	.87
0	0	16	0	14	0	1.00	.88	.88
0	0	17	0	16	0	1.00	.94	.94
0	0	7	0	5	0	1.00	.71	.71
0	0	18	0	15	0	1.00	.83	.83
0	0	3	0	2	0	1.00	.67	.67
0	0	5	0	4	0	1.00	.80	.80
0	0	15	0	11	1	1.00	.80	.80
0	0	17	0	16	0	1.00	.94	.94
0	0	18	0	10	0	1.00	.56	.56
0	0	14	0	11	0	1.00	.79	.79
0	0	4	0	3	0	1.00	.75	.75
0	0	63	0	57	0	1.00	.90	.90
0	0	190	0	151	2	1.00	.81	.81
0	0	82	0	63	2	1.00	.79	.79
0	17	0	12	0	0	1.00	.71	.71
0	3	0	1	0	0	1.00	.33	.33
0	22	0	18	0	0	1.00	.82	.82
0	500	.	310	1	0	1.00	.	.
0	4	0	4	0	0	1.00	1.00	1.00
0	4	0	4	0	0	1.00	1.00	1.00
0	19	0	15	0	0	1.00	.79	.79
0	1	0	0	0	0	1.00	0.00	0.00
0	9	0	9	0	0	1.00	1.00	1.00
0	10	0	7	0	0	1.00	.70	.70
0	3	0	3	0	0	1.00	1.00	1.00
0	37	0	33	0	0	1.00	.89	.89
0	1	0	1	0	0	1.00	1.00	1.00
0	5	0	5	0	0	1.00	1.00	1.00
0	28	0	25	0	0	1.00	.89	.89

Population 3			Number of		Ep (0) Or Pps (1)	Selected	
Country	Stratum Number	Stratum Name	Schools	Students		Using Schools	Non-use Schools
India							
	14	Using; U/G/G	21	.	0	21	0
	15	Using; U/G/C	101	.	0	101	0
	16	Using; U/LB/B	5	.	0	5	0
	17	Using; U/LB/G	1	.	0	1	0
	18	Using; U/LB/C	8	.	0	8	0
	19	Using; U/PA/B	91	.	0	91	0
	20	Using; U/PA/G	37	.	0	37	0
	21	Using; U/PA/C	71	.	0	71	0
	22	Using; U/PUA/B	13	.	0	13	0
	23	Using; U/PUA/G	7	.	0	7	0
	24	Using; U/PUA/C	82	.	0	82	0
	51	N-U UP; R/G/B	2	345	1	0	1
	52	N-U UP; R/G/G	6	234	1	0	1
	53	N-U UP; R/G/C	87	3957	1	0	4
	54	N-U UP; R/LB/B	2	153	1	0	1
	57	N-U UP; R/PA/B	293	41322	1	0	47
	58	N-U UP; R/PA/G	17	1153	1	0	1
	59	N-U UP; R/PA/C	223	31753	1	0	36
	63	N-U UP; U/G/B	21	3463	1	0	4
	64	N-U UP; U/G/G	21	2281	1	0	2
	65	N-U UP; U/G/C	6	467	1	0	1
	66	N-U UP; U/LB/B	5	356	1	0	1
	67	N-U UP; U/LB/G	4	336	1	0	1
	69	N-U UP; U/PA/B	259	50657	1	0	58
	70	N-U UP; U/PA/G	137	18680	1	0	21
	71	N-U UP; U/PA/C	16	3095	1	0	3
	72	N-U UP; U/PUA/B	2	184	1	0	1
	73	N-U UP; U/PUA/G	5	296	1	0	1
	74	N-U UP; U/PUA/C	18	1129	1	0	1
	151	N-U WB; R/G/B	1	91	1	0	1
	152	N-U WB; R/G/G	1	15	1	0	1
	157	N-U WB; R/PA/B	238	45177	1	0	27
	158	N-U WB; R/PA/G	24	4082	1	0	2
	159	N-U WB; R/PA/C	15	4431	1	0	2
	163	N-U WB; U/G/B	5	855	1	0	1

	Sent		Received					
Non-respons Schools	Using Schools	Non-use Schools	Using Schools	Non-use Schools	Unclear Schools	Partic. Rate	Return Rate	Response Rate
0	21	0	17	0	0	1.00	.81	.81
0	101	0	83	0	0	1.00	.82	.82
0	5	0	5	0	0	1.00	1.00	1.00
0	1	0	1	0	0	1.00	1.00	1.00
0	8	0	8	0	0	1.00	1.00	1.00
0	91	0	73	1	1	1.00	.82	.82
0	37	0	32	0	0	1.00	.86	.86
0	71	0	66	1	0	1.00	.94	.94
0	13	0	9	0	0	1.00	.69	.69
0	7	0	6	0	0	1.00	.86	.86
0	82	0	61	0	0	1.00	.74	.74
0	0	1	0	1	0	1.00	1.00	1.00
0	0	1	0	1	0	1.00	1.00	1.00
0	0	4	0	4	0	1.00	1.00	1.00
0	0	1	0	1	0	1.00	1.00	1.00
0	0	47	0	44	0	1.00	.94	.94
0	0	1	0	1	0	1.00	1.00	1.00
0	0	36	0	34	0	1.00	.94	.94
0	0	4	0	4	0	1.00	1.00	1.00
0	0	2	0	2	0	1.00	1.00	1.00
0	0	1	0	1	0	1.00	1.00	1.00
0	0	1	0	1	0	1.00	1.00	1.00
0	0	1	0	1	0	1.00	1.00	1.00
0	0	58	0	51	0	1.00	.88	.88
0	0	21	0	18	0	1.00	.86	.86
0	0	3	0	3	0	1.00	1.00	1.00
0	0	1	0	0	0	1.00	0.00	0.00
0	0	1	0	0	0	1.00	0.00	0.00
0	0	1	0	1	0	1.00	1.00	1.00
0	0	1	0	1	0	1.00	1.00	1.00
0	0	1	0	1	0	1.00	1.00	1.00
0	0	27	0	22	0	1.00	.81	.81
0	0	2	0	1	0	1.00	.50	.50
0	0	2	0	1	0	1.00	.50	.50
0	0	1	0	1	0	1.00	1.00	1.00

Country	Stratum Number	Stratum Name	Number of Schools	Number of Students	Ep (0) Or Pps (1)	Selected Using Schools	Selected Non-use Schools
Population 3							
India							
	164	N-U WB; U/G/G	4	730	1	0	1
	165	N-U WB; U/G/C	3	631	1	0	1
	169	N-U WB; U/PA/B	223	49457	1	0	29
	170	N-U WB; U/PA/G	96	19714	1	0	12
	171	N-U WB; U/PA/C	14	5647	1	0	3
	172	N-U WB; U/PUA/B	7	1067	1	0	1
	173	N-U WB; U/PUA/G	9	1838	1	0	1
	174	N-U WB; U/PUA/C	10	1211	1	0	1
	251	N-U TN; R/G/B	9	831	1	0	1
	252	N-U TN; R/G/G	13	1368	1	0	2
	253	N-U TN; R/G/C	178	15081	1	0	23
	255	N-U TN; R/LB/G	1	89	1	0	1
	256	N-U TN; R/LB/C	3	131	1	0	1
	257	N-U TN; R/PA/B	1	145	1	0	1
	258	N-U TN; R/PA/G	13	1482	1	0	2
	259	N-U TN; R/PA/C	52	4574	1	0	7
	262	N-U TN; R/PUA/C	1	110	1	0	1
	263	N-U TN; U/G/B	14	959	1	0	1
	264	N-U TN; U/G/G	8	709	1	0	1
	265	N-U TN; U/G/C	16	1319	1	0	2
	266	N-U TN; U/LB/B	12	1279	1	0	1
	267	N-U TN; U/LB/G	13	2031	1	0	3
	268	N-U TN; U/LB/C	5	545	1	0	1
	269	N-U TN; U/PA/B	49	5190	1	0	7
	270	N-U TN; U/PA/G	39	6157	1	0	9
	271	N-U TN; U/PA/C	40	4300	1	0	6
	272	N-U TN; U/PUA/B	1	95	1	0	1
	273	N-U TN; U/PUA/G	7	534	1	0	1
	274	N-U TN; U/PUA/C	54	3965	1	0	6
	356	N-U M; R/LB/C	13	714	1	0	1
	358	N-U M; R/PA/G	2	141	1	0	1
	359	N-U M; R/PA/C	319	35737	1	0	25
	362	N-U M; R/PUA/C	13	1094	1	0	1
	365	N-U M; U/G/C	9	1783	1	0	1
	366	N-U M; U/LB/B	1	200	1	0	1

	Sent		Received					
Non-respons Schools	Using Schools	Non-use Schools	Using Schools	Non-use Schools	Unclear Schools	Partic. Rate	Return Rate	Response Rate
0	0	1	0	0	0	1.00	0.00	0.00
0	0	1	0	0	0	1.00	0.00	0.00
0	0	29	0	13	0	1.00	.45	.45
0	0	12	0	7	0	1.00	.58	.58
0	0	3	0	1	0	1.00	.33	.33
0	0	1	0	0	0	1.00	0.00	0.00
0	0	1	0	0	0	1.00	0.00	0.00
0	0	1	0	0	0	1.00	0.00	0.00
0	0	1	0	1	0	1.00	1.00	1.00
0	0	2	0	2	0	1.00	1.00	1.00
0	0	23	0	22	0	1.00	.96	.96
0	0	1	0	0	0	1.00	0.00	0.00
0	0	1	0	1	0	1.00	1.00	1.00
0	0	1	0	1	0	1.00	1.00	1.00
0	0	2	0	1	0	1.00	.50	.50
0	0	7	0	6	0	1.00	.86	.86
0	0	1	0	1	0	1.00	1.00	1.00
0	0	1	0	1	0	1.00	1.00	1.00
0	0	1	0	0	1	1.00	1.00	1.00
0	0	2	0	2	0	1.00	1.00	1.00
0	0	1	0	1	0	1.00	1.00	1.00
0	0	3	0	3	0	1.00	1.00	1.00
0	0	1	0	1	0	1.00	1.00	1.00
0	0	7	0	5	0	1.00	.71	.71
0	0	9	0	7	0	1.00	.78	.78
0	0	6	0	6	0	1.00	1.00	1.00
0	0	1	0	1	0	1.00	1.00	1.00
0	0	1	0	1	0	1.00	1.00	1.00
0	0	6	0	4	0	1.00	.67	.67
0	0	1	0	1	0	1.00	1.00	1.00
0	0	1	0	1	0	1.00	1.00	1.00
0	0	25	1	21	0	1.00	.88	.88
0	0	1	0	1	0	1.00	1.00	1.00
0	0	1	0	1	0	1.00	1.00	1.00
0	0	1	0	1	0	1.00	1.00	1.00

Population 3			Number of		Ep (0)	Selected	
Country	Stratum Number	Stratum Name	Schools	Students	Or Pps (1)	Using Schools	Non-use Schools
India							
	367	N-U M; U/LB/G	2	191	1	0	1
	368	N-U M; U/LB/C	15	1342	1	0	1
	369	N-U M; U/PA/B	8	1443	1	0	0
	370	N-U M; U/PA/G	37	8101	1	0	7
	371	N-U M; U/PA/C	483	125435	1	0	91
	373	N-U M; U/PUA/G	1	73	1	0	0
	374	N-U M; U/PUA/C	33	4433	1	0	3
	451	N-U D; R/G/B	22	6398	1	0	1
	452	N-U D; R/G/G	23	2427	1	0	1
	453	N-U D; R/G/C	14	3181	1	0	1
	457	N-U D; R/ PA/B	4	516	1	0	1
	463	N-U D; U/G/B	145	28308	1	0	7
	464	N-U D; U/G/G	152	26767	1	0	6
	465	N-U D; U/G/C	11	1900	1	0	1
	466	N-U D; U/LB/B	2	344	1	0	1
	467	N-U D; U/LB/G	2	490	1	0	1
	468	N-U D; U/LB/C	1	177	1	0	1
	469	N-U D; U/PA/B	47	8235	1	0	2
	470	N-U D; U/PA/G	50	6915	1	0	1
	471	N-U D; U/PA/C	33	5005	1	0	1
	472	N-U D; U/PUA/B	1	447	1	0	1
	473	N-U D; U/PUA/G	6	1800	1	0	1
	474	N-U D; U/PUA/C	39	6485	1	0	1
Israel							
	.	.	.	.	.	.	.
	10	Jerusal newp	47	.	0	13	6
	11	Jerusal ewp	18	.	0	7	1
	20	North notewp	39	.	0	18	2
	21	North ewp	25	.	0	11	1
	30	Haifa notewp	37	.	0	15	2
	31	Haifa ewp	22	.	0	7	4
	40	Central newp	45	.	0	18	3
	41	Central ewp	37	.	0	19	2
	50	Tel Aviv newp	45	.	0	15	5

	Sent		Received					
Non-respons Schools	Using Schools	Non-use Schools	Using Schools	Non-use Schools	Unclear Schools	Partic. Rate	Return Rate	Response Rate
0	0	1	0	0	0	1.00	0.00	0.00
0	0	1	0	0	0	1.00	0.00	0.00
0	0	0	0	0	0	.	.	.
0	0	7	0	4	0	1.00	.57	.57
0	0	91	1	60	0	1.00	.67	.67
0	0	0	0	0	0	.	.	.
0	0	3	0	2	0	1.00	.67	.67
0	0	1	0	1	0	1.00	1.00	1.00
0	0	1	0	1	0	1.00	1.00	1.00
0	0	1	0	1	0	1.00	1.00	1.00
0	0	1	0	0	0	1.00	0.00	0.00
0	0	7	0	7	0	1.00	1.00	1.00
0	0	6	0	6	0	1.00	1.00	1.00
0	0	1	0	1	0	1.00	1.00	1.00
0	0	1	0	0	0	1.00	0.00	0.00
0	0	1	0	1	0	1.00	1.00	1.00
0	0	1	0	1	0	1.00	1.00	1.00
0	0	2	0	2	0	1.00	1.00	1.00
0	0	1	0	1	0	1.00	1.00	1.00
0	0	1	0	1	0	1.00	1.00	1.00
0	0	1	0	1	0	1.00	1.00	1.00
0	0	1	0	1	0	1.00	1.00	1.00
.	.	.	17	1	0	.	.	.
3	13	6	9	6	0	.86	.79	.68
0	7	1	6	1	0	1.00	.88	.88
1	18	2	14	1	0	.95	.75	.71
0	11	1	9	1	0	1.00	.83	.83
2	15	2	12	2	0	.89	.82	.74
0	7	4	3	3	0	1.00	.55	.55
2	19	3	13	3	0	.91	.73	.66
1	19	2	13	2	0	.95	.71	.68
4	17	5	11	5	0	.83	.73	.61

| **Population 3** | | | Number of | | Ep (0) | Selected | |
Country	Stratum Number	Stratum Name	Schools	Students	Or Pps (1)	Using Schools	Non-use Schools
Israel							
	51	Tel Aviv ewp	46	.	0	15	1
	60	South notewp	34	.	0	13	2
	61	South ewp	38	.	0	18	2
	70	Arabic lang	77	.	0	30	7
Italy							
	1	All schools	5598	330520	0	.	.
Japan							
	.	.	.	.	.	.	.
	11	Nat_pub_new	140	18617	1	4	10
	12	Nat_pub_low	1427	338333	1	125	175
	13	Nat_pub_midd	1118	419151	1	108	219
	14	Nat_pub_high	171	65643	1	20	32
	21	Private_new	33	3872	1	1	1
	22	Private_low	555	170979	1	45	52
	23	Private_midd	391	124687	1	26	51
	24	Private_high	213	74712	1	17	33
	61	Nat_pub_buss	925	125131	1	264	3
	62	Nat_pub_tech	1947	115331	1	244	2
	63	Nat_pub_othe	2228	96287	1	145	59
	71	Private_buss	397	62660	1	83	13
	72	Private_tech	376	32666	1	53	4
	73	Private_othe	430	25156	1	15	21
	82	Tech_college	224	9909	1	15	0
Netherlands							
	11	Sec/voc small	31	2201	0	13	11
	12	Sec/voc medium	66	8576	0	13	11
	13	Sec/voc large	34	7317	0	20	1
	21	Sec small	4	317	0	3	1
	22	Sec medium	10	1492	0	3	1
	23	Sec large	61	15445	0	44	3
	31	Voc small	5	393	0	2	2
	32	Voc medium	33	7577	0	22	2

	Sent		Received					
Non-respons Schools	Using Schools	Non-use Schools	Using Schools	Non-use Schools	Unclear Schools	Partic. Rate	Return Rate	Response Rate
0	15	1	12	1	0	1.00	.81	.81
3	13	2	11	1	0	.83	.80	.67
0	18	2	15	1	0	1.00	.80	.80
2	30	7	23	6	0	.95	.78	.74
.	.	.	278	69	1	.	.	.
.	.	.	17	4	0	.	.	.
1	4	2	5	0	1	.93	1.00	.93
7	125	0	103	1	11	.98	.92	.90
4	108	22	99	9	16	.99	.95	.94
0	20	1	12	3	6	1.00	1.00	1.00
1	1	0	1	0	0	.67	1.00	.67
38	45	9	22	1	3	.72	.48	.35
21	26	13	16	1	2	.79	.49	.38
9	17	7	11	1	1	.85	.54	.46
1	105	0	95	0	0	1.00	.90	.90
1	106	0	101	0	1	1.00	.96	.96
2	97	0	66	7	10	.99	.86	.85
38	44	0	20	1	1	.72	.50	.36
13	22	0	12	0	0	.81	.55	.44
18	20	0	4	4	0	.67	.40	.27
6	15	0	15	0	0	.71	1.00	.71
2	7	3	5	2	0	.92	.70	.65
5	10	6	9	3	3	.83	.94	.78
3	20	0	19	0	0	.88	.95	.83
0	3	0	3	0	0	1.00	1.00	1.00
1	2	0	2	0	0	.80	1.00	.80
3	36	0	34	0	0	.94	.94	.89
1	1	0	1	0	0	.80	1.00	.80
1	17	0	17	0	0	.96	1.00	.96

			Number of		Ep (0)	Selected	
	Stratum				Or	Using	Non-use
Country	Number	Stratum Name	Schools	Students	Pps (1)	Schools	Schools
Netherlands							
	33	Voc large	46	18518	0	40	2
	41	Ind/voc small	26	1223	0	2	12
	42	Ind/voc medium	145	15436	0	15	24
	43	Ind/voc large	369	72828	0	96	108
New Zealand							
	1	Small_sta_co	81	658	1	6	0
	3	Small_sta_bo	2	31	1	0	0
	4	Sm_in_pr_co	28	408	1	4	0
	5	Sm_in_pr_gi	27	628	1	7	0
	6	Sm_in_pr_bo	16	552	1	5	0
	10	Med_sta_co	77	2890	1	27	0
	11	Med_sta_gi	7	486	1	5	0
	12	Med_sta_bo	8	578	1	5	0
	13	Med_in_pr_co	7	344	1	3	0
	14	Med_in_pr_gi	11	711	1	7	0
	15	Med_in_pr_bo	14	986	1	9	0
	19	Large_sta_co	83	7360	1	69	0
	20	Large_sta_gi	18	1738	1	16	0
	21	Large_sta_bo	17	1794	1	17	0
Poland							
	.	.	.	.	.	.	.
	1	Small nonuse	150	.	0	0	104
	2	Large nonuse	108	.	0	0	108
	3	Small use	125	.	0	125	0
	4	Large use	497	.	0	408	0
Portugal							
	.	.	.	.	.	.	.
	13	Small use	40	2620	1	17	18
	14	Medium use	91	13232	1	55	28
	15	Large use	139	51491	1	100	18
	16	Small non-use	28	1837	1	4	20

Population 3

	Sent		Received					
Non-respons Schools	Using Schools	Non-use Schools	Using Schools	Non-use Schools	Unclear Schools	Partic. Rate	Return Rate	Response Rate
4	32	0	30	0	0	.91	.94	.86
1	2	9	2	4	1	.93	.64	.59
12	11	19	11	13	3	.76	.90	.69
35	52	81	54	33	29	.85	.87	.74
0	6	0	6	0	0	1.00	1.00	1.00
0	0	0	0	0	0	.	.	.
0	3	0	2	0	0	1.00	.67	.67
0	5	0	5	0	0	1.00	1.00	1.00
0	5	0	5	0	0	1.00	1.00	1.00
0	25	0	24	0	0	1.00	.96	.96
0	5	0	5	0	0	1.00	1.00	1.00
0	3	0	3	0	0	1.00	1.00	1.00
0	1	0	1	0	0	1.00	1.00	1.00
0	6	0	6	0	0	1.00	1.00	1.00
0	8	0	8	0	0	1.00	1.00	1.00
0	52	0	50	0	0	1.00	.96	.96
0	14	0	14	0	0	1.00	1.00	1.00
0	15	0	15	0	0	1.00	1.00	1.00
.	.	.	10	2	0	.	.	.
46	0	104	0	64	0	.69	.62	.43
0	0	108	1	77	0	1.00	.72	.72
0	125	0	85	0	0	1.00	.68	.68
89	408	0	338	1	1	.82	.83	.68
.	.	.	1	2	0	.	.	.
5	17	18	16	10	3	.88	.83	.73
8	55	28	54	14	4	.91	.87	.79
21	100	18	85	7	0	.85	.78	.66
4	4	20	3	15	1	.86	.79	.68

Population 3			Number of		Ep (0)	Selected	
Country	Stratum Number	Stratum Name	Schools	Students	Or Pps (1)	Using Schools	Non-use Schools
Portugal							
	17	Medium non-use	18	2055	1	5	12
	18	Large non-use	19	8677	1	9	8
Slovenia							
	1	The largest	43	1008	0	17	26
	2	Large	16	2510	0	6	10
	3	Medium	24	.	0	10	14
	4	Small	54	.	0	22	32
Switzerland							
	1	Kanton 1-29	217	57125	0	196	21
	2	Kanton 30-32	97	92153	0	97	0
	3	Kanton 40-42	102	56503	0	102	0
United States of America							
	1	All schools	24377	12694000	1	439	5

Notes: Remarks for specific countries:

CBC: No complete sampling information available. Weights have not been computed.
FRG: No complete sampling information available. Weights have not been computed.
HUN: No complete sampling information available. Weights have not been computed.
ITA: No complete sampling information available. Weights have not been computed.
USA: Extended sampling information about all 81 strata is available in the 'Final Sampling Report for the USA'. Computation of weights took place in the USA.

	Sent		Received					
Non-respons Schools	Using Schools	Non-use Schools	Using Schools	Non-use Schools	Unclear Schools	Partic. Rate	Return Rate	Response Rate
1	5	12	4	8	2	.94	.82	.78
2	9	8	8	6	1	.89	.88	.79
0	17	26	33	6	1	1.00	.93	.93
0	6	10	5	4	0	1.00	.56	.56
0	10	14	9	1	1	1.00	.46	.46
0	22	32	44	2	1	1.00	.87	.87
0	196	21	186	11	2	1.00	.92	.92
0	97	0	62	1	1	1.00	.66	.66
0	102	0	79	0	0	1.00	.77	.77
17	439	5	413	4	17	.96	.98	.94

Population 3

Stratum Extended

Country Number Stratum Name

Austria		
	2	Kärnten, HBLA für landwirtsch. Berufe
	3	Niederösterreich, HBLA für landwirtsch. Berufe
	4	Oberösterreich, HBLA für landwirtsch. Berufe
	5	Salzburg, HBLA für landwirtsch. Berufe
	6	Steiermark, HBLA für landwirtsch. Berufe
	7	Tirol, HBLA für landwirtsch. Berufe
	9	Wien, HBLA für landwirtsch. Berufe
	11	Burgenland, AHS-Oberstufe
	12	Kärnten, AHS-Oberstufe
	13	Niederösterreich, AHS-Oberstufe
	14	Oberösterreich, AHS-Oberstufe
	15	Salzburg, AHS-Oberstufe
	16	Steiermark, AHS-Oberstufe
	17	Tirol, AHS-Oberstufe
	18	Vorarlberg, AHS-Oberstufe
	19	Wien, AHS-Oberstufe
	71	Burgenland, HTL/HGL Höhere techn. LA
	72	Kärnten, HTL/HGL Höhere techn. LA
	73	Niederösterreich, HTL/HGL Höhere techn. LA
	74	Oberösterreich, HTL/HGL Höhere techn. LA
	75	Salzburg, HTL/HGL Höhere techn. LA
	76	Steiermark, HTL/HGL Höhere techn. LA
	77	Tirol, HTL/HGL Höhere techn. LA
	78	Vorarlberg, HTL/HGL Höhere techn. LA
	79	Wien, HTL/HGL Höhere techn. LA
	81	Burgenland, HAK Handelsakademien
	82	Kärnten, HAK Handelsakademien
	83	Niederösterreich, HAK Handelsakademien
	84	Oberösterreich, HAK Handelsakademien
	85	Salzburg, HAK Handelsakademien
	86	Steiermark, HAK Handelsakademien
	87	Tirol, HAK Handelsakademien
	88	Vorarlberg, HAK Handelsakademien
	89	Wien, HAK Handelsakademien
	91	Burgenland, HBLA für wirtschaftl. Berufe

Population 3

Stratum Extended
Country Number Stratum Name

Austria

	92	Kärnten, HBLA für wirtschaftl. Berufe
	93	Niederösterreich, HBLA für wirtschaftl. Berufe
	94	Oberösterreich, HBLA für wirtschaftl. Berufe
	95	Salzburg, HBLA für wirtschaftl. Berufe
	96	Steiermark, HBLA für wirtschaftl. Berufe
	97	Tirol, HBLA für wirtschaftl. Berufe
	98	Vorarlberg, HBLA für wirtschaftl. Berufe
	99	Wien, HBLA für wirtschaftl. Berufe

Belgium-Flemish

.

	1	State education, type I, doorstroming
	2	State education, type I, kwalificatie techniek & kunst
	4	Local & provincial education, type I, doorstroming
	5	Local & provincial education, type I, kwalificatie techniek & kunst
	8	Local & provincial education, type II, TSO
	10	Catholic education, type I, doorstroming
	11	Catholic education, type I, kwalificatie techniek & kunst
	13	Catholic education, type II, ASO
	14	Catholic education, type II, TSO

Belgium-French

.

	1	State education
	2	Catholic education
	3	Local boards

Canada-British
Columbia

	1	All schools

China

	11	Introduced computers before 31 dec. 1985, in cities, Beijing
	12	Introduced computers after 1 jan. 1986, in cities, Beijing
	13	Introduced computers before 31 dec. 1985, in counties, Beijing
	14	Introduced computers after 1 jan. 1986, in counties, Beijing

Population 3

Stratum Extended
Country Number Stratum Name

China

	15	Non-using school, located in cities, Beijing
	16	Non-using school, located in counties, Beijing
	21	Introduced computers before 31 dec. 1985, in cities, Neimong
	22	Introduced computers after 1 jan. 1986, in cities, Neimong
	25	Non-using school, located in cities, Neimong
	26	Non-using school, located in counties, Neimong
	31	Introduced computers before 31 dec. 1985, in cities, Jiling
	32	Introduced computers after 1 jan. 1986, in cities, Jiling
	34	Introduced computers after 1 jan. 1986, in counties, Jiling
	35	Non-using school, located in cities, Jiling
	36	Non-using school, located in counties, Jiling
	41	Introduced computers before 31 dec. 1985, in cities, Shanghai
	42	Introduced computers after 1 jan. 1986, in cities, Shanghai
	43	Introduced computers before 31 dec. 1985, in counties, Shanghai
	44	Introduced computers after 1 jan. 1986, in counties, Shanghai
	45	Non-using school, located in cities, Shanghai
	46	Non-using school, located in counties, Shanghai
	51	Introduced computers before 31 dec. 1985, in cities, Anhui
	52	Introduced computers after 1 jan. 1986, in cities, Anhui
	53	Introduced computers before 31 dec. 1985, in counties, Anhui
	55	Non-using school, located in cities, Anhui
	56	Non-using school, located in counties, Anhui
	61	Introduced computers before 31 dec. 1985, in cities, Xinxiang
	62	Introduced computers after 1 jan. 1986, in cities, Xinxiang
	64	Introduced computers after 1 jan. 1986, in counties, Xinxiang
	65	Non-using school, located in cities, Xinxiang
	66	Non-using school, located in counties, Xinxiang
	71	Introduced computers before 31 dec. 1985, in cities, Shichuan
	72	Introduced computers after 1 jan. 1986, in cities, Shichuan
	73	Introduced computers before 31 dec. 1985, in counties, Shichuan
	74	Introduced computers after 1 jan. 1986, in counties, Shichuan
	75	Non-using school, located in cities, Shichuan
	76	Non-using school, located in counties, Shichuan
	81	Introduced computers before 31 dec. 1985, in cities, Guangxi
	82	Introduced computers after 1 jan. 1986, in cities, Guangxi
	83	Introduced computers before 31 dec. 1985, in counties, Guangxi

Population 3

Stratum Extended
Country Number Stratum Name

China

84	Introduced computers after 1 jan. 1986, in counties, Guangxi
85	Non-using school, located in cities, Guangxi
86	Non-using school, located in counties, Guangxi
91	Introduced computers before 31 dec. 1985, in cities, Guangdong
92	Introduced computers after 1 jan. 1986, in cities, Guangdong
93	Introduced computers before 31 dec. 1985, in counties, Guangdong
94	Introduced computers after 1 jan. 1986, in counties, Guangdong
95	Non-using school, located in cities, Guangdong
96	Non-using school, located in counties, Guangdong

France

1	Rural Lycées (academic teaching)
2	Rural LT (technical schools)
3	Rural LEP (vocational schools)
4	Urban Lycées (academic teaching)
5	Urban LT (technical schools)
6	Urban LEP (vocational schools)
7	Region Paris Lycées (academic teaching)
8	Region Paris LT (technical schools)
9	Region Paris LEP (vocational schools)

Federal Republic
of Germany

3	Gymnasium SII
4	Gesamtschule SII
5	Vocational full times

Greece

1	N-Users; Athens, center of city
2	N-Users; Athens, eastern and northern regions
3	N-Users; Athens, western region
4	N-Users; Attika, excepting the Athens region
5	N-Users; Thessaloniki city

Population 3

Country | Stratum Number | Extended Stratum Name

Greece		
	6	N-Users; Thessaloniki Prefecture (excepting the city)
	7	N-Users; Patras
	8	N-Users; Urban areas (501-800 students in grade 12)
	9	N-Users; Urban areas (301-500 students in grade 12)
	10	N-Users; Urban areas (201-300 students in grade 12)
	11	N-Users; Semi-urban areas (101-200 students in grade 12)
	12	N-Users; Semi-urban areas (<100 students in grade 12)
	13	N-Users; Rural areas (<100 students in grade 12)
	23	N-Users; Technical vocational highschools
	24	N-Users; Technical vocational secondary schools
	26	Users; Technical vocational highschools
	27	Users; Technical vocational secondary schools
	28	Users; Unified comprehensive schools
Hungary		
	1	All schools
India		
	1	Using schools; Rural, Govern, Boys
	2	Using schools; Rural, Govern, Girls
	3	Using schools; Rural, Govern, Co-educational
	4	Using schools; Rural, Local Body, Boys
	6	Using schools; Rural, Local Body, Co-educational
	7	Using schools; Rural, Private Aided, Boys
	8	Using schools; Rural, Private Aided, Girls
	9	Using schools; Rural, Private Aided, Co-educational
	10	Using schools; Rural, Private UnAided, Boys
	12	Using schools; Rural, Private UnAided, Co-educational
	13	Using schools; Urban, Govern, Boys
	14	Using schools; Urban, Govern, Girls
	15	Using schools; Urban, Govern, Co-educational
	16	Using schools; Urban, Local Body, Boys
	17	Using schools; Urban, Local Body, Girls
	18	Using schools; Urban, Local Body, Co-educational
	19	Using schools; Urban, Private Aided, Boys
	20	Using schools; Urban, Private Aided, Girls

Population 3

Stratum Extended
Country Number Stratum Name

India

	21	Using schools; Urban, Private Aided, Co-educational
	22	Using schools; Urban, Private UnAided, Boys
	23	Using schools; Urban, Private UnAided, Girls
	24	Using schools; Urban, Private UnAided, Co-educational
	51	Non-Use Uttar Pradesh; Rural, Govern, Boys
	52	Non-Use Uttar Pradesh; Rural, Govern, Girls
	53	Non-Use Uttar Pradesh; Rural, Govern, Co-educational
	54	Non-Use Uttar Pradesh; Rural, Local Body, Boys
	57	Non-Use Uttar Pradesh; Rural, Private Aided, Boys
	58	Non-Use Uttar Pradesh; Rural, Private Aided, Girls
	59	Non-Use Uttar Pradesh; Rural, Private Aided, Co-educational
	63	Non-Use Uttar Pradesh; Urban, Govern, Boys
	64	Non-Use Uttar Pradesh; Urban, Govern, Girls
	65	Non-Use Uttar Pradesh; Urban, Govern, Co-educational
	66	Non-Use Uttar Pradesh; Urban, Local Body, Boys
	67	Non-Use Uttar Pradesh; Urban, Local Body, Girls
	69	Non-Use Uttar Pradesh; Urban, Private Aided, Boys
	70	Non-Use Uttar Pradesh; Urban, Private Aided, Girls
	71	Non-Use Uttar Pradesh; Urban, Private Aided, Co-educational
	72	Non-Use Uttar Pradesh; Urban, Private UnAided, Boys
	73	Non-Use Uttar Pradesh; Urban, Private UnAided, Girls
	74	Non-Use Uttar Pradesh; Urban, Private UnAided, Co-educational
	151	Non-Use West Bengal; Rural, Govern, Boys
	152	Non-Use West Bengal; Rural, Govern, Girls
	157	Non-Use West Bengal; Rural, Private Aided, Boys
	158	Non-Use West Bengal; Rural, Private Aided, Girls
	159	Non-Use West Bengal; Rural, Private Aided, Co-educational
	163	Non-Use West Bengal; Urban, Govern, Boys
	164	Non-Use West Bengal; Urban, Govern, Girls
	165	Non-Use West Bengal; Urban, Govern, Co-educational
	169	Non-Use West Bengal; Urban, Private Aided, Boys
	170	Non-Use West Bengal; Urban, Private Aided, Girls
	171	Non-Use West Bengal; Urban, Private Aided, Co-educational
	172	Non-Use West Bengal; Urban, Private UnAided, Boys
	173	Non-Use West Bengal; Urban, Private UnAided, Girls
	174	Non-Use West Bengal; Urban, Private UnAided, Co-educational

Population 3

Stratum Extended

Country Number Stratum Name

India

	251	Non-Use Tamil Nadu; Rural, Govern, Boys
	252	Non-Use Tamil Nadu; Rural, Govern, Girls
	253	Non-Use Tamil Nadu; Rural, Govern, Co-educational
	255	Non-Use Tamil Nadu; Rural, Local Body, Girls
	256	Non-Use Tamil Nadu; Rural, Local Body, Co-educational
	257	Non-Use Tamil Nadu; Rural, Private Aided, Boys
	258	Non-Use Tamil Nadu; Rural, Private Aided, Girls
	259	Non-Use Tamil Nadu; Rural, Private Aided, Co-educational
	262	Non-Use Tamil Nadu; Rural, Private UnAided, Co-educational
	263	Non-Use Tamil Nadu; Urban, Govern, Boys
	264	Non-Use Tamil Nadu; Urban, Govern, Girls
	265	Non-Use Tamil Nadu; Urban, Govern, Co-educational
	266	Non-Use Tamil Nadu; Urban, Local Body, Boys
	267	Non-Use Tamil Nadu; Urban, Local Body, Girls
	268	Non-Use Tamil Nadu; Urban, Local Body, Co-educational
	269	Non-Use Tamil Nadu; Urban, Private Aided, Boys
	270	Non-Use Tamil Nadu; Urban, Private Aided, Girls
	271	Non-Use Tamil Nadu; Urban, Private Aided, Co-educational
	272	Non-Use Tamil Nadu; Urban, Private UnAided, Boys
	273	Non-Use Tamil Nadu; Urban, Private UnAided, Girls
	274	Non-Use Tamil Nadu; Urban, Private UnAided, Co-educational
	356	Non-Use Maharashtra; Rural, Local Body, Co-educational
	358	Non-Use Maharashtra; Rural, Private Aided, Girls
	359	Non-Use Maharashtra; Rural, Private Aided, Co-educational
	362	Non-Use Maharashtra; Rural, Private UnAided, Co-educational
	365	Non-Use Maharashtra; Urban, Govern, Co-educational
	366	Non-Use Maharashtra; Urban, Local Body, Boys
	367	Non-Use Maharashtra; Urban, Local Body, Girls
	368	Non-Use Maharashtra; Urban, Local Body, Co-educational
	369	Non-Use Maharashtra; Urban, Private Aided, Boys
	370	Non-Use Maharashtra; Urban, Private Aided, Girls
	371	Non-Use Maharashtra; Urban, Private Aided, Co-educational
	373	Non-Use Maharashtra; Urban, Private UnAided, Girls
	374	Non-Use Maharashtra; Urban, Private UnAided, Co-educational
	451	Non-Use Delhi; Rural, Govern, Boys
	452	Non-Use Delhi; Rural, Govern, Girls

Population 3

Stratum Extended
Country Number Stratum Name

India

	453	Non-Use Delhi; Rural, Govern, Co-educational
	457	Non-Use Delhi; Rural, Private Aided, Boys
	463	Non-Use Delhi; Urban, Govern, Boys
	464	Non-Use Delhi; Urban, Govern, Girls
	465	Non-Use Delhi; Urban, Govern, Co-educational
	466	Non-Use Delhi; Urban, Local Body, Boys
	467	Non-Use Delhi; Urban, Local Body, Girls
	468	Non-Use Delhi; Urban, Local Body, Co-educational
	469	Non-Use Delhi; Urban, Private Aided, Boys
	470	Non-Use Delhi; Urban, Private Aided, Girls
	471	Non-Use Delhi; Urban, Private Aided, Co-educational
	472	Non-Use Delhi; Urban, Private UnAided, Boys
	473	Non-Use Delhi; Urban, Private UnAided, Girls
	474	Non-Use Delhi; Urban, Private UnAided, Co-educational

Israel

	10	Jerusalem, not educational welfare program
	11	Jerusalem, educational welfare program
	20	North, not educational welfare program
	21	North, educational welfare program
	30	Haifa, not educational welfare program
	31	Haifa, educational welfare program
	40	Central, not educational welfare program
	41	Central, educational welfare program
	50	Tel Aviv, not educational welfare program
	51	Tel Aviv, educational welfare program
	60	South, not educational welfare program
	61	South, educational welfare program
	70	Arabic Language

Italy

	1	All schools

Population 3

Stratum Extended

Country Number Stratum Name

Japan

11	National public new schools
12	National public low student-computer ratio schools (<35%)
13	National public middle student-computer ratio schools (35-65%)
14	National public high student-computer ratio schools (>=65%)
21	Private new schools
22	Private low student-computer ratio schools (<35%)
23	Private middle student-computer ratio schools (35-65%)
24	Private high student-computer ratio schools (>=65%)
61	National public business schools
62	National public techinical schools
63	Other national public schools
71	Private business schools
72	Private techinical schools
73	Other private schools
82	Technical College

Netherlands

11	General secondary/vocational schools, small (<400)
12	General secondary/vocational schools, medium (400-800)
13	General secondary/vocational schools, large (>=800)
21	General secondary schools, small (<400)
22	General secondary schools, medium (400-800)
23	General secondary schools, large (>=800)
31	Vocational schools, small (<400)
32	Vocational schools, medium (400-800)
33	Vocational schools, large (>=800)
41	Individual vocational schools, small (<400)
42	Individual vocational schools, medium (400-800)
43	Individual vocational schools, large (>=800)

New
Zealand

1	Small, state, co-educational schools
3	Small, state, single sex boys schools
4	Small, integrated or private, co-educational schools

Population 3

Stratum Extended
Country Number Stratum Name

New
Zealand

	5	Small, integrated or private, single sex girls schools
	6	Small, integrated or private, single sex boys schools
	10	Medium size, state, co-educational schools
	11	Medium size, state, single sex girls schools
	12	Medium size, state, single sex boys schools
	13	Medium size, integrated or private, co-educational schools
	14	Medium size, integrated or private, single sex girls schools
	15	Medium size, integrated or private, single sex boys schools
	19	Large, state, co-educational schools
	20	Large, state, single sex girls schools
	21	Large, state, single sex boys schools

Poland

	1	Non-using small size highschools
	2	Non-using large size highschools
	3	Using small size highschools
	4	Using large size highschools

Portugal

	13	Small, using schools (grade 11)
	14	Medium size, using schools (grade 11)
	15	Large, using schools (grade 11)
	16	Small, non-using schools (grade 11)
	17	Medium size, non-using schools (grade 11)
	18	Large, non-using schools (grade 11)

Slovenia

	1	The largest schools
	2	Large schools
	3	Medium schools
	4	Small schools

Population 3

Stratum Extended
Country Number Stratum Name

Switzerland
        1   Kanton 1 - 29
        2   Kanton 30 - 32
        3   Kanton 40 - 42

United States
of America
        1   All schools

Appendix B

Content of self-rating scales

I know . . .(KNOWLEDGE)

1. Several advantages of computer use for instruction.
2. The difference between a word processor and a desktop publishing program.
3. Criteria to judge the quality of a printer.
4. The trends in hardware development in the past 20 years.
5. What 'file extensions' are.
6. What a 'loop' means in programming.
7. What a 'relational database' is like.
8. What a 'bit' is defined as.
9. The difference between 'RAM' and 'ROM'.

I can write a program for . . .(PROGRAMMING)

1. Adding up numbers.
2. Using arrays.
3. Storing data on a disk drive.
4. Sorting data into a certain sequence.
5. Printing the complete ASCII character set.

I am capable of . . .(CAPABILITY)

1. Exchanging data between different types of computers.
2. Copying files from one disk to another.
3. Editing documents with a word processor.
4. Loading a data set from a disk drive.
5. Creating a database-file.
6. Evaluating the usefulness of software for my lessons.
7. Adapting instructional software to my needs.
8. Writing courseware for my own lessons.

Appendix C

Topics for which teachers could indicate whether they learned about it during teacher and/or in-service training

Computers and society
  History/evolution
  Relevance
  Impact of applications
  Ethical issues

Applications
  Editing/word processing
  Drawing/painting etc.
  Spreadsheets
  Database management
  Statistical applic.
  Artificial intelligence
  Authoring languages
  Models and simulations
  Laboratory instrumentation
  Scanning/image processing
  CAD/CAM/process control
  Telecommunications etc.
  Educational/recreational games
  Music generation

Problem analysis and programming
  General concepts
  General procedures
  Structure of programs
  Programming languages
  Problem analysis

Principles of hard- and software structure
  Basic computer concepts
  Hardware
  Software

Pedagogical/instructional aspects
  Drill/practice programs
  Overviews of existing software
  Evaluation of software
  Integration of software in lesson
  Organization of computer use

Appendix D

Names and addresses of participants

Name and addresses of participating institutions, General Assembly members and National Project Coordinators involved in stage 1 of the Computers in Education Study.

Austria

National Project Center
Universität Salzburg
Institut für Erziehungswissenschaft
Akademiestr. 26
A-5020 Salzburg

General Assembly Member
V. Krumm

National Project Coordinator
G. Haider

Belgium-French

National Project Center
Université de Liège
(Sart Tilman) B32
4000 Liege 1

General Assembly Member
G.L. De Landsheere

National Project Coordinator
N. Deltour

Belgium-Flemish

National Project Center
Seminarie en Laboratorium
voor Didactiek
H. Dunantlaan 2
9000 Gent

General Assembly Member
J.A.P. Heene

National Project Coordinator
C. Brusselmans-Dehairs

Canada-British Columbia

National Project Center
Faculty of Education
University of British Columbia
2125 Main Mall
V6T 1Z5 Vancouver B.C.

General Assembly Member
D. Robitaille

National Project Coordinator
S. Donn

China

National Project Center
China's IEA national centre
Central Institute of
Educational Research
46 Bei San Huan Zhong Lu
Beijing

General Assembly Member
Teng Chung

National Project Coordinator
H. Zhenyong À

Federal Republic of Germany

National Project Center
Institut der Pedagogik
für Naturwissenschaften
(IPN) Universität Kiel
Olshausenstrasse 92

General Assembly Member
W. Tietze

National Project Coordinator
H. Hansen

Hungary

National Project Center
Orszagos Pedagogia Intezet
Pf. 338
Budapest 1445

General Assembly Member
Z. Báthory

National Project Coordinator
P. Vári

France

National Project Center
Department of Evaluation and
International Comparisons
1 Avenue Léon Journault
92 311 Sevres

General Assembly Member
D. Robin

National Project Coordinator
D.Robin, E. Barrier

Greece

National Project Center
Department of Education
University of Patras
Patras

General Assembly Member
G. Kontogiannopoulou-Polydorides

National Project Coordinator
G. Kontogiannopoulou-Polydorides

India

National Project Center
Council of Educational
Research and Training
Sri. Aurobindo Marg.
New Delhi 110016

General Assembly Member

National Project Coordinator
A.K. Jalaludin

Israel

National Project Center
School of Education
Hebrew University
Jerusalem

General Assembly Member
D. Nevo

National Project Coordinator
D. Davis

Japan

National Project Center
National Institute for Educational
Research of Japan
6-5-22 Shimomeguro
Meguro-Ku
Tokyo

General Assembly Member
H. Takizawa

National Project Coordinator
T. Sawada

Netherlands

National Project Center
Universiteit Twente
Department of Education
OCTO
P.O. Box 217
7500 AE Enschede

General Assembly Member
Tj. Plomp

National Project Coordinator
A.C.A. ten Brummelhuis

Italy

National Project Center
CEDE
Villa Falconieri
00044 Frascati RM

General Assembly Member
A. Visalberghi

National Project Coordinator
A.M. Caputo

Luxembourg

National Project Center
Institut Supérieur
d'Etudes et de Recherches
Pedagogiques
BP 002
7201 Walferdange

General Assembly Member
R. Dieschbourg

National Project Coordinator
R. Dieschbourg

New Zealand

National Project Center
Research and Statistics
Division
Ministry of Education
P.O. Box 1666
Wellington

General Assembly Member
R.A. Garden

National Project Coordinator
M. Chamberlain, J. Burns

Poland

National Project Center
Oddzial Doskonalenia
Nayczycieli IKN
ul. Garbaska, 1
31-131 Krakow

General Assembly Member
B. Niemierko

National Project Coordinator
H. Szaleniec

Portugal

National Project Center
Gabinette de Estudos
e Planeamento
Av. Miguel Bombarda 20
1093 Lisboa Codex

General Assembly Member
C. Climaco

National Project Coordinator
M. Maia, M.J. Rau

Slovenia

National Project Center
University Edvard Kardeijn
Ljubljana
Gerbiceva 62
P.P. 76

General Assembly Member
M. Setinc

National Project Coordinator
M. Setinc

Switzerland

National Project Center
Institut für Verhaltenswissenschaften
Turnerstrasse 1
ETH-Zentrum
8092 Zürich

General Assembly Member
A. Gretler

National Project Coordinator
K. Frey, R. Niederer, E. Ramseier

United States of America

National Project Center
Center for Social Organization of Schools
Johns Hopkins University
3505 N; Charles Street
Baltimore MD 21218

General Assembly Member
R.M. Wolf

National Project Coordinator
H. Becker

Names and Addresses of the Authors

Drs. A.C.A. ten Brummelhuis
University of Twente
OCTO
P.O. Box 217
7500 AE Enschede
The Netherlands

Dr. D. Davis
Hebrew University
School of Education
Jerusalem
Israel

Drs. I.A.M. Janssen-Reinen
University of Twente
OCTO
P.O. Box 217
7500 AE Enschede
The Netherlands

Dr. G. Kontogiannopoulou-Polydorides
University of Patras
Department of Education
University Campus
26110 Patras
Greece

Dr. W.J. Pelgrum
University of Twente
OCTO
P.O. Box 217
7500 AE Enschede
The Netherlands

Prof. Dr. Tj. Plomp
University of Twente
Faculty of Educational Science and
Technology
P.O. Box 217
7500 AE Enschede
The Netherlands

Dr. A.C. Tuijnman
OECD
2, rue André-Pascal
75775 Paris Cedex 16
France

Dr. R.M. Wolf
Columbia University
Teachers College
Box 165
New York, NY 10027
United States of America

Index

ABOUSOFT (software suited for learning
    about computers) 66, 67
administration
    policies regarding computer use in
      schools 170
    problems in implementing computer use
      109, 110, 111, 112, 169–70
    use of computers for 17, 151,152–9,
      233
Ajzen, I. and Fishbein, M.
    on attitude and behavior 159
Akker, van den, J.J.H., Keursten, P. and
    Plomp, Tj.
    on importance of training 143
    on integration of computers into
      curriculum 4
    on role of school administration 19
algebra, use of computers in teaching 83, 85,
    230
Anderson, R.E. and Collis, B. on
    "functionality" perspective
    on computer use 4, 235–6
    on shortages of software 49–50
Andrews, R.
    on role of school principal 147
Apple, M.
    on gender 174
Apple Macintosh computers 56, 58
applications
    training in
    teaching of 313
    arithmetic, use of computers in teaching
      83, 84, 230
Atari computers 56, 58
    attitudes to computer use 235
    principals 159–69, 182–7, 188, 232
    teachers 232
Austria
    CAD/CAM/robotics teaching 93, 99
    computer applications teaching 93
    plans for introduction of computers in
      near future 38
    reasons for introduction of computers
      38

    sampling information 247, 264, 274,
      278–80, 300–1
    software usage 99
    teaching of computers and society 91
    use of computers in foreign language
      teaching 79
    use of computers in technology teaching
      79
    USEWITH and USEABOUT locations
      48
availability and resource needs,
    as indicator in six-system study of
      computer use 193

Basic, use in schools 99, 122
Becker, H.J.

    on computer use in United States 47, 73
    on exemplary teachers 127–8, 230, 236
    on integration of computers into
      curriculum 4, 43
Belgium–Flemish
    educational background of parents 150
    equity-related policies for computer use
      173
    mother tongue teaching 75, 89
    principals' attitudes towards computers
      167, 168
    sampling information 247, 264–6, 274,
      280, 301
    teaching principles of hardware and
      software structure 98
Belgium–French computer education for
    female teachers 181
    computer-using teachers 128
    educational background of parents 150
    gender dominance in teaching staff 176,
      177
    location of computers in classrooms 59
    principals' attitudes towards computers
      160, 167, 168
    problem analysis and programming
      teaching 95

321

on gender issues in computer use 174
Makau, B.M.,
   on introduction of computers in
     developing countries 227
Makrakis, V.
   on approaches to computer use 47
mathematics
   topics covered in training 133
   use of computers in teaching 46, 47,
     74–86, 120–1, 230
measurement, use of computers in teaching
   83, 85
measurement error, and LISREL analyses
   203–4
methodology, in six-system study of
   computer use 195–9
Ministries of Education 140, 145
models and simulation, teaching of 92, 94
monitoring and evaluation procedures, as
   indicator of
   readiness for educational innovation
     190
Moskowitz, J.H. and Birman, F.,
   on importance of training 143
mother tongue
   topics covered in training 133
   use of computers in teaching 46, 47,
     74–82, 89, 120–1, 230

national context, and difficulties of
   integrating computers in education 4
Netherlands, The
   bottom-up initiatives for introduction of
     computers 36
   computer education for female teachers
     181
   computer use for enrichment and
     remedial teaching 103
   computer-using teachers 128
   educational background of parents 150
   equity-related policies for computer use
     173
   estimate of changes resulting from
     computer use 120
   external financial support for computer
     use 210
   and gender dominance in teaching staff
     176, 177
   homogeneity of hardware 51
   "inside-school" initiatives for computer
     use 34
   introduction of computers 37, 38
   principals' attitudes towards computers
     160, 167, 168, 169
   and representative nature of
     samples 14
   sampling information 250, 256, 261,
     270, 276, 294–6, 308

and six-system study of computer use
   189, 193, 194, 201–3, 206, 208, 218,
   224
student:computer ratio 51
teachers as initiators of computer use 33
use of computers in teaching mother-
   tongue 89
use of computers in technology teaching
   79
use of software 67
New Zealand
   bottom-up initiatives for introduction of
     computers 36
   computer applications teaching 93
   computer communication and control
     devices usage 99
   computer education for female teachers
     181
   educational background of parents 150
   emphasis on mathematics 78
   equity-related policies for computer use
     173
   location of computers in classrooms 59,
     229
   mother tongue teaching 75, 89
   policies for equity in computer use 181
   principals' attitudes towards computers
     167, 168
   problem analysis and programming
     teaching 95
   reasons for introduction of computers
     38
   sampling information 250–1, 256–8,
     261–2, 270–1, 276–7, 296, 308–9
   software usage 99
   student:computer ratio 51
   teachers as initiators of computer use
     32, 33
   teaching of computers and society 91
   teaching principles of hardware and
     software structure 98
   telecommunications/ networks teaching
     93
   use of computer for administration 158
   use of software 67
   word processing teaching 93
Niederer, R. and Frey, K.
   on location of computers 58–9

opportunistic rationale, for introduction of
   computers in education 3–4
Orlich, D.C.,
   on training 125, 141

parents
   educational background of 148–52
support for training activities 140
pedagogical rationale, and introduction of
   computers 3, 40, 41